MINE WARFARE VESSELS
OF THE ROYAL NAVY
1908 TO DATE

MINE WARFARE VESSELS OF THE ROYAL NAVY 1908 TO DATE

M. P. Cocker

Airlife

First published in the UK in 1993
by Airlife Publishing Ltd

British Library Cataloguing in Publication Data
   A catalogue record for this book
   is available from the British Library

ISBN 1 85310 328 4

Printed by Livesey Ltd, Shrewsbury.

Airlife Publishing Ltd
101 Longden Road, Shrewsbury SY3 9EB

Contents

Acknowledgements

I am deeply indebted to the following individuals and institutions for information and assistance during the compilation of this work. I am also grateful for permission to use drawings and photographs and for the provision of same.

In random order: A. M. Stirling — Henry Robb Ltd; K. G. Burdis — Swan Hunter Shipbuilders; J. Rosewarn — Royal Institution of Naval Architects; Lt-Cdr M. R. Wilson RN (Retd) — Naval Historical Dept; S. H. Reed (MOD(N)); P. Kemp — Imperial War Museum; P. J. Usher, CBE — Vosper Thornycroft (UK) Ltd; D. Thornley — Manchester Ship Canal Co, also M. Emerson; R. Forrest & Associates — Wright & Logan; Cdr W. Alexander RN (Retd) — HMS *Vernon;* J. M. Davis for J. Marr & Sons Ltd; Wg Cdr J. A. MacBean MBE, RAF (Retd) — Explosive Ordnance Disposal Techical Information Centre; Maj. A. S. Hogben QGM, RE — Defence Explosive Ordnance Disposal School; Cdr F. E. R. Phillips RN (Retd); British Hovercraft Corporation; Brian Ollington (Photographer); J. G. Bell — Richards (Shipbuilders) Ltd; British Aerospace Dynamics Division; M. Lennon; David Brindle; Phillip & Son (Shipbuilders) Ltd; South African Navy Archives; Cochrane (Shipbuilders) Ltd; W. C. MacMillan — Yarrow (Shipbuilders) Limited; Sealink Ltd; Australian War Memorial; Brazilian Navy Archives; N. R. Plevy — DS4 (MOD(N)

In particular I must thank my wife for the typescript and proofreading, not to forget the indexing. If, by chance, I have omitted mention of any source, I trust that my apology will be accepted and understood.

Notes

Except where otherwise stated, all line drawings are of the minelayer or minesweeper design as conceived, and photographs of the ship when built or converted for its mine warfare role. Notwithstanding this intention, however, some photographs show the ship(s) before and/or after this time, as a minelayer or minesweeper, but where the photograph or drawing is of a ship from a specifically designed class, such as the 'Halcyon' class of minesweepers, the photographs are of the ship as commissioned.

• **Dimensions** are imperial measure, ie feet (ft) and inches (in) and tons of 2,240lb
• **Class** is a vessel, or vessels, to the same intended design
• **Type** is the definition of the intended purpose of the vessel
• **Machinery** is the method of mechanical propulsion to and of the engines for propelling the vessel
• **Complement** is the total number of Naval personnel in the ship's company
• **Shaft** means propeller shaft
• **nm** means nautical miles
• **U-Boat** means any enemy submarine

The line drawings on several of the Class pages are reproduced by kind permission of the Royal Institution of Naval Architects and are taken from the paper *Warships 1860-1960* by the late President of the Institution Sir Alfred Sims, and are all to the same scale. Other drawings included are acknowledged separately.

Glossary

'A' Bracket   A metal bracket proud of the underwater hull holding the
outer propeller shaft rigid

AA   Anti-Aircraft

A/S   Anti-Submarine

BHP   Brake horsepower

Calibre   The diameter of a missile, eg: 4.7in, 21in

Class   A number of ships all to the same design

CMB   Coastal Motor Boat

Complement   The total number of persons in the ship's company

DCT   Director Control Tower/Depth Charge Thrower

Displacement tons   The amount of water in tons displaced by a ship

DP   dual purpose

E-Boat   A light tonnage (fast patrol boat) enemy surface craft

Full Load tons   The displacement tonnage of a warship plus the weight of
ammunition, fuel and stores

HA   high angle

HMAS   His Majesty's Australian Ship

HMCS   His Majesty's Canadian Ship, etc

HMS   His/Her Majesty's Ship

hp   horsepower

HSMS   High Speed Minesweeping

ihp   indicated horse power

LA   low angle

Lay   The actual number of mines laid by a minelayer at one time, but there
could be 2 or 3 lays per voyage, eg: 6 mines, 20 mines, 14 mines, being a
total of 40 mines laid on that voyage in 3 lays

LOA   length overall

mg   machine gun

MGB   motor gun boat

ML   Motor Launch

M/L   Minelayer

mm   millimetre

mined   The occurrence of damage or loss to a ship caused by striking,
contacting or detonating a mine

MOD(N)   Ministry of Defence (Navy)

M/S   Minesweeper, minesweeping

MMS   Motor Mine Sweeper

MTB   Motor Torpedo Boat

mtg   mounting

nm   nautical mile

pdr   pounder

P No   Pennant (Pendant) number

posn   position

pp   hull length between perpendiculars

qf   quick firing

RCN   Royal Canadian Navy

RNN   Royal Netherlands Navy

RNZN   Royal New Zealand Navy

R/T   radio telephone

SANF   South African Naval Force

SHP   shaft horsepower

S/M   submarine

SS   steam ship

Sweep   A device towed by, or used from, a M/S to expose and/or detonate a mine

TB   Torpedo Boat

TBD   Torpedo Boat Destroyer

TC   Torpedo Catcher

TD   Torpedo Destroyer

Tubes   torpedo tubes

U-Boat   Any enemy submarine

WL   water line (length on)

W/T   wireless telegraphy

YD   Yard (for shipbuilding yard)

1: Mine Warfare: The Danger Below

For many decades the navigable waters of the world have been traversed by ships of all nations in peace and in war, and during the peace ships have foundered by stress of storm far too often. With the commencement of war, the hazards of the sea are increased many times by reason of the weapon known as the sea mine, or mine. The evolution of the mine is dealt with briefly later in this chapter, but despite the swept channels, the seas are still dangerous today from mines that have been laid by ships of many nations.

In the early 20th century the British Admiralty decided that the threat from the weapon of the weaker power, for such was the mine described, was now too well known and foreseen on too large a scale to be ignored. Consequently, in 1908 the Board decided that a number of the smaller vessels of the Fleet such as ships of the 'Alarm', 'Dryad' and 'Sharpshooter' classes should be converted into minesweepers. From information gained by the trials and experimentation with the purchased trawler *Oropesa II* and its minesweeping gear, additional trawlers were purchased from commercial owners.

The other need was in the provision of minelayers; here, the Royal Navy has always depended on requisitioned vessels to a large extent, although a number of classes of minelayers have originated from Admiralty designs and conversions of existing ships of the Fleet.

Minelaying can be carried out from any surface ship, large or small; and also from submarines and aircraft. Likewise, minesweeping has been tried operationally from fixed-wing aircraft, towed wooden and concrete skids, three-ton lorries and landing craft afloat, detonating mines on shore, besides the more conventional ships and craft listed herein.

Some details of the mines laid and swept will be given later, and although the facts and figures of fission weapons and missiles are surprisingly easily available to the layman – even up to the latest devised items of devastation – particulars of the sea mine are harder to acquire, for reasons best known to the powers that be. When the authorities in North Vietnam were unable to clear the entrances of their own ports, it was ironic that their ex-enemy, the United States of America, was the only nation which had the requisite knowhow to desensitise the mines laid by US Forces in the Vietnam War up to 1976.

The minesweeper was further developed with the use in 1915 of shallow draught inshore vessels such as the American/Canadian-built motor launches and also trawlers acquired from the ex-Tsarist Imperial Russian Navy. Other trawlers captured by the Royal Navy were put to good use by a Fleet desperate for more minesweepers.

Inshore minesweeping was of paramount importance and as paddle vessels had been requisitioned, it was decided to build the 'Ascot' and 'Improved Ascot' paddle minesweepers with their shallow draught, and one or two survived to fulfil the same task again in World War II, likewise with the screw-propelled 'Hunt' and 'Aberdare' class sweepers.

Another World War I class of shallow draught minesweeper were the conversions of the so-called 'Tunnel Tugs', built for Army use in the Persian Gulf, but which were commissioned as the 'Dance' class. As the years passed, from the cessation of hostilities on the 11 November 1918, the minesweeping task was by no means completed, but it was not until the late 1920s that thought was given by the Admiralty to new designs of minesweeping vessels. Two original craft but of small tonnage were motor minesweepers Nos 1 and 2, followed some time later by motor minesweeper No 51. Messrs Thornycroft also constructed a class of dual-purpose Patrol Boat/Motor Minesweeper which I have described as (Straits) MMS.

In the early 1930s, plans were made and put into operation for the requisitioning of fishing trawlers both for A/S and M/S use, and all of these trawlers were renamed and grouped into the 'Berberis' class, followed by requisitioned whalers which formed the 'Lake' class. Similar to these last mentioned vessels, the well-known Admiralty Naval Trawlers were designed and built under the 'Dance', 'Fish', 'Hills', 'Military', 'Round Table', 'Shakespearian', 'Tree' class names, and the largest class of all, the 'Western Isles' (abbreviated to 'Isles') class.

There never were sufficient trawlers in commission, so in 1942 a further class of naval trawlers was built in Brazilian yards and a similar class in Portugal, comprising 12 vessels, six of which were steel and six of timber construction.

The shortage of steel had some influence on the construction of minesweepers and the large classes of MMS, mainly built in Canada and the USA, were of the 119ft and 140ft lengths, but of all-timber construction, as were the MMS 'ZZ' class of converted Army 'A' Lighters built in India. Similarly, minesweepers built in the USA and designated YMS were turned over to the Fleet as BYMS, followed by the steel-hulled Ex-American 'Catherine' class.

In UK yards, the mercantile conversions of colliers and such like for use as Mine Destructor Vessels (MDVs) was underway and the 'Algerine' class of Fleet sweepers were rapidly being commissioned. Then followed the 'Bangor' class, which had two or three methods of propulsion according to the availability of turbines, diesel engines and reciprocating engines.

Specialist vessels were pressed into use for displacement minesweeping, these being Steam Gunboats (SGBs) and salvage tugs of the 'Assurance' and 'Bustler' classes.

As World War II continued, many landing craft types were fitted out for inshore sweeping, including the LCAs with their 'Hedgerow' weapons, the LCM Mk I, III and VII, the LCP (Large), LCT Mk IV, LCT Mk V, LCV M/S and the 75 ft MFV. In the early part of World War II, a number of 'Flower' class corvettes were relieved of convoy escort duties and converted to Fleet sweepers.

As the war in Europe closed, there was a tremendous minesweeping task, and ships of all nations took part for a number of years to attempt to clear the countless creeks, rivers, harbours and estuaries of Europe. Many German minesweepers were used, some were also brought to the UK for evaluation.

The rebuilding of our minesweeping fleets began in the early 1950s with the 'Ton' class which had many characteristics of the old BYMS, but inshore sweepers featured largely on the new construction list, with the 'Ham' class, followed by the 'Ley' class, the first two types being constructed of wood with the 'Leys' of composite build.

In the search for a substance strong enough to absorb a mine detonation, the man-made glass-reinforced plastic (GRP) was tried and is now afloat in the form of HMS *Wilton,* being the UK's first 'plastic' minesweeper: the design was a near-copy from the 'Ton' class and included 90 per cent of the basic parts.

The 'Hunt' class of mine countermeasures vessels commenced building in 1975 with the first of the class, HMS *Brecon,* commissioning in 1979. Like *Wilton,* the new 'Hunts' are designed for both hunting and sweeping mines, and the hull is constructed of GRP.

With the ever-increasing threat from nuclear submarines with their ability for deep diving, two stern trawlers were purchased in 1978 for the evaluation of deep minesweeping. They have been navalised and are forming the basis of the 'Venturer' class. Further vessels of a smaller type are planned. Lately, the advantages of the minimum draught minesweeper on the hovercraft hull have become evident, and although the endurance of the 'VT2' and 'BH7' are very low, they can sweep in any course or direction in the shallowest of water. The latest vessel to be considered for mine countermeasures, is the hydrofoil HMS *Speedy,* which commissioned in 1979 and was built in the USA but fitted out by Vosper Thornycroft in the UK. In 1984 HMS *Waveney,* the first of a class of 12 'River' class Fleet minesweepers built of steel, was completed and commissioned.

A follow-up Single-Role Mine Hunter (SRMH) design was announced in 1984, with the first of the class named *Sandown,* and launched in 1988. She is of GRP construction with a displacement of about 450 tons.

Minelayers

The first minelayers were conversions/adaptations of existing ships of the Fleet, such as the 'Apollo' class cruisers of 1890 vintage, followed by requisitioned passenger/cargo vessels, including the paddle steamers which frequented the coastline of the UK. Even the mighty HMS *Courageous* was converted into a minelayer but never employed as such.

As World War I progressed, cruisers of the 'Diadem' class joined the ranks of the minelayers, together with the much smaller Thornycroft 55 ft Coastal Motor Boats (CMB) and the 70ft CMBs, being especially built for minelaying. Additionally, the Ex-American/Canadian motor launches and British 'X' Lighters were employed. Further cruisers were from the 'Arethusa' and 'Boadicea' classes, followed by HMS *London* (Battleship) and ships of the 'Cressy' class. Quite a number of requisitioned trawlers and drifters were also used as minelayers in World War I.

Four vessels which were converted between the wars were from the 'M' class of monitors and at the conclusion of their conversion were then named, but two outstanding new buildings were the handsome HMS *Adventure* cruiser minelayer and the smaller but longer-lasting HMS *Plover*. There were controlled minelayers of the 'Linnet' class, and coastal forces provided the new Vosper 72½ ft motor torpedo boats (MTBs), together with the well-known 'Fairmile A', 'B' and 'D' vessels, which rapidly earned a good reputation for this skilled occupation.

In 1939, controlled minelayers M1 to M8 were launched but M7 was under construction at Singapore and was lost to the Japanese. More fishing vessels and passenger/cargo vessels were requisitioned to fulfil the same task as in World War I.

In 1940 the first of the new fast minelayers was launched, being HMS *Abdiel*, to be followed by five more of the same class. These vessels, although 418ft in length and displacing 2,650 tons, could make 40kts with no pressing of engineroom power. Some vessels from the 'Fish' class and 'Isles' class of naval trawlers were also converted as minelayers.

With the conclusion of World War II, minelayers were no longer needed, the emphasis being on minesweepers to clear the oceans of the world, but nevertheless, evaluation continued with the commissioning of several Ex-German minelaying tenders and the Japanese minelayer *Wakataka* which was renamed *Laburnum*. It was not until 1967 that the new building exercise minelayer HMS *Abdiel* was completed and she was in 1984 the only minelayer in the Fleet. Experiments have continued with the Sealink ferry *Ailsa Princess* and Royal Navy patrol vessels of the 'Castle' class.

Mines

The mine is effective against any type of ship. From the history of Royal Navy mine warfare which commenced in 1908, the mine – or sea mine – was constructed with an outer steel case for buoyancy and an inner container, which contained the charge, with its associated detonators, fuses, primers and triggers of various types. The mine case, with the firing mechanisms, are designed to be complementary to each other, and the charge in the mine to explode when the appropriate sequence of events occur:

- The magnetic mine is attracted to the built-in magnetism of a ship with a steel hull, and when the ship is sufficiently close, the detonation occurs.
- The acoustic mine is similar in construction, but is detonated by the sound of a ship, whether steel or otherwise, approaching within acoustic range.
- The contact mine may be drifting free (which is contrary to International Law), or moored and weighted with its own sinker, so that flotation occurs below the surface. For detonation, the ship must contact the mine. The contact is generally actuated by the impact of the ship's hull crushing one of the mine horns, inside which is the cover for a glass phial containing acid, which flows onto terminals and completes the firing circuit, so causing the detonation.
- Controlled mines are moored to protect harbours and anchorages but connected by underwater cable to an observation post on-shore, where the mine-firing switch is positioned. With controlled minefields, loops of cable which cross the navigable channel lie on the sea bed and are connected to a power supply with meters in the observation posts. The theory is that a steel vessel crossing the loop creates a current, or reverse current, which is indicated by the meter and signifies that an unknown ship or submarine has either entered or left the harbour. Consequently in a fraction of a second, one or more mines from the controlled field may be detonated at will, closest to the indicated position shown by the appropriate meter. (Combinations of all systems may be included in any mine.) In controlled fields, the detonation is usually manually or electrically actuated.
- A further type of mine which lay on the seabed included an arming delay clock device, so that sweepers could pass over many times, but after the clock in the mine had run its course, the fuse would be set and although the channel seemed to be clear, the next ship within acoustic or magnetic range could very well detonate the mine which until then had lain silent — possibly for weeks. Yet a further derivation on this theme was the 'ship clicker' mine with pulse delay mechanism which also lay on the seabed, permitting ships to steam overhead with the actuating device of the mine

'clicking up' on every passage until the detonating total was reached; then the next vessel would cause itself to be mined. Some mines had interrupter clocks to delay the arming of the mine for a short period of, say, 24 hours. Probably the ultimate in mines is still known as the pressure or oyster mine which is detonated by the pressure of water downwards, displaced by a moving or anchored vessel. Consequently, pressure mines are more reliably laid in the shallower navigational lanes. As the tidal flow varies, a device on the mine takes this into account by a punctured rubber diaphragm which permits ingress and egress of seawater which will not be sufficient to actuate the detonation cycle of the mine. The pressure mine is very largely unsweepable and hopefully decays in time.

A Short History of the Mine

The first recorded use of a mine was in 1585 by the Dutch against the Spaniards at Antwerp, then followed a lull with the next period of mining activities occurring in the American War of Independence from 1777. Twenty years later, in 1797, both sides fighting in the French Revolution made considerable use of shipping for transporting materials and reinforcements and mine warfare was carried out across the English Channel, although the Admiralty still maintained that the mine was a weapon of the weaker power. In 1814, during the British attack on Long Island (USA), mines were used against them but with little effect. A good example of controlled mining was in the defence of the Port of Kiel in the Schleswig-Holstein War of 1848. A few years later, the Crimean War broke out and the Tsarist military defended most of its ports with mines, and some casualties were caused to Royal Navy ships.

The American Civil War of 1864 brought forth mining by both the Confederate and Federal forces. Mine expertise grew with the Franco-Prussian War of 1870 and the Russo-Japanese War in 1904, when modern steel and iron-built ships sank with great rapidity from the effects of being mined.

At long last, the Admiralty did take an interest, and in 1900 the C-in-C Mediterranean was 'instructed to provide mines', but in 1903 this project was cancelled for twelve months. When the details of the Russo-Japanese War filtered through, and it was proved that mines were such a danger, then the first plans were laid to create a minesweeping force for the Royal Navy. In 1908, the Admiralty purchased a number of trawlers and drifters for conversion into sweepers, but it was not until six years later, in the November of 1914, that the Royal Navy laid the first mines in the English Channel to begin the Channel Barrage.

Minesweeping

The earliest method of sweeping a contact mine was to sever its mooring cable by a cutter suspended from the centre of a sweep cable, the ends of which were connected to two minesweepers. The width of the sweep was maintained by the distance apart of the sweepers and the depth of the cutter was maintained by the floats from which it was suspended. When the cutter (which was of sharp-toothed steel) contacted the cable, the cable was cut and gave, and the mine floated to the surface where it was exploded by rifle fire from the sweepers.

With experimentation and the inclusion of otter boards and kites, it was found that one sweeper could, with overlapping and steering a steady course, clear its own lane with the greatest of danger to the foremost ship only. The principle of kite and otter sweeps originated from the methods used to hold open the mouth of a trawler's net.

The acoustic mine was swept by a sweeper using a device which produced an underwater sound louder and more penetrating than the sound of the ships' engines. The magnetic mine was overcome by de-magnetising ships and using where possible non-magnetic sweepers, such as the MMSs, which have been mentioned previously. The de-magnetising of a steel vessel was accomplished by placing a coil of wire lengthways around its hull and then passing a current through it; this was known was 'wiping'. For ships under construction, a permanent cable was secured around the hull which was kept constantly charged from the ship's own generators whilst she was at sea. Both systems were known as 'de-gaussing', but 'wiping' only lasted for up to six months and had to be repeated.

For the oyster mine, no method of sweeping has yet been devised, but a ship is safer at dead-slow speed, similarly with the acoustic mine. Whilst the mine destructor vessels were reasonably effective against the magnetic mine, they were very expensive and needed their own flotilla of supporting vessels to deal with other types of mine in the same field. The great breakthrough came with the sweep known as the LL or Double-L sweep. This consisted of two buoyant cables of unequal length lashed together and streamed from a cable drum on the minesweeper's stern into the sea. The minesweeper pulsed electric power from its own generators through the cables intermittently, so creating a magnetic field which detonated the mines.

Today, the most effective way to deal with pressure mines is to use a swim team (one or two divers) from the mine countermeasures vessels to place a small explosive charge on the casing of the mine and, in a short time, a controlled explosion takes place.

The latests tests of Royal Navy minesweeping skills were during and after the liberation of the Falkland Islands in 1982 and the Anglo-French-USA

MCM force to clear the Suez Canal of a clandestine lay by the Libyan Ro-Ro vessel *Ghat* in 1984. In 1987 again, MCM vessels of the Royal Navy were deployed in the Gulf of Hormuz and Persian Gulf to clear mines layed from various Iranian vessels. In August 1988, the United Nations negotiated a truce between the warring states and the MCM vessels, by this time including other ships of NATO, were gradually withdrawn.

On 2 August 1990, the armed forces of Iraq invaded and a few days later annexed the sovereign state of Kuwait. The reaction of the European states and the USA was straightaway to condemn this action and resolutions of the UN Security Council included a blockade of shipping to and from Iraqi ports. It was possible that mines could be laid against the vessels of the blockade and in consequence three 'Hunt' MCM vessels were despatched to the Persian Gulf. Others followed for service in the Red Sea and the Gulf of Aquaba through which port supplies were landed for transit, via the Joint Jordan-Iraq highways. The Iraqi pipelines with terminals on the coast of Saudi Arabia and Turkey were cut by UN resolution by those nations.

The devices which may be incorporated into a mine include anything from anti-handling to submarine-attract systems, and the secrets beneath the waves cause considerable thought in the minds of the Naval Staffs of every maritime nation.

It is said that the first shot to be fired at sea in World War I was from HMS *Lance* (Destroyer) upon sighting the German passenger liner *Königen Louise* which had been converted to a minelayer, but was still in her peacetime colours in the English Channel. Peace has been with us for many years, not withstanding many 'incidents', but still the old corroded, rusty mines from wars long ago break the surface or are dragged from their moorings by trawlers' nets and create some of the havoc which they were originally intended to do.

'Mines reported in the fairway
warn all traffic and detain.
Send up UNITY, CLARIBEL, ASSYRIAN
STORMCOCK and GOLDEN GAIN.'

(From *Minesweepers,* by Rudyard Kipling)

2: HM Minelayers

'Adventure' Class Cruiser Minelayer

HMS	Commenced	Completed	Builder
Adventure	1923	1925	HM Dockyard Devonport/Vickers Armstrong (Tyne)

SPECIFICATION

Displacement:	6,740 tons (Full load: 7,260 tons)
Dimensions:	500pp 520 × 59 × 19
Armament:	4 (4 × 1) 4.7in QF LA
	4 × 3pdr QF
	12 × mg
Machinery:	4 shaft geared turbines all giving 40,000shp, with diesel-electric for cruising
Boilers:	2
Fuel:	1,550 tons of fuel oil
Speed:	28½kts
Complement:	383
Minelaying capacity:	280 large or 340 small
Mines actually laid:	12,401

Notes:

HMS *Adventure* was rather lightly armoured but was built with a torpedo bulge. She was the first cruiser to be designed with a transom stern which had to be rebuilt for better positioning of the stern minelaying doors. During World War II she was mined twice and in 1943 was converted to a repair ship.

HMS Adventure *at anchor with modified minelaying doors.* (National Maritime Museum)

HMS Plover. *A profile view of* Plover. *She has a 20mm AA on the bow and a 3in DP in 'X' positions.* (Imperial War Mueum)

'Plover' Class Coastal Minelayer

HMS	Launched	Builder
Plover	1937	Denny

SPECIFICATION

Displacement:	805 tons (Full load: 1,020 tons)
Dimensions:	180pp 195½ × 37½ × 8½
Armament:	1 × 12 pdr DP AA
	2 × 20mm on single mountings
Machinery:	2 shaft triple expansion all giving 1,400ihp
Fuel:	65 tons
Speed:	12½kts
Complement:	69
Minelaying capacity:	80
Mines actually laid:	15,327

Notes:
HMS *Plover* was accepted by the Royal Navy on the 25 September 1937, being commissioned the same day. She was continuously in commission until 1969.

'Linnet' Class Controlled Minelayers

HMS	Launched	Builder
Linnet	1938	Ardrossan
Redstart	1938	Robb
Ringdove	1938	Robb

HMS Ringdove *at her mooring.* (Imperial War Mueum)

SPECIFICATION

Displacement:	498 tons
Dimensions:	145pp 163¾ × 27¼ × 8
Armament:	1 × 20mm and 2 × mg all DP
Machinery:	2 shaft triple expansion all giving 400ihp
Speed:	10½kts
Complement:	24
Minelaying capacity:	12

Loss:

HMS *Redstart* was scuttled by own forces at Hong Kong on the 19 December 1941 in the face of the Japanese advance.

'M' Class Controlled Minelayers

HMS	Launched	Builder
M1 (later *Miner I*)	1939	Philip
M2 (later *Miner II*)	1939	Philip
M3 (later *Miner III*)	1939	Philip
M4 (later *Miner IV*)	1940	Philip
M5 (later *Miner V*)	1940	Philip
M6 (later *Miner VI*)	1942	Philip
M7	**	Singapore Dockyard
M7(II) (later *Miner VII*)	1944	Philip
M8 (later *Miner VIII*)	1943	Philip

HMS M2, *shown disarmed in the Portsmouth area.* (Wright & Logan)

SPECIFICATION

Displacement:	364 tons
Dimensions:	110¼ pp × 26½ × 8
Armament:	1 × 20mm AA 2 × .303in mg on single mtgs
Machinery:	2 shaft diesel engines all giving 720bhp
Speed:	10kts
Complement:	32
Mines carried:	10

Loss:

M7 whilst under construction at Singapore but incomplete, was seized in February 1942 by Japanese forces. **

'Abdiel' Class Fast Minelayers

HMS	Commenced	Completed	Builder
Abdiel GROUP 1	1939	1940	White
Latona	1939	1940	Thornycroft
Manxman	1939	1940	Stephen
Welshman	1939	1940	Hawthorne Leslie
Apollo GROUP 2	1941	1944	Hawthorne Leslie
Ariadne	1941	1943	Stephen

HMS Manxman *leaving harbour.* (Wright & Logan)

SPECIFICATION

Displacement:	2,650 tons (Full load: 3,700 tons)
Dimensions:	418 × 40 × 11¼ (16ft deep draught)

Armament:	*GROUP 1*	*GROUP 2*
	6 (3 × 2) 4in DP AA on twin mtgs at A, B and X posn	4 (2 × 2) 4in DP AA on twin mtgs at A and Y posn
	4 (1 × 4) 2pdr Pom Pom on 1 quad mtg	4 (2 × 2) 40mm DP AA on twin mtgs
	8 × 5in mg AA on 2 quad mtgs	12 × 20mm AA on 6 twin mtgs
	4 × 20mm AA on single mtgs	

Machinery:	2 shaft geared turbines all giving 72,000shp
Boilers:	4
Speed:	40kts+
Fuel:	750 tons of oil fuel
Range:	1,000nm at 40kts
Complement:	156
Minelaying capacity:	150 but varied according to type
Mines actually laid:	*Abdiel* 2,007
	Apollo 8,561
	Ariadne 1,352
	Latona Nil
	Manxman 3,111
	Welshman 3,275

Notes:
The speeds attained by these ships is legendary. *Manxman* is reputed to have cruised at 44kts, *Latona* to have exceeded 49kts; suffice it to say that although *Ariadne* at one period was only

capable of 33kts all of this class were able to outpace any comparable ship. HMS *Latona* and others were used for rapid replenishments of various ports and locations, depending on their speed for protection.

Losses:

HMS *Abdiel* was mined off Taranto on 9 September 1943; HMS *Latona* was bombed by Italian aircraft off the Libyan coast on 25 October 1941; HMS *Welshman* was torpedoed by U-617 on 1 February 1943 off Crete.

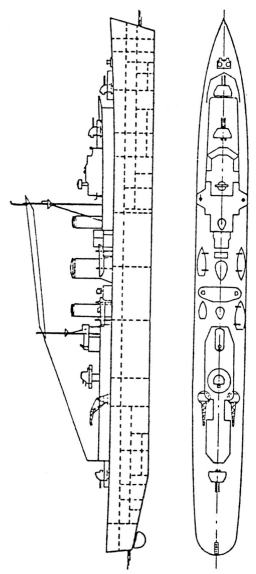

HMS Redshank. *This Controlled Minelayer is moored. Note her minelaying rails aft.*
(Wright & Logan)

'Fish' Class, *Corncrake* Type Controlled Minelayer

HMS	Launched	Builder
Corncrake (ex-*Mackerel*)	1942	Cochrane
Redshank (ex-*Turbot*)	1942	Cochrane

SPECIFICATION
Displacement:	670 tons (Full load: 900 tons)
Dimensions:	116 × 25 × 12½
Armament:	1 × 4in DP. 3 × 20mm AA on single mtgs
Machinery:	1 shaft triple expansion giving 700ihp
Boiler:	1
Speed:	11kts
Fuel:	200 tons fuel oil
Complement:	35

Notes:
These two Naval Trawlers were converted when under construction to operate as Controlled Minelayers. Upon completion they exchanged their 'Fish' names for 'Bird' names.

Loss:
HMS *Corncrake* on 25 January 1943 whilst in the North Atlantic foundered due to heavy weather.

'Western Isles' Class, *Blackbird* Type Controlled Minelayers

HMS	Launched	Builder
Blackbird (ex-*Sheppey* (I))	1943	CWG
Dabchick (ex-*Thorney*)	1943	CWG
Stonechat	1944	CWG
Whitethroat	1944	CWG

SPECIFICATION
Displacement:	545 tons (Full load: 790 tons)
Dimensions:	164 × 27½ × 10½
Armament:	1 × 12pdr DP, 3 × 20mm AA on single mtgs
Machinery:	1 shaft triple expansion giving 850ihp
Boiler:	1
Speed:	12kts
Complement:	40

HMS Blackbird *making weigh. Notice her camouflage, which was normal in wartime.* (Not known)

Notes:
These four Naval Trawlers were laid down to the design of the 'Western Isles' class but were re-named/named after birds on conversion, whilst under construction, to Controlled Minelayers.

'Abdiel' Class MCM Vessel and Exercise Minelayer

HMS	**Completed**	**Builder**
Abdiel	1967	Vosper Thornycroft

SPECIFICATION

Displacement:	1,375 tons (Full load: 1,500 tons)
Dimensions:	265 × 38½ × 10
Armament:	Not normally carried
Machinery:	2 shaft diesel engines all giving 2,690bhp
Speed:	16kts
Complement:	77
Minelaying capacity:	44

Notes:
HMS *Abdiel* was the first minelayer completed since World War II from the experience gained with HMSs *Adventure* and *Plover,* but was for disposal at March 1989. The function of the ship was to act as a support vessel for Mine Counter Measures vessels and in a lesser way as a Depot Ship for Minesweepers. Nevertheless, her prime purpose is to lay mines of various types.

During the Armilla patrol up to 1988, 1 × 30mm DP AA was sited on the forecastle and 1 × 20mm P & S aft of the bridge.

Footnote: For details of other of HM ships designed as Minelayers but not necessarily employed in that role, see *Destroyers of the Royal Navy 1893-1981, Royal Navy Submarines 1901-1982,* and *Frigates, Sloops and Patrol Vessels of the Royal Navy 1900 to date,* by this author.

HMS Abdiel *in commission in the Clyde exercise area.* (Vosper Thornycroft)

3: HM Ships and Other Vessels Converted for Minelaying

'Apollo' Class *Intrepid* Type Minelayers

HMS	Launched	Converted	Builder
Intrepid	1891	1910	London & Glasgow
Iphigenia	1891	1907	London & Glasgow

HMS Iphigenia *leaving harbour with a small run of mines on her port quarter.*

SPECIFICATION

Displacement:	3,500 tons
Dimensions:	300pp × 43¼ × 18
Armament:	4 × 4.7in QF LA on single mtgs
Machinery:	2 shaft triple expansion all giving 9,000ihp
Boilers:	5
Fuel:	580 tons of coal
Speed:	20kts
Complement:	276
Mines carried:	100 *Intrepid*, 140 *Iphigenia*
Mines actually laid:	1,439 *Intrepid*, 640 *Iphigenia*

Notes:

These two ships with *Apollo* and *Andromache* (see below) were the minelaying squadron which laid the first minefield between 3-5 October 1914 from the Dutch Coast NW to the Goodwin Sands to create the cross-channel mine barrier in which numbers of U-Boats met their timely end.

Losses:

HMS *Intrepid* and *Iphigenia* were both sunk as block ships on 23 April 1918 by own forces at Zeebrugge.

'Apollo' Class *Andromache* Type Minelayers

HMS	Launched	Converted	Builder
Andromache	1890	1909	HM Dockyard Chatham
Apollo	1891	1909	HM Dockyard Chatham
Latona	1890	1908	Vickers
Naiad	1890	1910	Vickers
Thetis	1890	1907	Vickers

SPECIFICATION

Displacement:	3,400 tons
Dimensions:	300pp × 43¼ × 18
Armament:	4 × 4.7in QF LA on single mtgs
	1 × 12pdr QF AA (*Andromache* only)
Machinery:	2 shaft triple expansion all giving 9,000ihp
Boilers:	5
Fuel:	560 tons of coal

HMS Apollo *in peacetime colours prior to her conversion as a minelayer.* (Imperial War Mueum)

Speed:	20kts
Complement:	273
Mines carried:	100
Mines actually laid:	1,425 *Andromache* 1,600 *Apollo*
	2,499 *Latona* 800 *Naiad*
	800 *Thetis*

Notes:
The last of class of the 'Apollo' class to remain in the fleet were the minelaying conversions as listed above. All at least 20 years old and being past their prime were hard put to maintain 16/17 kts, however their role as Minelayers was not in doubt.

Loss:
HMS *Thetis* was sunk as a block ship on 23 April 1918 by own forces at Zeebrugge.

Ex-Mercantile World War I Auxiliary Minelayers

HMS	Tons	Built	Speed	Armament	Minelaying capacity	Mines actually laid
Angora	4,288	1911	17kts	3 × 4.7in single, 2 × 6pdr AA	320	14,729
Biarritz	2,465	1915	23kts	2 × 12pdr single	180	5,673
Gazelle	613	1889	20kts	2 × 12pdr single	Not known	243
Old Colony	4,779	1907	Not known	Although selected for conversion she was never completed as a Minelayer and there is little information regarding this ship		
Orvieto	12,130	1909	18kts	4 × 4 7in single, 1 × 3pdr AA	600	3,131
Paris	1,774	1913	25kts	1 × 4in, 1 × 12pdr, 1 × 6pdr AA	140	6,236
Perdita	543	1910	10½kts	1 × 12pdr, 1 × 6pdr AA	100	1,332
Princess Irene	5,934	1914	23kts	2 × 4.7in single, 2 × 12pdr single, 2 × 6pdr AA	500	723
Princess Margaret	5,938	1910	23kts	2 × 4.7in single, 2 × 12 pdr single	500	25,242
Wahine	4,436	1913	21kts	2 × 14pdr, 2 × 6pdr AA	180	11,378

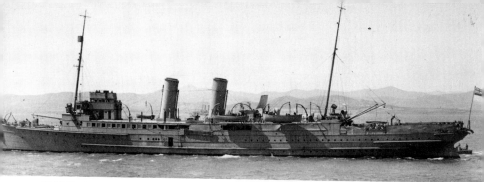

HMS Biarritz *with a large White Ensign at the stern and canvas dodgers painted in grey, both sides aft of the main mast to hide the minelaying rails, the turnout of which may be seen at the counter stern.* (Imperial War Mueum)

Notes:
These ships were requisitioned by the Admiralty from the Mercantile Marine and brief details follow below:

HMS *Angora* prior to requisition was an ocean-going passenger/cargo ship on the UK to India run;

HMS *Biarritz* was a short-range, cross-channel passenger ship, normally employed Newhaven/Dieppe;

HMS *Gazelle* was a short-range converted Channel Islands steamer;

HMS *Orvieto* was an ocean-going passenger liner, with adequate space for mine stowage, being able to carry two lays below decks, in addition to the mines already on the tram tracks. Her disadvantages were lack of speed and deep draught;

HMS *Paris,* particulars and remarks, similar to *Biarritz;*

HMS *Perdita* was a coaster which had been routed to Gallipoli with naval stores, and although small in size and slow, she was converted at Mudros. She had a capacity of 50 additional mines to be stowed below, in addition to her lay;

HMS *Princess Irene* was a passenger ship designed for the Seattle-Vancouver run. Consequently, her design gave her shallow draught and high speed, plus adequate magazine capacity;

HMS *Princess Margaret,* as *Princess Irene;*

HMS *Wahine* was a passenger ship previously on the New Zealand coastal trade. She replaced the *Orvieto* and became a very successful minelayer, despite her limited range.

Loss:
On 20 January 1915 whilst taking on mines at Sheerness, HMS *Princess Irene* was destroyed by what has been described as an internal explosion.

Landing Craft 'X' Lighter, as a Minelayer

HM 'X' Lighter	Completed	Builder
149	1915	Doxford

Dimensions:	105½ pp × 21 × 2½
Displacement:	160 tons
Machinery:	Diesel engine of 60bhp (average)

Notes:
'X' Lighters were designed as an early form of Landing Craft for the Gallipoli landings and over 100 were built. They were versatile craft, some ending their service careers having acted as fuel carriers, water carriers and coal lighters.

This is a photograph of X 224 in peacetime rig as a duty boat, flying the Blue Ensign. No known photograph exists of X 149. (National Maritime Mueum)

'X' Lighter *149* was converted to a minelaying craft and was based at Sheerness. She was engaged in completing the fields near Heligoland, together with CMBs and MLs;

HM 'X' Lighter *149* served throughout World War I and during the interwar period until 1939, thence her career is unknown.

Requisitioned Paddle (Controlled) Minelayers

HMS	Tons	Built	Armament	Minelaying Capacity	Remarks
Albert Victor	128	1883	Not known	8	Ex-*Lass O'Gowrie* Tug
America	244	1891	Not known	8	Tug
Flying Fish	187	1886	Not known	8	Conversion not completed. Tug
Ireland	245	1891	Not known	10	Tug
Queen	169	1883	Not known	8	Later *Quince*. Tug
The Lady Carmichael	376	1871	Not known	10	Paddle vessel
Golden Eagle	793	1909	Not known		Aircraft transport in World War I selected for conversion to a minelayer in 1940 to carry 10 mines but not completed
Medlar	194	1891	Not known	10	Ex-*The Mermaid*

This photograph shows HMS Golden Eagle *as a paddle steamer awaiting conversion to her designated role as a Controlled Minelayer. (National Maritime Mueum)*

Notes:
All of these requisitioned paddle steamers were converted to Controlled Minelayers. They very seldom steamed any distance and were mainly concerned with the maintenance of the controlled minefield at the port or harbour where they normally berthed. Their armament, although described as 'not known', would most likely have consisted of a number of 3 and/or 6pdr QF guns together with depth charges, to act as a gun platform to engage any entrapped U-Boat etc.

A controlled minefield consists of one or more lays across the entrance to the estuary and/or navigable channel to a port or harbour. The mines were connected by underwater cable to the shore, with provision for detonation, either singly or in multiples, when it appeared that an enemy vessel was in the vicinity of the port or harbour. Visual and hydrophone systems were used in World War I to indicate if a U-Boat was entering the harbour; late in World War I, but certainly in World War II, magnetic loops (electrified cables) were stretched across the harbour mouth for further advice of entry of a suspect vessel.

'Glorious' Class *Courageous* Type Minelayer

HMS	Launched	Converted	Builder
Courageous	1916	1917	Armstrong

HMS Courageous *prior to conversion to a minelayer.* (Imperial War Mueum)

SPECIFICATION

Dimensions:	735 pp 786½ × 81 × 22¼
Displacement:	18,800 tons
Full Load:	22,700 tons
Armament:	4 × 15in 42 Cal in 2 twin turrets in 'A' and 'Y' positions; 18 × 4in guns in 6 triple mountings, 2 × 3in singles, 4 × 3pdr singles, 5 × mg singles,
Torpedo Tubes:	2 × submerged 21in, 12 × 21in on triple mountings, 2 either beam and aft of the funnel
Machinery:	4 shaft geared turbines all giving 90,000shp
Boilers:	18
Fuel oil:	Minimum 750 tons
Speed:	31kts
Complement:	842
Minelaying capacity:	202

Note:
Although *Courageous* was converted to lay mines, she was never so employed.

'Diadem' Class *Amphitrite* Type Minelayers

HMS	Launched	Converted	Builder
Amphitrite	1898	1917	Vickers
Ariadne	1898	1917	Thomson

HMS Amphitrite *leaving harbour painted in streaky dazzle camouflage. The turnout for the minelaying rails can be seen at the stern.* (Imperial War Mueum)

SPECIFICATION

Displacement:	11,000 tons
Dimensions:	450 × 69 × 27
Armament:	4 × 6in on single mtgs, 1 × 4in DP AA
Machinery:	2 shaft triple expansion all giving 16,500ihp
Boilers:	30
Fuel:	1,730 tons coal
Speed:	22½kts
Complement:	480

Minelaying capacity:	*Amphitrite*	*Ariadne*
	354	400
Mines actually laid:	5,053	708

Notes:
Cruisers of the 'Diadem' Class when serving in their original role were somewhat similar to other cruisers of this period, having guns in shields.

They were reasonably armoured from 2in to 4½in giving long range protection from light to medium shot.

Loss:
HMS *Ariadne* on 26 July 1917 was torpedoed by *UC-65* when off Beachy Head.

Thornycroft Coastal Motor Boats 55ft (CMB)

A number of these CMBs were used for a period as Minelayers.
Coastal Motor Boats Nos *14A, 15A, 16A, 17A, 18A* and *21B* — **Builder:** J. I. Thornycroft, 1917;
Coastal Motor Boats Nos *24A, 25BB, 26B, 27A, 29A, 31BB, 33A, 34A, 36A, 65A, 75A, ·78E, 80C, 82C, 83CE, 87B, 93E, 94E, 95E, 96E* and *97E, 118CK* and *120F* (the latter 3 were not completed) — **Builder:** J. I. Thornycroft, 1918;

This is an aerial photograph of a 55 ft CMB, showing the launching trough for the torpedoes aft of the wheelhouse. This CMB is carrying seven depth charges. The aircraft recognition rondel is prominent on the bow. (Imperial War Mueum)

Coastal Motor Boats Nos *19A, 68B, 73B, 74B, 84C* and *86BD* — **Builder:** Taylor & Bates, 1918;
Coastal Motor Boats Nos *114D* and *115DE* — **Builder:** Taylor & Bates, 1919;
Coastal Motor Boats Nos *20A, 37A, 39B, 69A, 70A, 72A, 75B, 77A, 79A* and *81C* — **Builder:** Camper & Nicholson, 1918;
Coastal Motor Boats Nos *98ED* and *99ED* — **Builder:** Camper & Nicholson, 1919;
Coastal Motor Boats Nos *118D* and *119D* — **Builder:** Camper & Nicholson, 1920;
Coastal Motor Boats Nos *22B, 30B, 63BD* and *64BD* — **Builder:** Wills & Packham, 1918;
Coastal Motor Boats Nos *116D* and *117D* — **Builder:** Wills & Packham, 1919;
Coastal Motor Boats Nos *23B, 62BB* and *67A* — **Builder:** Salter Bros, 1918;
Coastal Motor Boats Nos *29A* and *35A* — **Builder:** Rowhedge Iron Works, 1918;
Coastal Motor Boats Nos *90BD, 91BD* and *92BD* — **Builder:** Rowhedge Iron Works, 1919;
Coastal Motor Boats Nos *32A, 38B, 66BB* and *71A* — **Builder:** F. Maynard, 1918;
Coastal Motor Boats Nos *85C* and *88BD* — **Builder:** F. Maynard, 1919;
Coastal Motor Boat No *89BD* — **Builder:** not known.

SPECIFICATION
Displacement: 11 tons
Dimensions: 55pp × 11 × 3
Armament: 4 × mg AA, 4 depth charges
Torpedo armament: 1 or 2 × 18in in troughs. If these craft were used for minelaying, neither torpedoes nor depth charges were carried
Machinery: 2 petrol engines to 2 shafts (see note below)
Complement: 3/5

Notes:
The letter codes after the number of the CMB gave a visual indication of the make of the engine which propelled that particular boat, as follows:

Engine Type & No		BHP	Speed	Torpedo Capacity
A 2	Thornycroft V12	each 250bhp	35¼kts	1
B 2	Green 12	each 275bhp	37kts	1
C 2	Sunbeam	each 450bhp	41kts	1
D 2	Green 18	each 450bhp	-	1
E 2	Thornycroft Y12	each 350bhp	41kts	1
F 2	Not known			1
BD 2	Green 12	each 275bhp	35kts	2
CE 2	Not known			2

CK 2 Not known			2
DE 2 Green 18	each 450bhp	40½kts	2
ED 2 Thornycroft Y12	each 350bhp	-	2

Losses:
HM CMB *18A* on 12 April 1918 was in collision off the Belgian coast;
HM CMB *24A* on 18 August 1919 in the attack on the Bolshevik Naval Base at Kronstadt;
HM CMB *33A* sank on 12 April 1918 in a surface action off Ostend;
HM CMB *82C* sank in 1923 whilst on passage to Portsmouth;
HM CMB *114D* caught fire in April 1923 off the Nab and sank;
HM CMB *39B* caught fire on 28 April 1918 at Dunkirk;
HM CMB *79A* was lost on 18 September 1919 in the attack on the Bolshevik Naval Base at Kronstadt;
HM CMB *99ED* caught fire at Portsmouth in 1920;
HM CMB *62BD* was lost on 18 September 1919 in the attack on the Bolshevik Naval Base at Kronstadt. Likewise HM *CMB 67A*;
HM CMB *90BD* was sunk in 1923 as a target;
HM CMB *71A* on 15 October 1918, missing possibly foundered, after collision off the Belgian coast.

Thornycroft Coastal Motor Boats 70ft (CMB) as Minelayers

HM CMB	Completed	Builder
100M	1919	Thornycroft
102MT	1919	Thornycroft
101M	1919	Thornycroft
103MT	1920	Camper & Nicholson
104MT	1920	Camper & Nicholson

These were the only completed boats of an intended class of 12.

SPECIFICATION
Displacement: 24 tons
Dimensions: 72½ × 14 × 3½
Armament: 6 × .303in Lewis mg

This is a post-war photograph of 100M, *but not carrying mines.* (Imperial War Mueum)

Anti-submarine:	4 × depth charges or torpedoes
Machinery:	2 petrol engines of 375bhp to each shaft
Speed:	28kts
Complement:	6
Minelaying capacity:	6

Notes:
Engine rating for M boats gave 25.96kts; engine rating for MT boats gave 36.60kts.
It is doubtful if larger naval craft with hydroplane-type hulls were ever seen in service. This length of CMB, with its emphasis from the design onwards on minelaying, would have been a useful craft, being more seaworthy than the 55fts and capable of carrying more mines. Nevertheless, they never saw action.

Ex-American/Canadian Motor Launches 75ft & 80ft (ML)

Builder:	Electric Boat Co	Canadian Vickers
Motor Launch Nos:	*1–50* inc	*51–550* and *551–580* inc
Displacement:	34 tons	37 tons
Dimensions:	75 × 12 × 4	80 × 12¼ × 4
Armament:	1 × 13pdr or 1 × 3pdr	1 × 3in
	1 or 2 mg	1 or 2 mg
Machinery:	Petrol engines	Petrol engines
	440hp to 2 shafts	440hp to 2 shafts
Anti-submarine:	depth charges	depth charges
Range:	1,000nm at 15kts	1,000nm at 15kts
Speed:	18-20kts	18-20kts
Complement:	8	10

This photograph of ML 260 *shows her carrying two mines at the rear of the mid-ships cabin – one either beam. The mines are of the contact type.* (Imperial War Mueum)

Notes:
The Motor Launch (ML) was a new type of craft for the Royal Navy and was used for many and varied tasks including inshore minesweeping, coastal mine laying, hydrophone vessels, smokescreen generators and anti-submarine tasks. The evolution of the ML was as a direct result of the great success resulting from the patrols of requisitioned Motor Boats which had been formed into the Motor Boat Reserve and were mainly craft of ex-private ownership, varying from 3 to 75 tons displacement and armed according to capacity.

The first 50 MLs were ordered from Elco in the USA with a length of 75ft with further orders for 530 launches of 80ft length from Canadian Vickers. They were too small for transatlantic delivery and so crossed to the UK on merchant ships as deck cargo.

Losses:

HM ML *19* on 31 January 1916 caught fire at Harwich;

HM ML *40* caught fire on 18 May 1916 whilst making way in the Suez Canal;

HM ML *149* on 10 September 1916 was destroyed by fire at Taranto;

HM ML *230, 253* and *255* were deck cargo on the freighter *Inververbie,* which on 14 September 1916 was torpedoed in the Gulf of Squillace;

HM ML *197* on 31 January 1917 was wrecked near Ballincourty Lighthouse;

HM ML *534* on 13 April 1917 was destroyed by fire at Taranto;

HM ML *431* on 22 April 1917 was destroyed by fire at Poole;

HM ML *540* and *541* were deck cargo on the freighter *Hunstrick,* when it was torpedoed on 8 June 1917, off Tangier;

HM ML *474* was shelled on 23 July 1917 near Chios;

HM ML *52* on 29 November 1917 was destroyed by fire in Sandown Bay;

HM ML *278* on 15 January 1918 was wrecked on Dunkirk Pier;

HM ML *55* on 28 January 1918, whilst undergoing refit was destroyed by fire in a shipyard at Sittingbourne;

HM ML *421* on 6 April 1918 was wrecked in Seaford Bay;

HM ML *356* was in collision with an unknown vessel off Dover on 11 April 1918;

HM ML *110* and *424* on 23 April 1918 were lost in action at Zeebrugge;

HM ML *254* on 10 May 1918 was sunk by own forces whilst off Ostend to avoid her falling into the hands of the enemy;

HM ML *64* was destroyed by fire in Granton Harbour on 10 June 1918;

HM ML *403* whilst endeavouring to salve a floating German torpedo in Runswick Bay contacted the pistol and blew up;

HM ML *247* on 29 September 1918 was wrecked off St Ives;

HM ML *561* was mined on 21 October 1918 off Ostend;

HM MLs *18, 62* and *191* were lost on 29 September 1919 due to heavy weather off the Norwegian coast;

HM ML *98* was lost, date, cause and place unknown;

HM ML *121* was in collision with another vessel on 22 December 1918 off the Seine Bank;

HM ML *152* took the ground on 2 January 1920 off Southern Oland;

HM ML *196* caught fire, date and place unknown;

HM ML *434* caught fire on the Danube, date and cause unknown;

HM ML *521* caught fire at Portsmouth, date and cause unknown;

HM ML *566* sank in heavy weather on 22 December 1918 off Cape Barfleur;

HM MLs *97, 127* and *229* became constructive total losses, dates, causes and places unknown.

Note:

That so many MLs should be lost by fire deserves a comment regarding their fuel. This of course was petrol and at any time was very dangerous and presumably, and in consequence thereof, 'brew ups' were not uncommon. It is surprising that only two MLs were lost by mining, but the shallow draught of these craft should be remembered.

Requisitioned Trawlers and Drifters as Minelayers WW I

HMS	Tons	Built	Armament	Remarks
Carmania II	250	1907	1 × 6pdr	
Erna	330	1915	1 × 6pdr	Was employed as a minesweeper in World War II
Hero	226	1907	1 × 6pdr	Was employed as a minesweeper in World War II under the name *Heroine*

HMS Shackleton *is shown carrying twenty-four mines (twelve either beam). She also wears her Fishery registration number with the White Ensign aft.* (Imperial War Museum)

Kate Lewis	207	1916	1 × 6pdr AA	After World War I was purchased by the Admiralty for use as a tender to HMS *Vernon*
King Emperor	246	1914	1 × 3pdr	Was employed as a minesweeper in World War II
Osta	230	1915	1 × 6pdr AA	Was employed as a minesweeper in World War II
Ostrich (later *Ostrich II*)	244	1903	1 × 6pdr AA	
Pitfour	227	1916	1 × 6pdr AA, 1 × 7½in Bomb Thrower	Was later employed as a minesweeper
Russell II	246	1906	1 × 6pdr AA	
St Maurice	251	1903	1 × 6pdr AA, 1 × 7½in Bomb Thrower	Was later employed as a minesweeper
Scott	288	1913		Struck a mine and sank on 22 October 1915 off the Tongue Light Vessel (LV)
Shackleton	288	1913	1 × 3pdr	
Strathcoe	215	1916	1 × 6pdr AA	After World War I was purchased by the Admiralty for use as a tender to HMS *Vernon,* with the name of *Vernon*
The Norman	225	1908	1 × 6pdr AA, 1 × 7½in Bomb Thrower	Was later employed as a minesweeper
Welbeck	302	1915	1 × 6pdr AA	Was in Naval Service in World War II

Note:
The above vessels were all modified to carry 24 mines.

'Arethusa' Class, *Aurora* Type Minelayers

HMS	**Launched**	**Converted**	**Builder**
Aurora	1913	1917	HM Dockyard Devonport
Galatea	1914	1917	Beardmore
Inconstant	1914	1917	Beardmore
Penelope	1914	1917	Vickers
Phaeton	1914	1917	Vickers

| *Royalist* | 1915 | 1917 | Beardmore |
| *Undaunted* | 1914 | 1917 | Fairfield |

HMS Aurora *moored at a buoy.* (Imperial War Mueum)

Displacement:	3,512 tons
Dimensions:	436 × 39 × 13½/15½
Armament:	2 × 6in on single mtgs,
	6 × 4in on single mtgs,
Undaunted	1 × 4in AA & 2 × 2pdr AA,
Aurora	2 × 3in AA
Galatea	3 × 6in on single mtgs,
Inconstant	4 × 4in on single mtgs,
Phaeton	2 × 3in AA on single mtgs
Royalist	
Penelope	3 × 6in on single mtgs,
	4 × 4in on single mtgs,
	1 × 4in AA
Torpedo tubes:	4 × 21in (all listed)
Machinery:	4 shaft turbines all giving 40,000shp
Boilers:	8
Fuel:	490 tons plus oil fuel
Speed:	28½kts
Complement:	320
Minelaying capacity:	*Penelope, Undaunted* (70); *Aurora, Galatea, Inconstant, Phaeton, Royalist* (74).
Mines actually laid:	*Aurora* 212, *Galatea* 220, *Inconstant* 370, *Penelope* 210, *Phaeton* 358, *Royalist* 1,183, *Undaunted* 0.

Notes:
Some of these cruisers were fitted with a Kite Balloon and the armour varied from 1in on the midships deck to 6in on the control tower. Later in the war a dwarf mast was fitted aft of the third funnel to carry the ends of the telegraphy aerials.

HMS Blanche *moored at a buoy. Note the canvas mine screens on the aft main deck.*

'Boadicea' Class *Bellona* Type Minelayer

HMS	Launched	Converted	Builder
Bellona	1909	1917	HM Dockyard Pembroke
Blanche	1909	1917	HM Dockyard Pembroke
Blonde	1910	1917	HM Dockyard Pembroke
Boadicea	1908	1917	HM Dockyard Pembroke

SPECIFICATION

Displacement:	*Boadicea* — 3,300, *Bellona*, *Blanche* and *Blonde* — 3,350 tons	
Dimensions:	405¼ × 41½ × 15½	
Armament:	*Blanche, Blonde*	*Bellona, Boadicea*
	8 × 4in on single mountings,	10 × 4in on single mountings,
	1 × 4in AA,	1 × 4in AA,
	4 × 3pdr,	4 × 3pdr,
	1 × mg	1 mg
Torpedo Tubes:	2 × 18in on single mountings, 1 either beam of the third funnel	2 × 18in on single mountings, 1 either beam of the third funnel
Machinery:	2 shaft turbines all giving 18,000shp	2 shaft turbines all giving 18,000shp
Boilers:	12	12
Fuel:	450 tons coal plus 190 tons oil	450 tons coal plus 200 tons oil
Speed:	24kts	25kts
Complement:	270-330	

	Minelaying capacity	Mines actually laid
HMS *Bellona*	66	305
HMS *Blanche*	65	1,238
HMS *Blonde*	66	0
HMS *Boadicea*	66	184

Notes:
Cruisers of this type were ideal for the minelaying role by reason of their long exposed main deck from the forward funnel, aft. They were only lightly armoured with 1½in on the deck to 4in on the conning tower.

Ex-Mercantile Channel Packets

HMS	Requisitioned	Builder
Anglesey (Ex-*Anglia*)	1918	Denny
Sheppey (Ex-*Hibernia*)	1918	Denny

Dimensions:	392 × 45 × 27
Displacement:	3,475 tons
Machinery:	Geared turbines 15,000shp to 2 shafts giving 25kts

Notes:
The above two ships were requisitioned by the Admiralty from the London & North Western Railway Company when under construction. They were designed as Irish Sea cross-channel steamers but Messrs Denny rapidly commenced to convert them into fast minelayers. Unfortunately they were requisitioned too late to see active service but 80 per cent of the conversion work had already been completed. No photographs are available.

'Cressy' Class *Euryalus* Type Minelayer

HMS	Launched	Converted	Builder
Euryalus	1901	1918	Vickers

HMS Euryalus *after conversion for minelaying.* (Imperial War Mueum)

SPECIFICATION
Dimensions:	472 × 69½ × 27¼
Displacement:	12,000 tons
Armament:	2 × 9.2in in single turrets,
	2 × 6in in single mtgs,
	2 × 6pdr AA, 2 × 3pdr AA
Machinery:	2 shaft triple expansion all giving 21,000ihp
Boilers:	30
Fuel:	1,600 tons coal
Speed:	21kts
Complement:	387

Notes:
HMS *Euryalus* was one of a class of six armoured cruisers. Surprisingly, the armour was supplied by Krupp and varied from 2in on the bow to 12in on the conning tower, the likely weight of armour when she was built was approximately 2,100 tons. She was built for flag duties with an Admiral's gallery at the stern.

This cruiser was in reserve at the end of World War I, but had been under conversion by Hong Kong Dockyard as a minelayer.

'London' Class *London* Type Minelayer

HMS London, *dazzle-painted, perhaps to aid her in the task of minelaying.* (Imperial War Mueum)

HMS	Launched	Converted	Builder
London	1899	1918	HM Dockyard Portsmouth

SPECIFICATION

Displacement:	15,000 tons
Dimensions:	413¼ × 75 × 28 max
Armament:	3 × 6in on single mountings,
	1 × 4in single AA, 2 mg
Torpedo Tubes:	4 × 18in submerged
Machinery:	2 shaft triple expansion all giving 15,000ihp
Boilers:	20
Fuel:	2,000 tons coal
Speed:	18kts
Complement:	481
Minelaying capacity:	240

Notes:
HMS *London* was one of a class of three battleships, and for her time was an expensive ship — the completion cost being over one million pounds — but modern ideas were incorporated with electric hoists for the ammunition; the training and elevating of the main armament was by a hydraulic system. She carried a complete set of anti-torpedo nets but the resistance from these was to reduce her speed by at least 5kts. She was armoured once again by Krupp with 3in on the deck, 12in on the after bulkhead, barbettes and conning tower, giving an estimated tonnage for the armour alone of 4,300.

HMS Medusa, *converted from her role as monitor into a minelayer. She appears to have a lay of forty mines.* (Not known)

'Medea' Class Coastal Minelayers

HMS	Launched	Converted	Builder
Medea (ex-*M22*)	1915	1922-25	Raylton Dixon
Medusa (ex-*M29*)	1915	1922-25	Harland & Wolff
Melpomene (ex-*M31*)	1915	1922-25	Harland & Wolff
Minerva (ex-*M33*)	1915	1922-25	Workman Clark

SPECIFICATION (as built)

	Medusa *Melpomene* *Minerva*	*Medea*
Displacement:	580 deep tons	610 deep tons
Dimensions:	177¼ × 31 × 6¼	173 × 31 × 6½
Armament:	Nil	Nil
Machinery:	2 shaft triple expansion all giving 400ihp	2 shaft triple expansion all giving 650ihp
Range:	1,440nm at 8kts	660nm at 9½kts
Fuel:	45 tons oil	32 tons oil
Speed:	10kts (designed)	12kts (designed)
Complement:	52	52
Minelaying capacity:	52	44

Notes:
These minelayers were conversions from a class of 15 Coastal Monitors. They were surprisingly modern in design, and were good seaboats. Normally, mine types 52 'H' or 15 'L' were carried.

HMS *Vernon* — Tenders as Minelayers

HMS	Launched	Builder
Kate Lewis	1916 (Purchased)	Cochrane
Nightingale	1931	HM Dockyard — Portsmouth
Strathcoe (later *Vernon*)	1916 (Purchased)	Hall Russell

HMS Vernon, *with minelaying stern and sheaved bow.* (National Maritime Mueum)

SPECIFICATIONS

	Kate Lewis	Nightingale	Strathcoe
Dimensions:	117½ × 22 × 12½	106 × 25½ × 6½	117½ × 22 × 15
Displacement:	325 tons	255 tons	436 tons
Armament:	Nil	Nil	Nil
Machinery:	1 shaft triple expansion of 475ihp	1 shaft triple expansion of 400ihp	1 shaft triple expansion of 430ihp
Fuel:	110 tons coal	115 tons coal	110 tons coal
Speed:	11kts	10kts	10kts
Complement:	15	12	15
Minelaying capacity:	24	20	24

Notes:
HMS *Kate Lewis* was a requisitioned trawler from World War I; HMS *Vernon* (ex-*Strathcoe*) was a hired trawler from World War I; HMS *Nightingale* was built as an HM ship (mining tender).

Vosper 72.5ft Motor Torpedo Boats (MTB) as Minelayers

Dimensions:	72½ × 19¼ × 26¼
Displacement:	40 tons
Armament (as built):	2 × .5in mg, 2 × .303in mg
Torpedo tubes:	2 × 21in
Anti-submarine:	2 × depth charges
Machinery:	3 petrol engines of 1,400hp + 1 auxiliary of 10hp, to 3 shafts giving 38½kts
Range:	400nm at 20kts
Fuel capacity:	2,540gal petrol
Complement:	14

Losses:-
HM MTB *73* on 24 November 1943, whilst off Madalena was bombed by German aircraft;
HM MTB *74* on 28 March 1942 during the raid on St Nazaire was sunk by shellfire from German shore batteries;

A 72½ ft Vosper MTB as used for minelaying. (Imperial War Mueum)

HM MTB *77* on 8 September 1943 whilst off Vito Valencia was bombed by German aircraft;
HM MTB *80* was lost in 1943, place and cause unknown;
HM MTB *87* on 31 October 1942 was mined off Lowestoft;
HM MTB *93* was in collision with MTB *729* off Harwich on 18 April 1944 and foundered;
HM MTB *222* (as RNN *Sperwer*) on 10 November 1943 was mined in the North Sea;
HM MTB *230* on 9 November 1943 was lost in collision with HM MTB *222* in the North Sea;
HM MTB *237* on 7 August 1942 was sunk in a surface action when off Barfleur;
HM MTB *241* on 31 March 1944 was sunk in a surface action when off Ijmuiden;
HM MTB *242* in May 1945 foundered whilst in tow for Malta;
HM MTB *243* in July 1945 was expended as a target by own forces whilst off Malta;
HM MTBs *284* and *285* whilst in transit as cargo on the SS *Larchbank* were lost when the latter foundered on 9 September 1943 south of Italy;
HM MTB *287* on 24 November 1944 took the ground on Levrea Island in the Adriatic Sea, and was later blown up by own forces;
HM MTB *288* was bombed by German aircraft off Augusta on 22 July 1943;
HM MTB *347* on 1 October 1944 was sunk in a surface action when off Ijmuiden;
HM MTB *352* collided with an unknown vessel on 26 March 1944 in the North Sea;
HM MTB *365* on 16 October 1943 was sunk in a surface action when off Ijmuiden; likewise *360* on 1 October 1944;
HM MTB *357* on 23 December 1943 whilst engaged in a surface action with German light forces off the Dutch coast was severely damaged by gunfire and foundered the following day;
HM MTB *371* on 24 November 1944 took the ground on Levrea Island in the Adriatic Sea, and was later blown up by own forces;
HM MTB *372* on 24 July 1944 whilst crossing the Bay of Biscay sank from gunfire in a surface action from German light forces.

Fairmile 'A' Type Motor Launch

HM ML	Completed	Builder
100	1940	Woodnutt (St Helens)
101	1940	Macraft (Sarnia)
102	1940	Woodnutt (St Helens)
103	1940	Brooke Marine (Lowestoft)
104	1940	Dickie (Bangor)

105	1940	Macraft (Sarnia)
106	1940	Grew Boats
107	1940	Grew Boats
108	1940	Midland Boat Works
109	1940	Wm Osborne (Littlehampton)
110	1940	Minette Shields (Bracebridge)
111	1940	Le Blanc S B (Weymouth)

HM ML 103 *with a lay of ground mines.* (Imperial War Mueum)

SPECIFICATION
Displacement:	60 tons
Dimensions:	110 × 17½ × 4½/6½
Armament:	1 × 3pdr, 2 × .303in mg
Anti-submarine:	12 depth charges
Machinery:	Three shaft petrol engines 1,800bhp
Speed:	25kts
Complement:	16

Notes:
All of these MLs were converted to minelayers with an alternative armament of 3 × 20mm
in lieu of the .303in mg. Minelaying capacity was 9 contact or 6 ground mines.

Losses:
HM ML *103* on 24 August 1942 was mined in the Dover Straits;
HM ML *108* on 5 September 1943 was mined in the English Channel;
HM ML *109* on 30 October 1940 was mined in the Humber Estuary;
HM ML *111* on 25 November 1940 was mined off the Humber Light Vessel.

Fairmile 'B' Type Motor Launch

Motor Launches *112-311, 336-500, 511-600, 801-933, 4001-4004, 050-129* (ex-*001-080*), all
built 1940-44 inclusive.

Two Fairmile B MLs, with the inboard one loaded with nine sinker mines and the outer ML with six ground mines. (Imperial War Mueum)

SPECIFICATION

Displacement tons:	65 to No *123*, 73 thereafter
Dimensions:	112 × 18¼ × 3¾/4¼
Armament:	1 × 3pdr and 2 × .303in mg
Anti-submarine:	Up to 12 depth charges
Machinery:	Twin shaft petrol engines 1,200bhp
Speed:	20/16¾kts
Complement:	16

Notes:
The 'B' MLs were used all over the many theatres of operations and for such tasks as Rescue MLs, Ambulance MLs, Minesweeping MLs, Minelaying MLs, and in 1940 some were armed with 2 × 21in torpedo tubes as anti-invasion attack craft. They sustained many losses as listed below;

Losses:
HM ML *130* on 7 May 1942 was sunk in action by Italian surface craft off Malta;
HM ML *132* whilst on patrol off Bone was taken by the enemy on 22 March 1942;
HM ML *133* on 11 May 1943 was lost by fire in Scottish waters;
HM ML *126* was torpedoed by a U-Boat off the west coast of Italy on 27 November 1943;
HM ML *127* on 22 November 1940 was mined in the Thames Estuary;
HM ML *129* was lost in a surface action with Italian craft off Cape Bon on 22 March 1942;
HM ML *267* when Free French-manned was lost by damage from shore batteries at St Nazaire on 28 March 1942, likewise ML *268* and ML *270,* excepting that the latter was sunk by own forces that same day;
HM ML *298* as ML 268;
HM ML *306* was damaged by shore batteries at St Nazaire on 28 March 1942 and abandoned, later she was recovered and recommissioned by the German Navy as RA9 and on 16 August 1944 was attacked by Allied aircraft off Le Havre and sank;
HM MLs *446, 447* and *457* as ML *268;*
HM ML *144* on 22 September 1941 was mined off Dungeness;
HM ML *156* on 28 March 1942 during the raid on St Nazaire was severely damaged by German shore batteries and later sunk by own forces;

HM ML *160* was bombed by German aircraft whilst in Brixham Harbour on 6 May 1942;

HM ML *169* whilst at Gibraltar on 15 February 1942 was lost by fire;

HM ML *177* on 28 March 1942 during the raid at St Nazaire was severely damaged by German shore batteries;

HM ML *183* whilst manoeuvring in Dieppe Harbour on 11 February 1945 was lost by collision;

HM ML *192* on 28 March 1942 during the raid on St Nazaire was severely damaged by German shore batteries;

HM ML *210* on 15 February 1944 was mined off Dieppe;

HM ML *216* on 19 September 1944 was mined in the North Sea and later foundered on 28 September 1944;

HM ML *219* on 21 November 1941 whilst on passage in bad weather was wrecked off Stornoway;

HM ML *230* on 17 August 1945 was in collision off the coast of Ceylon;

HM ML *242* on 29 November 1942 whilst in Freetown Harbour was lost by fire;

HM ML *251* on 6 March 1943 whilst off the Gambia river was in collision with an unknown vessel;

HM ML *258* when off Rimini was mined on 16 September 1944;

HM ML *262* on 28 March 1942 during the raid on St Nazaire was severely damaged by German shore batteries;

HM ML *265* on 1 July 1944 whilst in Freetown Harbour was lost by fire;

HM ML *287* on 1 July 1944 whilst in Freetown Harbour was lost by fire;

HM ML *288* on 11 October 1941 in bad weather foundered off West Hartlepool;

HM ML *301* on 9 August 1942 whilst in Freetown Harbour was lost by fire;

HM ML *310* on 15 February 1942 was lost during a surface action with Japanese forces off Tjebia Island;

HM ML *311* on 14 February 1942 was lost during a surface action with Japanese forces off the Banka Strait;

HM ML *339* was torpedoed by an E-Boat in the North Sea on 7 October 1942;

HM ML *352* and *353* were lost after an air attack by German aircraft on Tobruk Harbour on 14 September 1942;

HM ML *358* when off Leros on 12 November 1943 was lost in a surface action;

HM ML *387* on 5 March 1944 was destroyed by fire in Beirut Harbour;

HM ML *443* on 12 July 1944 was mined off Vada;

HM ML *444* on 22 May 1944 was lost by fire at Maddalena;

HM ML *466* on 25 March 1945 was mined off the Island of Walcheren;

HM ML *562* after an engagement with shore batteries sank off Ischia on 31 October 1944;

HM ML *563* on 16 August 1944 was mined off Frejus;

HM ML *579* was bombed on 12 October 1943 by German aircraft at Leros;

HM ML *591* took the ground and later sank in the Sittang river on 9 May 1945;

HM ML *835* was bombed on 12 October 1943 by German aircraft at Leros;

HM ML *870* on 15 October 1944 was mined off Piraeus;

HM ML *147* became a constructive total loss off Portsmouth on 3 November 1944;

HM ML *385* caught fire and became a constructive total loss off Alexandria in 1944;

HM ML *460* on 2 April 1945 became a constructive total loss off Malta;

HM ML *890* was mined off Ramree Island on 21 January 1945;

HM ML *905* took the ground and later sank on 9 May 1945 in the Sittang river;

HM ML *916* was mined off Walsoorden on 8 November 1944;

MLs *362, 363, 364, 365, 372, 373, 374, 375, 432* and *433* were destroyed by own forces whilst building in the face of the Japanese advance at Singapore in February 1942;

MLs *376* and *377* were destroyed on the stocks at Hong Kong in the face of the Japanese advance in December 1941;

MLs *436* and *437* were destroyed on the stocks at Rangoon in April 1942 in the face of the Japanese advance.

Transfers:
HM MLs *050-129* to the RCN; *829-832* and *848-857* to the SANF;
HM MLs *390-391, 412-423,* and *436-441* to the RIM;
HM MLs *400-411* to the RNZN; *424-431* and *801-827* to the RAN;
HM MLs *138, 143, 162* and *164* to the RNN;
HM MLs *123, 182, 205, 245-247, 267-269, 303, 244, 271, 266, 302, 052, 062* and *063* to the
Free French.

Builders (Craft built in the UK):
Aldous Successors (Brightlingsea): Nos *138, 170, 206, 225, 278, 301, 463, 492, 519, 559;*
Austin's (East Ham): Nos *227, 287, 450, 482, 514, 542, 549, 570, 925, 933;*
Boat Construction Co (Falmouth): Nos *137, 164, 187, 226, 261, 271, 336, 446, 471, 491;*
Brooke Marine (Oulton Broad): Nos *114, 127, 142, 147, 186, 211, 230, 248, 270, 281, 290, 344, 443, 527, 562;*
Cardnell Bros (Maylandsea): Nos *215, 288, 461, 534;*
Collins (Lowestoft): Nos *180, 262, 341, 479, 515, 541, 569, 926;*
Curtis (Looe): Nos *123, 130, 131, 139, 140, 143, 145, 146, 161, 172, 173, 174, 241, 242, 249, 250, 251, 256, 257, 276* (Par), *280, 295, 307, 308, 458, 465, 480, 481, 490, 493, 513, 521, 525, 530, 533, 566, 568;*
Dickie (Bangor): Nos *122, 162, 183, 212, 235, 460, 500, 537, 565;*
Dickie (Tarbert): Nos *124, 188, 217, 234, 337;*
Diesel Constructors (Isleworth): No *345;*
HM Dockyard (Sheerness): Nos *150, 151, 245, 246;*
Doig (Grimsby): Nos *125, 222, 286, 464, 512;*
Dorset Yacht (Hamworthy): Nos *135, 144, 189, 229, 258, 268, 293, 296, 298, 462;*
Harris (Appledore): Nos *128, 152, 184, 233, 263, 279, 303, 450, 451;*
Itchenor Shipyard: Nos *132, 191, 282, 466, 524, 558, 913;*
Johnson & Jago (Leigh-on-Sea): Nos *194, 207, 264, 274, 305, 342, 457, 469, 486, 487, 522, 532, 543, 548, 564, 572, 575, 577, 580, 581, 584, 587, 590, 593, 597, 901, 903, 907, 909, 911, 915, 918, 923;*
Wm King (Burnham-on-Crouch): Nos *169, 221, 226, 302;*
Kris Cruisers (Isleworth): No *165;*
Lady Bee (Southwick): No *117;*
Mashford Bros.(Cremyll): Nos *129, 141, 213, 255, 292, 452;*
Jas Miller (St Monance): Nos *108, 126, 159, 196, 203, 303, 313, 346, 483, 489, 518, 529, 546, 552, 573, 574, 578, 579, 585, 586, 592, 598, 902, 904, 910, 914, 919, 924, 928;*
Wm Osborne (Littlehampton): Nos *175, 210, 219, 273, 291;*
H. J. Percival (Horning): Nos *153, 193, 244, 283, 447, 470, 523, 531, 567, 917;*
Alex Robertson (Sandbank): Nos *136, 160, 197, 223, 238, 454;*
Leo Robinson (Oulton Broad): Nos *163, 178, 182, 259, 340* (Tewkesbury), *258;*
J. Sadd (Maldon): Nos *181, 253, 294, 456, 517;*
Jas Silver (Rosneath): Nos *200, 201, 232, 384;*
Solent Shipyard (Sarisbury Green): Nos *134, 177, 190, 239, 267, 285, 306, 459, 472, 526, 563;*
Southampton Steam Joinery: No *252;*
Sussex Sbdg (Shoreham): Nos *133, 148, 202, 216, 231, 299, 488, 496;*
Jas Taylor (Chertsey): Nos *185, 205, 209, 453, 520, 571, 576, 588, 905, 908, 922;*
Thomson & Balfour (Bo'ness): Nos *240, 275, 478, 494;*
Thornycroft (Hampton): Nos *157, 195, 260, 343;*
Tough Bros (Teddington): Nos *113, 171, 199, 220, 228, 448;*
J. W. & A. Upham (Brixham): Nos *166, 167, 179, 236, 237, 247, 254, 277, 297, 309, 445, 511;*
Wallasea Bay Yacht Stn.: Nos *224, 272, 289, 339;*
Wm. Weatherhead (Cockenzie): Nos *168, 218, 243, 269, 300, 455, 473, 495, 516, 535;*
Woodnutt (St. Helen's): Nos *112, 155, 198;*
          (Portsmouth): No *149;*

(Dumbarton): Nos *121, 154, 176;*
(Rochford): No *156;*
(Southampton): Nos *158, 192, 208, 265, 338, 449, 467, 468, 497;*
(Northam): Nos *204, 498, 499;*
(Blyth): No *214;*
Builders unknown: Nos *115, 116, 118, 119, 120, 347, 444, 484, 485, 536, 538, 539, 540, 544, 545, 547, 551, 553, 554, 555, 556, 557, 560, 561, 582, 583, 589, 591, 594, 595, 596, 599, 600, 906, 912, 916, 920, 921, 927, 929, 930, 931, 932.*

Builders (Craft built abroad):
Anglo-American Nile Tourist Co (Cairo): Nos *360, 361, 386, 387, 835, 836;*
Assoc Boat Bldr (Auckland): Nos *403, 404, 405, 406;*
Bailey (Auckland): Nos *400, 401, 402;*
Belmont Dock (Jamaica): Nos *378, 379, 422, 423, 858, 859;*
A. C. Benson (Vancouver): Nos *068, 069, 128, 129;*
C. L. Burland (Bermuda): Nos *368, 369, 370, 371;*
Burn & Co (Calcutta): No *441;*
Thos Cook (Cairo): Nos *384, 385;*
Garden Reach (Calcutta): Nos *412, 413, 414, 415, 418, 439, 440, 477;*
Greavette Boats (Gravenhurst): Nos *054, 055, 056, 077, 078, 114;*
Green Point Boatyard (Sydney): Nos *424, 425, 426, 427, 428, 429, 430, 431, 801, 802, 803, 804, 805, 806, 807, 808, 809, 810, 811, 812;*
Grew Boats (Penatanguishene): Nos *072, 073, 098, 099, 100, 106, 107, 117;*
Halvorsen (Sydney): Nos *813, 814, 817, 818, 819, 820, 821, 822, 823, 824, 825;*
Hunter Boats (Orillia): Nos *060, 061, 085, 092, 093, 109, 116;*
Indian General Nav & Rly Co (Calcutta): Nos *438, 474, 475, 476;*
Le Blanc Sbdg (Weymouth): Nos *064, 065, 083, 084, 120, 121;*
Louw & Halvorsen (Capetown): Nos *383, 829, 830, 831, 832, 846, 847, 854, 855;*
MacCraft (Sarnia): Nos *062, 063, 115;*
Midland Boat Works: Nos *050, 051, 081, 082, 094, 095, 118;*
Minette Shields (Bracebridge): Nos *057, 058, 059, 074, 075, 076, 096, 097, 110, 119;*
H. Mahatta (Karachi): Nos *843, 844, 845;*
Rangoon Dockyard: contracts transferred to Calcutta;
Shipbuilding Ltd (Auckland): Nos *407, 408, 409;*
Star Shipyard (New Westminster): Nos *070, 071, 125, 126, 127;*
Singapore Harbour Board: Nos *310, 311, 432, 433;*
Taikoo Dock (Hong Kong): Nos *376, 377, 434, 435;*
Task Rly & Port Service (Dar-es-Salaam): Nos *366, 367, 833, 834;*
J. J. Taylor (Toronto): Nos *052, 053, 079, 080, 086, 088, 089, 090, 091, 112, 113;*
Vancouver Shipyard: Nos *066, 067, 122, 123, 124;*
Voss Ltd (Auckland): Nos *410, 411;*
    (Singapore): Nos *362, 363, 364, 365, 372, 373, 374, 375, 388, 389;*
    (Alexandria): Nos *348, 349, 350, 351, 352, 353, 354, 355, 356, 357, 358, 359, 837, 838, 839, 840, 841, 842, 860, 861, 862, 863, 864, 865, 866, 867, 868, 869, 870, 871, 872;*
    (Bombay): Nos *390, 391, 420, 421;*
    (Calcutta): Nos *416, 417, 419, 436 & 437,* (both ex-Rangoon);
    (East London): Nos *848, 849, 850, 851, 856, 857;*
    (Knysna): Nos *852, 853;*
    (East Africa): Nos *4001, 4002, 4003, 4004;*
Norman Wright (Brisbane): Nos *815, 816, 826;*
Builders unknown: Nos *380, 381, 382, 392, 393, 394, 395, 396, 397, 398, 399, 442, 828, 873, 874, 875, 876, 877, 878, 879, 880, 881, 882, 883, 884, 885, 886, 887, 888, 889, 890, 891, 892, 893, 894, 895, 896, 897, 898, 899, 900.*

Fairmile 'D' Type Motor Gun Boats (MGB), Motor Torpedo Boats (MTB), Interchangeable

A Fairmile D (MGB 642) of the type used for minelaying. (Imperial War Mueum)

All built 1942-1944. Motor Gun Boats (MGB) and Motor Torpedo Boats (MTB) interchangeable and described in this text as MTB except as otherwise stated. MTBs *601–800*.

SPECIFICATION	MGB	MTB	MGB/MTB
Displacement:	90 tons	95 tons	105 tons
Dimensions:	all craft 11Owl 115 × 21¼ × 5		
Armament:	all craft 1 × 2pdr, 2 × 20mm, 4 × .5in mg, 4 × .303in mg		
Torpedo tubes:	Nil	2 × 21in	4 × 18in
Depth charges:	2+	2+	2+
Machinery:	all craft 4 shaft petrol engines 5,000bhp		
Speed:	31/27½kts	31/27½kts	29/26kts
Complement:	24	24	30

Notes:
Designed for two roles and the hardest hitting of all Royal Navy coastal craft. Some hulls built with scallops on the bow for the better clearance of torpedoes when discharged.

Minelayers were in general of the Fairmile Modified 'D' Type but included boats Nos *725-800* above.

Losses:
HM MTB *601* caught fire at Dover on 4 July 1942;
HM MTB *605* foundered when off Ostend on 17 April 1945;

HM MTB *606* sank after surface action off the Dutch coast 14 November 1943;

HM MTB *622* sank after surface action from German light forces near Terschelling on 10 March 1943;

HM MTB *625* was lost in home waters in 1944, no other particulars available;

HM MTB *626* caught fire at Lerwick on 22 November 1943;

HM MTB *631* went aground on the Norwegian coast and was captured by German land forces, on 14 March 1943;

HM MTB *635* was damaged and expended as a target off Malta in July 1945;

HM MTB *636* on 15 October 1943 sank as a result of gunfire from enemy batteries on Elba;

HM MTB *639* sank after surface action with the Italian TB *Sagittario* when off Tunisia on 28 April 1943;

HM MTB *640* was mined on 27 June 1944 when off Spezia;

HM MGB *641* sank after severe gunfire from enemy batteries in the Straits of Messina, on 14 July 1943;

HM MGB *644* was mined west of Sicily on 26 June 1943 and sunk by own forces;

HM MGB *648* sank after air attack when off Pantellaria on 14 June 1943;

HM MTB *655* was mined in the Adriatic on 22 March 1945;

HM MTB *657* on 12 February 1944 was mined off Rimini;

HM MGB *663* on 10 October 1944 was mined off Rimini;

HM MTB *665* sank from gunfire of shore batteries when off Messina, on 15 August 1943;

HM MTB *666* sank after surface action with German light forces off the Dutch coast on 5 July 1944;

HM MTB *669* sank after surface action with German light forces off the Norwegian coast on 26 October 1943;

HM MTB *671* sank after surface action with German destroyers on 24 April 1944 when off Cape Barfleur;

HM MTB *672* was mined on 29 April 1944 when off Dartmouth;

HM MTB *681* sank after surface action with German light forces off the Dutch coast on 10 June 1944;

HM MTB *686* caught fire at Lerwick on 22 November 1943;

HM MTB *690* sank after colliding with a wreck off Lowestoft on 18 January 1945;

HM MTB *697* was mined in the Adriatic on 17 April 1945;

HM MTB *705* was mined in the Adriatic on 23 March 1945;

HM MTB *707* sank after colliding with the FFS *L'Escarmouche* off the coast of Ulster, on 18 August 1944;

HM MTB *708* was attacked in error by Allied aircraft in the English Channel and finally sunk by own forces on 5 May 1944;

HM MTB *710* was mined on 10 April 1945 when off Zara;

HM MTB *712* was lost off Scarpa and formally paid off on 19 July 1945;

HM MTB *715* sank after an explosion at Fosnavaag on 19 May 1945;

HM MTB *732* was attacked in error by FFS *La Combattante* on 28 May 1944 in the English Channel;

HM MTB *734* on 26 June 1944 was attacked in error by an Allied aircraft but the still floating hull was sunk by units of the Royal Navy in the North Sea;

HM MTBs *776, 789, 791* and *798* were lost in the Port of Ostend as a result of an explosion and later fire, from unsafe ordnance on 14 February 1945;

HM MTB *782* on 19 December 1944, was mined in the Scheldt Estuary.

Builder:

Austins (East Ham):	Nos *745, 773, 789;*
Boat Construction Co (Falmouth):	Nos *635, 650, 659;*
Brooke Marine (Lowestoft):	Nos *611, 622, 639, 660, 681, 695, 711, 729, 762;*
Collins (Lowestoft):	Nos *740, 783;*
Dickie (Bangor):	Nos *604, 620, 638, 647, 671, 679, 714, 717, 726, 750, 771, 777;*
Dickie (Tarbert):	Nos *615, 629, 664;*

Dorset Yacht (Hamsworthy):	Nos *619, 624, 633, 648, 662, 666, 685, 699, 713, 732, 752, 778, 800;*
J. Hall (Glampton):	*612, 613, 645, 652, 702;*
P. K. Harris (Appledore):	*618, 627, 642, 665, 687, 723, 757, 788;*
Wm King (Burnham-on-Crouch):	Nos *609, 631, 667;*
Kris Cruisers (Isleworth):	Nos *602, 632, 666;*
Lady Bee (Southwick):	No *654;*
Wm Osborne (Littlehampton):	Nos *605, 616, 617, 634, 655, 663, 700, 710, 728, 748, 749, 787, 795;*
Risdon Beazley (Northam):	Nos *646, 649;*
Leo A. Robinson (Lowestoft):	No *770;*
Alex Robertson (Sandbank):	Nos *625, 630, 637, 653, 661, 675, 691, 781, 731, 758;*
Jas A. Silver (Rosneath):	Nos *607, 608, 621, 636;*
Sussex Shipbuilding (Shoreham):	No *774;*
Thomson & Balfour (Bo'ness):	Nos *641, 668;*
Tough Bros (Teddington):	Nos *601, 603, 626, 644, 651, 673, 674, 703;*
J. W. & A. Upham (Brixham):	Nos *628, 658;*
Wallasea Bay Yacht Stn:	Nos *606, 623, 640, 658;*
Woodnutt (St Helen's):	Nos *610, 614, 643, 657, 684, 697, 715, 730, 759, 799;*
Builders unknown:	Nos *669, 670, 672, 676, 678, 680, 682, 683, 686, 688, 690, 692, 694, 696, 698, 701, 704, 709, 712, 716, 719, 722, 724, 725, 717, 733, 739, 741, 744, 746, 751, 753, 756, 760, 761, 763, 769, 772, 775, 776, 779, 782, 784, 786, 794, 797.*

Modified Fairmile 'D' Type, Interchangeable MGBs and MTB

HM MGB/MTB	Completed	Builder
5001	1944	Woodnutt (St Helen's)
5002	1944	Not known
5003	1944	Not known
5004	1944	Not known
5005	1944	Wm Osborne (Littlehampton)
5006	1944	Not known
5007	1944	Not known
5008	1944	Not known
5009	1944	Not known
5010	1944	Dickie (Bangor)
5011	1944	Not known
5012	1944	Austins (East Ham)
5013	1944	Austins (East Ham)
5014	1944	Woodnutt (St Helen's)
5015	1944	Not known
5016	1944	Not known
5017	1944	Not known
5018	1944	Not known
5019	1944	Not known
5020	1944	Wm Osborne (Littlehampton)
5021	1944	Not known
5022 (ex-785)	1944	Brooke Marine (Lowestoft)
5024	1944	Dickie (Bangor)
5025	1944	Not known
5026	1944	Not known
5027	1944	Not known
5028	1944	Woodnutt (St Helen's)
5029	1944	Not known

SPECIFICATION

Displacement tons:	as for Fairmile 'D' Type
Dimensions:	110wl 115 × 21¼ × 5
Armament:	2 × 6pdr and 2 × 20mm
Torpedo tubes:	2 × 21in excepting Minelayers which had 4 × 18in
Machinery:	4-shaft petrol engines, 5,000bhp
Speed:	as for Fairmile 'D' Type
Range:	1,200nm at 10kts
Complement:	as for Fairmile 'D' Type

Notes:
Some of this type were completed as Long Range Rescue Craft for the RAF. Forty 'D' and Modified 'D' completed as minelayers.

Loss:
HM MGB *5001* on 7 April 1945 sank after a surface action with an E-Boat.

Ex-Mercantile World War II Auxiliary Minelayers

HMS Agamemnon *at a mooring.* (Imperial War Mueum)

HMS	Built	Converted	Builder
Agamemnon	1929	1940	Workman Clark
Tons gross:	7,593		
Deep displacement:	13,735		
Dimensions:	460pp × 59½		
Armament:	2 × 4in AA, 2 × 2pdr AA, 4 × 20mm AA, 2 × twin .5in mg AA		
Machinery:	2 shaft diesel		
Speed:	16kts		
Minelaying capacity:	520		
Mines actually laid:	24,216		

HMS	Built	Converted	Builder
Kung Wo	1921	1941	Hong Kong & Whampoa Dockyard
Tons gross:	4,636		
Dimensions:	362½ × 48½		
Armament:	2 × 4in AA		
Machinery:	2 shaft triple expansion		
Speed:	14kts		
Minelaying capacity:	240		

Loss:
On 20 and 21 January 1942 *Kung Wo* was bombed by Japanese aircraft at Singapore and again on 14 February 1942 when off the Linnga Archipeligo and became a constructive total loss.

HMS	Built	Converted	Builder
Hampton			
(ex-*Hampton Ferry*)	1934	1939	Swan Hunter
Tons gross:	2,839		
Dimensions:	347pp × 60¼		
Armament:	1 × 4in AA, 2 × .5in mg AA		
Machinery:	2 shaft geared turbines		
Speed:	15kts		
Minelaying capacity:	270		
Mines actually laid:	5,190		

HMS	Built	Converted	Builder
Menestheus	1929	1939	Caledon (Dundee)
Tons gross:	7,494		
Deep displacement:	13,735		
Dimensions:	460pp × 59½		
Armament:	2 × 4in AA, 2 × 2pdr AA, 4 × 20mm AA, 4 × .5in AA		
Machinery:	2 shaft diesel		
Speed:	15kts		
Minelaying capacity:	410		
Mines actually laid:	22,866		

HMS Menestheus *at her moorings in a Scottish loch. Note her two level mine doors.*
(Imperial War Mueum)

HMS	Built	Converted	Builder
Port Napier	1940	1940	Swan Hunter
Tons gross:	9,847		
Dimensions:	524 × 69		
Armament:	2 × 4in AA, 2 × 2pdr AA		
Machinery:	1 shaft diesel		
Speed:	16kts		
Minelaying capacity:	550		
Mines actually laid:	6,331		

Loss:
HMS *Port Napier* caught fire and was abandoned on 27 November 1940 in Loch Alsh.

HMS	Built	Converted	Builder
Port Quebec	1939	1939	Thompson
Tons gross:	5,936		
Deep displacement:	8,490		
Dimensions:	468 × 59½		
Armament:	2 × 4in AA, 2 × 2pdr AA, 4 × 20mm AA, 2 × .5in AA mg		
Machinery:	1 shaft diesel		
Speed:	15kts		
Minelaying capacity:	548		
Mines actually laid:	33,494		

HMS	Built	Converted	Builder
Princess Victoria	1939	1939	Denny
Tons gross:	2,197		
Dimensions:	305¼ × 48 × 12		
Armament:	2 × 12pdr AA		
Machinery:	2 shaft diesel		
Speed:	20½kts		
Minelaying capacity:	244		
Mines actually laid:	2,756		

Loss:
HMS *Princess Victoria* on 19 May 1940 was mined off the Humber.

HMS	Built	Converted	Builder
Shepperton (ex-*Shepperton Ferry*)	1935	1939	Swan Hunter
Tons gross:	2,839		
Dimensions:	347pp × 60¼		
Armament:	1 × 4in AA, 2 × .5in AA mg		
Machinery:	2 shaft turbines		
Speed:	15kts		
Minelaying capacity:	270		
Mines actually laid:	2,742		

Loss:
HMS *Shepperton* on 5 May 1941 became a constructive total loss during an air-raid on Belfast.

HMS Southern Prince *at her moorings taking on mines from a Lighter.* (Imperial War Mueum)

HMS	Built	Converted	Builder
Southern Prince	1929	1939	Lithgow
Tons gross:	10,917		
Dimensions:	496pp × 64¼ × 26½		
Armament:	2 × 4in AA, 2 × 2pdr AA, 4 × 20mm AA, 4 × .5in AA mg		
Machinery:	2 shaft diesel		
Speed:	16kts		
Minelaying capacity:	560		
Mines actually laid:	23,762		

HMS	Built	Converted	Builder
Teviot Bank	1938	1939	Readhead
Tons gross:	5,087		
Dimensions:	429 × 58½ × 25		
Armament:	1 × 12pdr AA, 2 × .5in mg AA		
Machinery:	1 shaft triple expansion		
Speed:	15kts		
Minelaying capacity:	272		
Mines actually laid:	15,865		

Minelayer Base Ships but Served as Minelayers

HMS	Built	Builder
Alca	1927	Caledon (Dundee)
Tons gross:	3,712	
Deep displacement:	4,200	
Dimensions:	320pp × 46¼ × 23	
Armament:	4 × 20mm AA	
Machinery:	1 shaft triple expansion	
Minelaying capacity:	234	

HMS	Built	Builders
Atreus	1911	Scotts (Greenock)
Tons gross:	6,546	
Deep displacement:	10,000	
Dimensions:	443½pp × 52¼ × 22½	
Armament:	1 × 12pdr AA, 4 × 20mm AA, 8 × .5in mg AA	
Machinery:	1 shaft triple expansion	
Minelaying capacity:	246	

HMS	Built	Builders
Helvig	1937	Helsingfors
(Seized 1940)		
Tons gross:	2,252	
Deep displacement:	2,800	
Dimensions:	325pp × 45¼	
Armament:	4 × 20mm AA	
Machinery:	1 shaft diesel	
Minelaying capacity:	258	

HMS	Built	Builders
Manchester City	1937	Blythswood
Tons gross:	5,600	
Deep displacement:	11,791	
Dimensions:	446½ × 57 × 26	
Armament:	1 × 12pdr AA, 4 × .303in mg Lewis	
Machinery:	1 shaft turbine	
Minelaying capacity:	590	

Miscellaneous Vessels Requisitioned as Minelayers

HMS	Tons	Built	Converted
Alsey	416	1932	1940
Blue Tit	53	1936	1940
(Ex-*Anna Leopold*)			
Jay	352	1926	1940
(Ex-*Nautilus*) (later *Sandmartin*)			
Snakefly	310	1930	1939
(Ex-*Fane*)			

Notes:
HMS *Blue Tit* was employed as an Observation Minelayer. These trawlers were all returned to their owners at the end of World War II.

HMS	Completed	Builder
Loch Nevis	1934	W. Denny
Tons gross:	568	
Tons nett:	228	
Dimensions:	171¼ × 31 × 8½	
Armament:	Not known	
Machinery:	Diesel-electric, two 6-cylinder diesels of 1,300bhp and two electric motors of 1,050bhp to 2 shafts giving 15kts	

HMS Loch Nevis, *very comprehensively converted from her peacetime role. Note the bow sheaves and working derricks.* (Imperial War Mueum)

Note:
HMS *Loch Nevis* was built for service on the Clyde as a passenger ferry but served from the outbreak of war until 1944 as a minelayer.

HMS	Tons	Converted	Completed
Rhu	254	1941	1940

Note:
HMS *Rhu* was in Singapore Dockyard in January 1942 and taken over by the Japanese Navy. She was commissioned as Anti-Submarine Vessel No 21 and served at least until 1944.

HMS	Ex-French
Chaffinch	*Nacqueville*
Greenfinch	*Lama*
Hawfinch	*Honfleurais*

	Ex-Belgian
Goldfinch (I)	*Antwerp 33*
later *Greenfinch (II)*	

Notes:
The above four vessels were tugs taken over in June 1940 and used as Observation Minelayers. There were no losses.

Ex-Japanese 'Hatsutaka' Class *Laburnum* Type Minelayer

HMS	Ex-Japanese	Completed	Builder
Laburnum	*Wakataka*	1941	Harima Dockyard

This photograph shows a sister ship of HMS Laburnum, *which was the appropriated Japanese minelayer/netlayer* Wakataka. *The ship in the photograph is* Hatsutaka. (Imperial War Mueum)

SPECIFICATION
Displacement: 1,608 tons
Dimensions: 269½pp × 37 × 13½
Original Armament: 2 × 3in on single mountings
4 × 40mm AA as above
4 × 25mm AA on two twin mtgs

Machinery:	2 shaft geared turbines all giving 6,000shp
Boilers:	3
Speed:	20kts
Minelaying capacity:	360

Notes:
The *Wakataka* was built as a dual purpose Minelayer/Netlayer and in the latter role could dispense up to 25 anti-submarine nets. By 1944, however, her minelaying rails had been removed and she was employed as an A/S convoy escort, and in the same year was torpedoed but repaired. At the Japanese surrender she was under Allied control as a repatriation transport until October 1947 when she was re-named and commissioned into the Royal Navy for use by the Malayan Division of the Royal Naval Volunteer Reserve. She served in that role until 1967 being then disposed of. Her Japanese name meant 'Young Hawk'.

Photographic Note:
The photograph is of the *Hatsutaka,* sister ship of the *Wakataka.*

Ex-German Minelaying Tenders

HMS	Ex-German
Dipper	*C 30*
Diver	*C 28*
Displacement:	120 tons
Dimensions:	60 × 16½
Machinery:	Diesel
Speed:	9kts

HMS Dipper. *This photograph shows the German C30 as commissioned under the White Ensign.* (Wright & Logan)

Note:
These craft were used in the 1950s as diving tenders for HMS *Lochinvar,* the experimental minesweeping establishment.

HMS	Ex-German
Clearwater	*Lumme*
Displacement:	62 tons
Dimensions:	85 × 15 × 4½
Machinery:	1 diesel 180bhp giving 9kts
Complement:	9

Notes:
This craft was used in the 1950s as a tender to HMS *Vernon* for harbour diving instruction.
   All three craft when in the German Navy were designated Minelaying Tenders.

Ex-German (Prize)

HMS	Ex-German	Captured by
Sprindrift	2623	HMS *Arrow*
	(Schiff 26)	
Displacement:	926 tons	
Dimensions:	160 × 26	

Notes:
This German trawler was boarded by a party from HMS *Arrow* in position 62°37' North 00°40' East on 26 April 1940 and escorted to the UK by HMS *Griffin*. She was commissioned into the Royal Navy as a Controlled Minelayer and at the close of World War II was transferred to SANF.

'Dark' Class MTBs, Interchangeable as Minelayers

HMS Dark Rover *at speed in the Solent. She is not armed and the rails for the torpedo tubes, which would be removed for minelaying, are visible on deck.* (Vosper Thornycroft)

HMS	Completed	Builder
Dark Adventurer	1954	Saunders Roe (Anglesey)
Dark Aggressor	1954	Saunders Roe (Anglesey)
Dark Antagonist	1955	Saunders Roe (Anglesey)
Dark Avenger	1955	Saunders Roe (Anglesey)
Dark Biter	1955	Saunders Roe (Anglesey)

Dark Buccaneer	1954	Vosper
Dark Clipper	1955	Vosper
Dark Fighter	1955	Taylor
Dark Gladiator	1956	Taylor
Dark Hero	1957	McGrue Boats
Dark Highwayman	1955	Vosper
Dark Hunter	1954	Miller
Dark Hussar	1957	J. I. Thornycroft
Dark Intruder	1955	Morgan Giles
Dark Invader	1955	Morgan Giles
Dark Killer	1956	J. I. Thornycroft
Dark Rover	1954	Vosper
Dark Scout	1958	Saunders Roe (Anglesey)

SPECIFICATION

Displacement:	64 tons
Dimensions:	71½ × 19¼ × 3¼ mean
Armament (as MGB):	1 × 4.5in 25 cal, 1 × 40mm Bofors or 2 × 40mm Bofors
(as MTB):	1 × 40mm Bofors, 4 × 21in torpedo tubes
Anti-submarine:	1 or 2 depth charge racks were fitted on some boats
Mines:	HMS *Dark Antagonist* and possibly others of this Class were used for minelaying with a capacity of 6 ground mines
Machinery:	Twin diesel engines, 5,000shp
Speed:	47kts
Sea Speed:	40kts
Fuel:	8 tons oil
Complement:	15

Notes:
Built of composite aluminium and wood. HMS *Dark Scout* was, however, built entirely of aluminium.

Cancellations:
The following boats of the 'Dark' class were under construction to a greater or lesser extent but all cancelled; *Dark Attacker, Dark Battler* and *Dark Bowman* by Saunders Roe (Anglesey) Ltd; *Dark Chaser, Dark Chieftain* and *Dark Crusader* by Vosper Ltd; *Dark Defender* and *Dark Explorer* by J. I. Thornycroft & Co; and *Dark Horseman* by McGrue Boats Ltd.

'Brave' Class, Fast Patrol Boats as Minelayers

HMS	**Completed**	**Builder**
Brave Borderer	1960	Vosper
Brave Swordsman	1960	Vosper

SPECIFICATION

Displacement:	89 tons (Full load: 114 tons)
Dimensions:	99pp 96wl 98¼ × 25½ × 6¼
Armament (as MGB):	2 × 40mm Bofors and 2 × 21in side-launched torpedoes
(as MTB):	1 × 40mm Bofors and 4-21in side-launched torpedoes
Machinery:	3 gas turbine propulsion units, 10,500shp
Speed:	50kts plus (trials)
Fuel:	25 tons oil
Complement:	20 or 22 as Senior Officer's Ship

HMS Brave Borderer. *A profile view, showing five ground mines either beam.*

Note:
Built with an aluminium hull and sheathed with glass fibre below the water line.

Gunnery Note:
The designed armament was one 3.3in turret-mounted gun with built-in stabilisation, also 1 × 40mm Bofors and 2 × 21in torpedo tubes. Designed for high-speed minelaying.

Passenger Vehicle Ferry *Ailsa Princess* as a Minelayer

	Completed	Converted	Builder
Ailsa Princess	1971		Cantiere Navale Breda Venezia
		1982	Cammell Laird

SPECIFICATION
Gross tons:	3,715
Nett registered:	1,442
Dimensions:	369½ × 55½ × 12¼
Machinery:	2 shaft diesel engines all giving 15,560bhp
Fuel:	117 tons heavy 1000 seconds oil
Speed:	19½kts
Range:	12,000nm at 12kts
Complement:	48
Naval Party:	40
Minelaying capacity:	For a ship of this size and type, possibly 500

Notes:
MV *Ailsa Princess* was chartered to MOD(N) in November 1982 and converted to an Experimental Minelayer by Cammell Laird. She took on and laid practice mines during her Naval requisition and has since reverted to her normal trade. Whilst on charter, *Ailsa Princess* wore the Blue Ensign.

MV Ailsa Princess *as chartered by MOD(N) for temporary conversion to a minelayer.*

'Castle' Class OPV2 as Minelayers

HMS Leeds Castle *in the Firth of Forth, spring 1983. She has been modified to carry and lay mines, eight of which may be seen on the main deck before the stern.* (MOD(N))

HMS	Launched	Completed	Builder
Dumbarton Castle	1981	1982	Hall Russell
Leeds Castle	1980	1982	Hall Russell

SPECIFICATION

Displacement:	1,450 tons
Dimensions:	265¼ × 37¼ × 11¼
Armament:	1 × 40mm 40/60 AA Bofors in lieu of the intended Oto Melera 76mm
Machinery:	Two diesel engines with an MCR of 2,820bhp with each driving a variable pitch propeller.
Speed:	20kts
Range:	12,000nm at 12kts
Fuel:	180 tons
Auxiliary Machinery:	Three diesel alternator sets plus one emergency set
Helicopter:	The OPV2 (Ocean Patrol Vessel Mk 2) is designed with a helicopter flight deck, consequently there is provision for landing, take-off and servicing of either a Sea King or Lynx aircraft.
Stabilisers:	Fitted with non-retractable active fin type

Class Note:
These vessels are the logical development of the OPV1 'Island' class vessels built for fishery protection and North Sea patrol work.

Minelaying:
In April 1983 both HMSs *Dumbarton Castle* and *Leeds Castle* were temporarily fitted with twin sets of minelaying rails for over a month to prove their capability as minelayers.

'Tornado' Class Torpedo Recovery Vessels as Minelayers

HMS/RMAS	Commenced	Completed	Builder
Torch	1978	1980	All by Hall Russell
Toreador	1979	1980	

Tormentor	1979	1980
Tornado	1978	1979

HMS Tornado, *prior to conversion to a minelayer. Note the hydraulic mechanism for the stern door.* (J. W. Goss)

Specification as built

Displacement:	660 tons
Full load:	698 tons
Dimensions:	155½ × 28 × 10
Armament:	Small arms
Machinery:	2 shaft diesel engines all giving 2,200bhp
Range:	3,000nm at 10kts
Fuel:	110 tons of diesel oil
Complement:	As a TRV, 14

Construction Note:
All built with a stern ramp for easier handling of recovered torpedoes.

Minelaying Note:
It was announced in October 1991 that the above TRVs would be converted as and when required to act as practice minelayers.

Minelaying Capacity:
20 or 16 mines will be carried according to type, on minelaying rails installed either beam of the vessel. Sponsons will be fitted outboard of each set of rails with associated handling and laying equipment. The installation, which is removable, is designated FEMS (Fleet Exercise Minelaying System).

Manning:
Originally manned by the Royal Maritime Auxiliary Service but may become RN-manned and HM ships.

4: HM Minesweepers

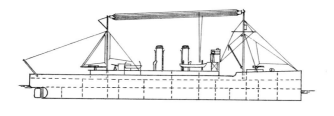

ACACIA CLASS 1915

HMS Acacia. *This is a good view of the nameship of this Class, and apart from photographic distortion on the bows, very little comment is needed. The bow gun is unshielded, there are canvas dodgers on the bridge wings with one searchlight either beam and the minesweeping davit is right aft; a very good telegraphy aerial is fitted.* (Imperial War Museum)

'Acacia' Class Fleet Sweeping Sloop

HMS	Launched	Builder
Acacia	1915	Swan Hunter
Anemone	1915	Swan Hunter
Aster	1915	Earle
Bluebell	1915	Scotts
Daffodil	1915	Scotts
Dahlia	1915	Barclay Curle
Daphne	1915	Barclay Curle
Foxglove	1915	Barclay Curle
Hollyhock	1915	Barclay Curle
Honeysuckle	1915	Lobnitz
Iris	1915	Lobnitz
Jonquil	1915	Connell
Laburnum	1915	Connell
Larkspur	1915	Napier & Miller
Lavender	1915	McMillan
Lilac	1915	Greenock
Lily	1915	Barclay Curle
Magnolia	1915	Scotts
Mallow	1915	Barclay Curle
Marigold	1915	Bow McLachlan
Mimosa	1915	Bow McLachlan
Primrose	1915	Simons
Sunflower	1915	Henderson
Veronica	1915	Dunlop Bremner

SPECIFICATION
Displacement: 1,200 tons
Dimensions: 262½ × 33 × 11¼
Armament: 2 × single 12pdr, in 'A' and 'X' positions, and 2 × 3pdr AA
Machinery: 1 shaft triple expansion (4 cyl) giving 2,200ihp
Boilers: 2

Fuel:	130 tons coal minimum
Speed:	17kts
Range:	2,000nm at 15kts
Complement:	77

Notes:

The first class of sloops to be built this century and for World War I, being dual-purpose vessels and officially described as Fleet Sweeping Sloops. The construction of the bows is understood to have involved triple hulls with the intention of resistance to exploding mine-pressure and detonations. Being fuelled by coal these ships were renowned for their prowess in giving off great clouds of smoke, and after dark, streams of sparks from their funnels. They were also known as the 'Flower' class, 'Cabbage' class and/or 'Herbaceous Borders'.

Losses:

HMS *Aster* on 4 July 1917 struck a mine and sank off Malta;

HMS *Laburnum* in February 1942, whilst on the Far East station and based at Singapore, was overtaken by the Japanese advance and lost at the fall of Singapore;

HMS *Lavender* on 4 May 1917 was torpedoed by the German submarine *UC-75* in the English Channel;

HMS *Mallow* was transferred to the Royal Australian Navy in 1919 and sunk as a target ship on 1 August 1935 off Sydney Heads.

'Azalea' Class Fleet Sweeping Sloop

HMS	Launched	Builder
Azalea	1915	Barclay Curle
Begonia	1915	Barclay Curle
Camellia	1916	Bow McLachan
Carnation	1916	Greenock & Grangemouth
Clematis	1915	Greenock & Grangemouth
Heliotrope	1915	Lobnitz
Jessamine	1916	Swan Hunter
Myrtle	1915	Lobnitz
Narcissus	1915	Napier & Miller
Peony	1916	McMillan
Snowdrop	1915	McMillan
Zinnia	1915	Swan Hunter

HMS Myrtle *looking in need of a coat of paint and seemingly having lost 'X' gun.*

(Imperial War Museum)

SPECIFICATION
Displacement:	1,200 tons
Dimensions:	262½ × 33 × 11¼
Armament:	2 × 4.7in LA QF or 2 × 4in DP AA, 2 × 3pdr QF
Machinery:	1 shaft triple expansion (4 cyl) giving 2,200ihp
Boilers:	2
Fuel:	130 tons of coal minimum
Speed:	17kts
Complement:	80

Note:
Apart from a difference in armament, similar vessels to the 'Acacia' class.

Losses:
HMS *Begonia* as Q 10 (*Dolcis Jessop*) was in collision with *U-151* off Casablanca on 2 October 1918, and did not make port;
HMS *Myrtle* on 16 July 1915 was mined in the Gulf of Finland.

'Arabis' Class Fleet Sweeping Sloop

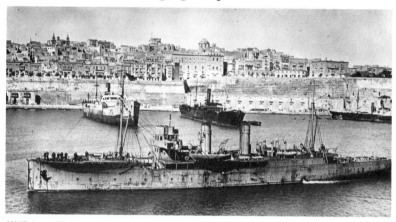

HMS Amaryllis, *entering Valetta harbour and looking very woebegone. The main armament is without shields and she is fitted with a towing bridle aft of the main mast. There are also protrusions which could be minelaying rails.* (Imperial War Museum)

HMS	**Launched**	**Builder**
Alyssum	1915	Earle
Amaryllis	1915	Earle
Arabis	1915	Henderson
Asphodel	1915	Henderson
Berberis	1916	Henderson
Buttercup	1915	Barclay Curle
Campanula	1915	Barclay Curle
Celandine	1916	Barclay Curle
Cornflower	1916	Barclay Curle
Crocus	1915	Lobnitz
Cyclamen	1916	Lobnitz
Delphinium	1915	Napier & Miller

Genista	1916	Napier & Miller
Gentian	1915	Greenock & Grangemouth
Geranium	1915	Greenock & Grangemouth
Gladiolus	1915	Connell
Godetia	1916	Connell
Hydrangea	1916	Connell
Lobelia	1916	Simons
Lupin	1916	Simons
Marguerite	1915	Dunlop Bremner
Mignonette	1916	Dunlop Bremner
Myosotis	1916	Bow McLachlan
Nasturtium	1915	McMillan
Nigella	1915	Hamilton
Pansy	1916	Hamilton
Pentstemon	1916	Workman Clark
Petunia	1916	Workman Clark
Poppy	1915	Swan Hunter
Primula	1915	Swan Hunter
Rosemary	1915	Richardson Duck
Snapdragon	1915	Ropner
Valerian	1916	C. Rennoldson
Verbena	1915	Blyth
Wallflower	1915	Irvine
Wistaria	1915	Irvine

SPECIFICATION

Displacement:	1,250 tons
Dimensions:	267¼ × 33½ × 11¼
Armament:	2 × single 4.7in or 2 × single 4in, and 2 × 3pdr AA
Machinery:	1 shaft triple expansion (4 cyl) giving 2,400ihp
Boilers:	2
Fuel:	130 tons of coal minimum, normally 250 tons
Speed:	17kts
Range:	2,200nm at 15kts
Complement:	79

Notes:
Vessels of the 'Arabis', 'Azalea' and 'Acacia' Classes were fitted to tow a Kite Balloon. Where this balloon was installed then 'X' gun was suppressed and the main mast removed. For the benefit of improved wireless telegraphy, some sloops had their topmasts heightened by 20ft and some by 40ft.

Losses:
HMS *Alyssum* on 18 March 1917 struck a mine and sank in St Georges Channel;
HMS *Arabis* on 10 February 1916 was torpedoed and sank after attack by German torpedo boats off the Dogger Bank;
HMS *Cornflower* on 19 December 1941 was captured by Japanese forces at the fall of Hong Kong;
HMS *Genista* on 23 October 1916 was torpedoed by the German submarine *U-57* in the Western Approaches;
HMS *Gentian* on 16 July 1919 struck a mine and sank in the Gulf of Finland;
HMS *Mignonette* on 17 March 1917 struck a mine and sank off Galley Head, South West Ireland;
HMS *Nasturtium* on 27 April 1916 struck a mine and sank off Malta;
HMS *Primula* on 1 March 1916 was torpedoed by the German submarine *U-35* off Alexandria;
HMS *Valerian* in heavy weather foundered on 22 October 1916 off Bermuda.

'24' Class Fleet Sweeping Sloops

HMS	Launched	Builder
Ard Patrick	1918	Swan Hunter
Bend Or	1918	Barclay Curle
Cicero	1918	Swan Hunter
Donovan	1918	Greenock & Grangemouth
Flying Fox	1918	Swan Hunter
Harvester	1918	Barclay Curle
Iroquois	1918	Barclay Curle
Isinglass	1919	Greenock & Grangemouth
Ladas	1918	Osbourne Graham
Merry Hampton	1918	Blyth SB
Minoru	1919	Swan Hunter
Orby	1918	Swan Hunter
Ormonde	1918	Blyth SB
Persimmon	1919	Osborne Graham
Rocksand	1918	Swan Hunter
Sanfoin	1918	Greenock & Grangemouth
Sefton	1918	Barclay Curle
Silvio	1918	Barclay Curle
Sir Bevis	1918	Barclay Curle
Sir Hugo	1918	Greenock & Grangemouth
Sir Visto	1918	Osborne Graham
Spearmint	1918	Swan Hunter

HMS *Ard Patrick is shown in broad chequered camouflage belching smoke and proving how difficult is was to differentiate between the bow and the stern. The after 4in gun is trained to port.*
(Imperial War Museum)

SPECIFICATION

Displacement:	1,320 tons
Dimensions:	276½ × 34½ × 12
Armament:	2 × single 4in 3pdrs were mounted for close range action, different numbers, different ships. 40 depth charges were carried
Machinery:	1 shaft triple expansion (4 cyl) giving 2,400ihp
Boilers:	2
Fuel:	260 tons coal
Speed:	17kts
Range:	3,000nm at 12½kts
Complement:	82

Notes:
This was a design of sloop to confuse the enemy, and it is indeed fortunate that our own watchkeepers were not confused by their appearance as the ships were built with straight stems and straight sterns and a very large level main-deck, with superstructure of symmetrical layout which gave a double-ended appearance. No two ships of this class were identical having only one mast, with the mast either before or aft of the funnel, and all were dazzle-painted.

Of this class, two ships were cancelled which had been named *Galtee More* by Osbourne Graham, and *Sunstar* by Swan Hunter.

Loss:
HMS *Merry Hampton* in 1923 was renamed *Herald* and used as a Survey Vessel in the Far East. In February 1942, to avoid the rapid advance of the Japanese forces, she was scuttled at Seltar, but later raised by Japanese salvage craft and renamed *Heiyo,* in October 1942, but struck a mine and sank off Singapore on 14 November 1944.

'Ascot' Class Paddle Minesweepers

HMS	Launched	Builder
Ascot	1916	Ailsa SB
Atherstone	1916	Ailsa SB
Chelmsford	1916	Ailsa SB
Cheltenham	1916	Ardrossan SB
Chepstow	1916	Ayrshire
Croxton	1916	Ayrshire
Doncaster	1916	Ayrshire
Eglington	1916	Ayrshire
Epsom	1916	George Brown
Eridge	1916	Clyde SB
Gatwick	1916	Dundee SB
Goodwood	1916	Dundee SB
Haldon	1916	Dunlop Bremner
Hurst	1916	Dunlop Bremner
Kempton	1916	Ferguson
Lingfield	1916	Fleming & Ferguson
Ludlow	1916	Goole SB
Melton	1916	Hamilton
Newbury	1916	Inglis
Plumpton	1916	McMillan
Pontefract	1916	Murdoch & Murray
Redcar	1916	Ayrshire
Sandown	1916	Dunlop Bremner
Totnes	1916	McMillan

HMS Atherstone. *This Paddle Minesweeper is probably on builders trials. Her paintwork is immaculate grey and perhaps the engineers are having trouble with stoking her boilers.*

(Imperial War Museum)

SPECIFICATION

Displacement:	810 tons
Dimensions:	235pp 245¼ × 29 × 6¼ mean
Armament:	1 × 6pdr in 'A' and 'Y' positions and 2 × 2pdr on single mtgs
Machinery:	Inclined compound, 1,400hp to 2 paddles
Fuel:	156 tons coal
Speed:	15kts
Complement:	50

Aircraft Note:
HMSs *Eridge* and *Melton* were adapted at some stage to operate seaplanes.

Losses:
HMS *Ascot* whilst off the Farne Islands on 10 November 1918 was torpedoed by *UB-67;*
HMS *Kempton* on 24 June 1917 was mined whilst off Dover;
HMS *Ludlow* on 29 December 1916 was mined whilst off the Shipwash light vessel;
HMS *Plumpton* was mined off the Belgian coast on 19 October 1918, beached off Ostend and was broken up there;
HMS *Redcar* on 24 June 1917 was mined in the Straits of Dover.

'Hunt' Class Minesweepers

HMS Belvoir. *This minesweeper is shown as Flotilla Leader and is in very dark grey paint.*
(Imperial War Museum)

HMS	Launched	Builder
Belvoir	1917	Ailsa SB
Bicester	1917	Ailsa SB
Blackmorevale	1917	Ardrossan SB
Cattistock	1917	Clyde SB
Cotswold	1916	Bow McLachlan
Cottesmore	1917	Bow McLachlan
Croome	1917	Bow McLachlan
Dartmoor	1917	Dunlop Bremner
Garth	1917	Dunlop Bremner
Hambledon	1917	Fleming & Ferguson
Heythrop	1917	Fleming & Ferguson
Holderness	1916	Henderson

Meynell	1917	Henderson
Muskerry	1916	Lobnitz
Oakley	1917	Lobnitz
Pytchley	1917	Napier & Miller
Quorn	1917	Napier & Miller
Southdown	1917	Simons
Tedworth	1917	Simons
Zetland	1917	Murdoch & Murray

SPECIFICATION

Displacement:	750 tons
Dimensions:	220pp 231 × 28 × 7 mean
Armament:	2 × 12pdr single in 'A' and 'X' positions, 2 × 2pdr single
Machinery:	2 shaft triple expansion all giving 1,890ihp
Boilers:	2
Fuel:	140 tons coal
Speed:	16kts
Complement:	71

Note:
Some of this class were armed as a temporary measure with 1 × 12pdr and 1 × 6pdr in 'A' and 'X' positions.

Losses:
HMS *Blackmorevale* on 1 May 1918 was mined off Montrose;
HMS *Tedworth* collided with *Rochester* on 1 June 1945 and became a constructive total loss.

'Sea Bird' Class Paddle Minesweepers

The above class were proposed new buildings as Improved ships of the 'Ascot' class, and would have been named:

HMS	**Builder**
Fulmar	Ailsa SB
Gadwall	Ailsa SB
Pochard	Ailsa SB
Stormy Petrel	Murdoch & Murray
Tern	Murdoch & Murray

Ordered in 1918 but cancelled December 1918, two additional names are believed to have been *Redshank* and *Shrike*, but builders not known.

Improved 'Ascot' Class Paddle Minesweepers

HMS	**Launched**	**Builder**
Banbury	1917	Ailsa SB
Harpenden	1918	Ailsa SB
Hexham	1917	Clyde SB
Lanark	1917	Fleming & Ferguson
Lewes	1918	Fleming & Ferguson
Shincliffe	1918	Dundee SB
Shirley	1917	Dunlop Bremner
Wetherby	1918	Murdoch & Murray

HMS Hexham. *This is an improved version of the Ascot Class Paddle Minesweeper.*

(National Maritime Museum)

SPECIFICATION

Displacement:	820 tons
Dimensions:	235pp 249¼ × 29½ × 7
Armament:	1 × 12pdr in 'A' position and 1 × 3in AA in 'X' position, also 2 × 2pdr on single mtgs
Machinery:	Diagonal compound, 1,400 (maximum 1,500) ihp to 2 paddles
Fuel:	156 tons coal
Speed:	15kts
Complement:	52

Notes:
Ships of this class were similar to the earlier 'Ascot' design and all built under the Emergency War Programme. A distinguishing feature is that the foremast is footed below the charthouse, whereas on the 'Ascot' class the foremast was stepped forward of the bridge.

'Aberdare' Class Minesweepers

HMS	Launched	Builder
Aberdare	1918	Ailsa SB
Abingdon	1918	Ailsa SB
Albury	1918	Ailsa SB
Alderburgh	1918	Ailsa SB
Alresford	1919	Ailsa SB
Ambleside (later *Beaufort*)	1919	Ailsa SB

HMS Kendal *in peacetime colours, with an air identification tricolour on 'A' gun shield.*

Amersham (later Collinson)	1919	Ailsa SB
Badminton	1918	Ardrossan SB
Bagshot	1918	Ardrossan SB
Banchory	1918	Ayreshire
Bantry (later Swindon)	1918	Ardrossan SB
Barnstaple	1919	Ardrossan SB
Blakeney (later Burslem)	1918	Ayreshire
Bradfield	1919	Ayreshire
Bridlington (later Goole)		
(later Irwell)	1919	Ayreshire
Buckie (later Bootle)	1918	Bow McLachlan
Burnham (later Blackburn)	1918	Bow McLachlan
Bury	1919	Eltringham
Caerleon	1918	Bow McLachlan
Camberley	1918	Bow McLachlan
Cawsand (later Carstairs)		
(later Dryad)	1919	Bow McLachlan
Caterham	1919	Bow McLachlan
Cheam	1919	Eltringham
Craigie	1918	Clyde SB
Dawlish (later Derby)	1918	Clyde SB
Dorking	1918	Clyde SB
Dundalk	1919	Clyde SB
Dunoon	1919	Clyde SB
Fairburn (later Forfar)	1918	Dundee SB
Fairfield	1919	Clyde SB
Fairham	1918	Dunlop Bremner
Faversham	1918	Dunlop Bremner
Fermoy	1919	Dundee SB
Filey (later Rugby)	1918	Dunlop Bremner
Fleetwood (later Ford)	1918	Dunlop Bremner
Fowey (later Forres)	1918	Clyde SB
Gaddesdon	1917	Eltringham
Gorleston		
(later Gainsborough)	1918	Eltringham
Gretna	1918	Eltringham
Harrow	1918	Eltringham
Havant	1919	Eltringham
Helmsdale (later Huntley)	1919	Eltringham
Ilfracombe (later Instow)	1919	Eltringham
Irvine	1917	Fairfield
Kendal	1918	Fairfield
Kinross	1918	Fairfield
Lydney (later Lydd)	1918	Fairfield
Mallaig	1918	Fleming & Ferguson
Malvern	1919	Fleming & Ferguson
Marlow	1918	Harkess
MacDuff (later Munlochy)	1918	Fleming & Ferguson
Maryport (later Mistley)	1918	Harkess
Minehead (later Longford)	1919	Harkess
Mullion (later Monaghan)	1919	Harkess
Newlyn (later Newark)	1918	Inglis
Newquay (later Nailsea)	1918	Inglis
Northolt	1918	Eltringham
Padstow (later Pangbourne)	1918	Lobnitz
Penarth	1918	Lobnitz

Polperro (later *Pontypool*)	1918	Lobnitz
Portmadoc (later *Petersfield*)	1919	Lobnitz
Portreath (later *Pinner*)		
(later *Fitzroy*)	1919	Lobnitz
Prestatyn (later *Porlock*)	1918	Lobnitz
Radley (later *Flinders*)	1919	Lobnitz
Ramsey (later *Ross*)	1919	Lobnitz
Rosslare (later *Cupar*)	1918	McMillan
Salcombe (later *Sutton*)	1918	McMillan
Saltash	1918	Murdoch & Murray
Saltburn	1918	Murdoch & Murray
Selkirk	1918	Murdoch & Murray
Shoreham (later *Salford*)	1919	Murdoch & Murray
Shrewsbury	1918	Napier & Miller
Sligo	1918	Napier & Miller
Southwold (later *Stoke*)	1918	C. Rennoldson
Staithes (later *Stafford*)	1918	C. Rennoldson
Stranraer (later *Clonmel*)	1918	Simons
Tarbert (later *Sherborne*)	1918	Simons
Teignmouth (later *Tring*)	1918	Simons
Tiverton	1918	Simons
Tonbridge	1918	Simons
Tralee	1918	Simons
Troon (later *Elgin*)	1919	Simons
Truro	1919	Simons
Uppingham (later *Kellett*)	1919	Simons
Ventnor (later *Verwood*)		
(later *Crozier*) (later *Protia*)	1919	Simons
Walmer (later *Wem*)	1919	Simons
Wexford	1919	Simons
Weybourne	1919	Inglis
Wicklow (later *Repton*)	1919	Inglis
Withernsea (later *Widnes*)	1918	Napier & Miller
Yeovil	1918	Napier & Miller

SPECIFICATION

Displacement:	800 tons
Dimensions:	220pp 231 × 28½ × 7½ mean
Armament:	This tended to vary between individual ships, but in general consisted of: 1 × 4in and 1 × 12pdr AA or 2 × 3pdr. Alternative, 1 × 6pdr or 3pdr
Machinery:	2 shaft triple expansion all giving 2,200ihp
Boilers:	2
Fuel:	185 tons coal
Speed:	16kts
Range:	1,500nm at 15kts
Complement:	74

Notes:

Of this class, 36 ships were cancelled. Their names and builders are given below:
Arbroath and *Ashburton* by Ailsa SB;
Beaumaris and *Bideford* by Ardrossan SB;
Cley, Clifton, Clovelly, Colwyn and *Crediton* by Bow McLachlan;
Atheleney, Bala and *Bathgate* by Clyde SB;
Beccles and *Blickling* by Dundee SB;
Curragh, Flint, Frome, Grays, Kew, Kinguissie, Knowle and *Naas* by Eltringham;

Northrepps, Okehampton, Oundle, Radnor, Reading, Retford, Ringwood, Runcorn, Shifnal
and *Smethwick* by Lobnitz;
Tain, Wembdon and *Yealmpton* by Simons;
Battle by Dundee SB and *Brixham* (later *Bloxham*) by Ayrshire, were broken up incomplete;
and two unnamed vessels by Fleming & Ferguson.

Losses:
HMS *Abingdon* on 5 April 1942 was bombed by Italian aircraft off the coast of Malta and
beached at Calcara. She was finally broken up in 1950;
HMS *Bagshot* whilst under the name *Medway II* and later sold for breaking up, was mined on
1 September 1951 whilst in tow, off the Island of Corfu;
HMS *Cupar* on 5 May 1919 was mined when entering the River Tyne;
HMS *Dundalk* on 17 October 1940 was damaged by a mine whilst off Harwich, and later in
the day sank from damage sustained;
HMS *Dunoon* on 30 April 1940 was mined off Great Yarmouth;
HMS *Fermoy* on 4 May 1941 whilst in Malta dockyard was the victim of an aircraft attack
and later sank;
HMS *Huntley* was attacked by aircraft on 31 January 1941 south of Cyprus, and later sank;
HMS *Kinross* on 16 June 1919 was mined in the Aegean Sea;
HMS *Penarth* on 4 February 1919 was mined off Great Yarmouth;
HMS *Petersfield* on 11 November 1931, took the ground in bad weather and became a
constructive total loss on Tung Yung Island;
HMS *Fitzroy* on 27 May 1942 was mined off Great Yarmouth;
HMS *Saltburn* was wrecked in tow to the breakers' yard in December 1946 off Hartland Point;
HMS *Stoke* on 7 May 1941 was sunk after aircraft attack near Tobruk harbour;
HMS *Widnes* was damaged by enemy aircraft on 20 May 1941 and beached at Suda Bay. She
was taken into the German Naval forces as *12V4* and later as *UJ2109*. On 17 October 1943
whilst in the Dodecanese she was engaged by HMS *Hursley* and sank off the Island of Kos.

'Halcyon' Class Minesweepers

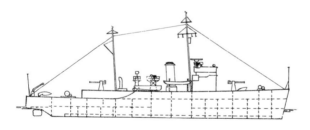

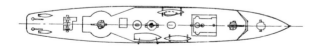

HALCYON CLASS 1934

HMS	Launched	Builder
Bramble	1938	HM Dockyard Devonport
Britomart	1938	HM Dockyard Devonport
Franklin	1937	Ailsa
Gleaner	1937	Grays
Gossamer	1937	Hamilton

Halcyon	1933	Clydebank
Harrier	1934	Thornycroft
Hazard	1937	Grays
Hebe	1936	HM Dockyard Devonport
Hussar	1934	Thornycroft
Jason	1937	Ailsa
Leda	1937	HM Dockyard Devonport
Niger	1936	White
Salamander	1936	White
Scott	1938	Caledon
Seagull	1937	HM Dockyard Devonport
Sharpshooter	1936	HM Dockyard Devonport
Skipjack	1934	Clydebank
Speedwell	1935	Hamilton
Speedy	1938	Hamilton
Sphinx	1939	Hamilton

SPECIFICATION

Displacement and Dimensions: *Halcyon, Harrier, Hussar, Niger, Salamander, Skipjack* and *Speedwell*, 815 tons/245 × 33½ × 6¾
Franklin, Gleaner, Gossamer, Hazard, Hebe, Jason, Leda, Seagull and *Sharpshooter*, 835 tons/245 × 33½ × 7¼
Bramble, Britomart, Scott, Speedy and *Sphinx*, 875 tons/245 × 33½ × 8

Armament: 1 × 4in QF and 1 × 4in DP AA *Halcyon, Harrier, Hussar, Niger, Salamander, Skipjack* and *Speedwell*
2 × 4in AA on single mtgs and 4 × 5in mg on single mtgs for the remainder of this class. The 2 × 4in of whatever type were at 'A' and 'X' positions

Machinery: 2 shaft reciprocating engines all giving 1,770ihp for *Halcyon, Harrier, Hussar, Niger* and *Salamander*
2 shaft reciprocating engines all giving 2,000ihp for *Skipjack* and *Speedwell*
2 shaft geared turbines all giving 1,750shp for the remaining ships of this class

Boilers: 2
Fuel: 220 tons oil

HMS Seagull *was the first all-welded major warship in the Royal Navy. From bow to stern the following items will be observed: the unshielded 4 in gun on the foredeck and the quadruple .5 in mg on the lower bridge just forward of a Carley float. The large director on the upper bridge, the searchlight and bandstand just above the break in the forecastle, a large M/S winch to the rear of the deckhouse with the M/S floats and kites right on the stern, together with one smoke generator.* (Imperial War Museum)

| Speed: | 17kts |
| Complement: | 80 |

Construction Notes:
HMS *Seagull* was the first all-welded warship in the Royal Navy and full particulars of this innovation may be found in the 1939 volume of the *Transactions of the Institution of Naval Architects*.

Losses:
HMS *Bramble* on 31 December 1942 was engaged by the *Admiral Hipper* in the Barents Sea;
HMS *Hebe* was mined off Bari on 22 November 1943;
HMS *Gossamer* on 24 June 1942 was attacked by German aircraft in the Kola Inlet;
HMS *Niger* when off Iceland was mined on 5 July 1942;
HMS *Leda* on 20 September 1942 when south of Greenland was torpedoed by *U-435;*
HMS *Sphinx* whilst in the Moray Firth was attacked by German aircraft on 3 February 1940 and foundered as a result of the attack the same day;
HMS *Skipjack* on 1 June 1940 whilst taking part in the evacuation of Allied troops from Dunkirk, was attacked and bombed by German aircraft.

The 1st Minesweeping Flotilla on 27 August 1944 was off Cap d'Antifer, their task at that time was to maintain the swept channel between Portsmouth and Arromanches. This took longer than expected and consequently the Commanding Officer of HMS *Jason* reported to Staff in the HQ ship that further time was needed and this signal, which would have cancelled the return of the Flotilla, was duly made.

But at noon, when all the ships were sweeping, they were observed by an RAF reconnaissance aircraft, which came down low, with their aircrew returning the waves from the ships company. Approximately one-and-a-half hours later, in beautiful summer weather, the ships were deliberately attacked by RAF Typhoon aircraft, with rocket and cannon fire with the following results: HMS *Britomart* was sunk, HMS *Hussar* was also sunk, HMS *Salamander* was a constructive total loss, HMS *Jason* and the 'Isles' class Danlayer *Colsay* were also damaged. From this attack by friendly aircraft, 78 of the ships' companies lost their lives and 149 were seriously wounded.

The official explanation as to this appalling mistake was that the signal to continue sweeping off Cap d'Antifer was not repeated to the Flag Officer, British Assault Area (FO-BAA), and notwithstanding, that the reconnaissance aircraft reported the ships as friendly and that the Squadron Leader of the Typhoons twice questioned his instructions to attack, back to base, the FO-BAA persisted with the strike as they assumed that the ships were enemy vessels in the approaches to Le Havre.

Thornycroft Type Motor Minesweepers

HM MMS	Completed	Builder
1	1937	Thornycroft (Singapore) Ltd
2	1937	Thornycroft (Singapore) Ltd

SPECIFICATION
Displacement:	32 tons
Dimensions:	75 × 14¼ × 5
Armament:	Nil (when built)
Machinery:	3 shaft petrol engines all giving 1,500bhp
Speed:	15kts
Sweeping speed:	10kts
Range:	270nm at 15kts
Complement:	11

HM MMS 1 *was the first Motor Minesweeper from a class of two. She is shown here with a mid-grey hull and dark varnished wheelhouse with the M/S gear at the stern and on the port side aft.* (Not known)

Notes:
These two vessels were the original prototypes for Motor Minesweepers but the design was not continued with.

Experimental Type Motor Minesweeper

HMS	Completed	Builder
MMS *51*	1938	British Power Boat Co
(later MTB *100*)		

Little is known of this craft but particulars are believed to be:
SPECIFICATION

Displacement:	22 tons
Dimensions:	60¼ × 13¼ × 3
Armament:	8 × mg in four twin 'dustbin' mtgs
Torpedo tubes:	2, one 18in tube on either beam facing forward of the wheelhouse
Machinery:	2 shaft petrol engines all giving 1,500bhp
Speed:	25kts
Complement:	9

Notes:
The particulars as given are of MMS *51* after her conversion to MTB *100* in 1939.

HM MMS 51 on builders trials. She was built as a one-off craft for minesweeping, but was not successful. (Wright & Logan)

Requisitioned Ex-Canadian Motor Minesweepers

HMCS MMS	HMS	Completed	Builder
119	Emberley	1941	Stone, St Johns
120	Oderin	1941	Stone, St Johns
121	Marticot	1942	Stone, St Johns
122	Merasheen	1942	Stone, St Johns

HMS Emberley. This is a censored photograph of Emberley by reason that the acoustic hammer box has been deleted from the bows. On port and starboard forward shrouds are secured two dan buoys and the Pennant No. FY1758 is displayed. (Imperial War Museum)

SPECIFICATION
Displacement: 219 tons
Dimensions: 116pp × 26 × 10
Armament: 2 × .303 mg on single mtgs
Machinery: 1 shaft diesel engine giving 275bhp
Speed: 9kts
Complement: 18

Class Notes:
In late 1942, all four of this class were converted to Danlayers.

'Cambus' Class Motor Minesweepers

HMS	Completed	Builder
Cambusdoon	1944	A. Zoghzochy (Beirut)
Cambuskenneth	1944	A. Moussali (Beirut)
Cambuslang	1943	A. Tahab (Tripoli)
Cambuslie	1943	A. Moussali (Beirut)

SPECIFICATION
Length: 115 and 100 pp
No other details of the individual vessels are known.

Historical Notes:
These four minesweepers of the 'Cambus' class were laid down in 1942 for the purpose of skid-towing vessels for magnetic minesweeping and were actually designated the 405th Minesweeping Group.

There were, however, considerable delays in completion and in 1943 they would have been manned from the Royal Hellenic Navy (RHN) with the vessels being renamed (in sequence) *Nafpaktia*, *Monemuassia*, *Amvrakia* and *Aegialia* and described as wooden Minesweeping Trawlers. It is uncertain if *Cambusdoon* ever was commissioned with the RHN and after the end of World War II the four vessels were returned to the Royal Navy and put up for disposal. During this period (1946), *Cambusdoon* was renamed *Pillar Box* when in use outside of naval service, but again information is virtually unavailable.

The greater part of the information related above was supplied by the Naval Historical Branch of the MoD.

Admiralty Type Motor Minesweepers 119ft (Short Boats)

This was the first of the Motor Minesweeper classes produced in quantity to combat the magnetic mine. They were of timber hull construction and their particulars are as below:

HM MMS 192 is shown with full sweeping gear including the acoustic hammer on the bows and the more conventional LL sweep at the stern. She is armed with two 20mm mg on a twin mounting. (Imperial War Museum)

SPECIFICATION
Displacement: 165 tons
Dimensions: 105pp 119 × 23 × 9½
Armament: 2 × 20mm on a twin mtg
Machinery: 1 shaft diesel engine giving 500bhp
Speed: 11kts
Complement: 20

Building Note:
Motor Minesweepers were built in the UK, Canada, India, Singapore, Hong Kong and Tel Aviv. All of this class commissioned into the Royal Canadian Navy (RCN) were named, but Royal Navy MMSs were numbered.

Numbers Built:
MMS Short Boats were built in sequence from *1-118*, and *123-313*, with a small number which were commissioned into the RCN being named.

Losses:
HM MMS *39* on 7 August 1941 was mined in the Thames Estuary;
HM MMS *180* whilst sweeping the war channel off the approaches to the River Tyne on 13 February 1942 was rammed whilst attempting to clear the path of a convoy;
HM MMS *51* on 4 March 1942 to prevent her falling into the hands of the Japanese Navy, was sunk by own forces South of Java;
HM MMS *174* during an attack by enemy aircraft on 12 July 1942 whilst in Brixham Harbour was sunk but subsequently raised and recommissioned;
HM MMS *89* when sweeping off Bizerta on 12 May 1943 was mined;
HM MMS *70* on 24 September 1943 was mined in the Gulf of Taranto;
HM MMS *229* on 13 June 1944 was mined off the Normandy Beaches;
HM MMS *8* on 14 June 1944 was lost in similar circumstances to HM MMS *229;*
HM MMS *55* on 10 July 1944 was lost in similar circumstances to HM MMS *229;*
HM MMS *117* on 1 September 1944 was mined off Civita Vecchia, Western Italy;
HM MMS *278* took the ground, being stranded on the rocky foreshore of Le Rance river, St Malo, on 14 September 1944;
HM MMS *170* on 12 October 1944 was mined whilst off Gorgona Island, Western Italy;
HM MMS *101* was mined on 29 November 1944 when off Salonika;
HM MMS *257* whilst clearing the Schelde was mined on 11 December 1944;
HM MMS *68* on 4 February 1945 when off the coast of Greece was mined close to Cephalonia;
HM MMS *248* on 30 January 1945 was mined whilst clearing the Schelde Estuary;
HM MMS *168* on 25 June 1945 whilst clearing Genoa Harbour was mined and sank;
HM MMS *58* whilst allocated to the Thames Division of the RNVR was lost by fire off Dunkirk on 17 April 1954;
HM MMS *288* on 21 October 1952 foundered in heavy weather when off Winterton Ness.
HM MMS *223* (later *Jade*) suffered storm damage in February 1951 and was scuttled on 24 February 1951 off Bermuda.

Notes:
The 'Short' MMS became a requirement in 1940 when the magnetic mine, which had just appeared in the War channels, seemed to be unsweepable. They commissioned in early 1941, but were found to have a lack of towing power for the sweep which in any weather was of considerable weight. The sweeps carried were the wire sweep, the LL sweep and they were retrofitted with the SA hammer box, which was mounted on the boom. Notwithstanding the inadequacies of their design, it will be observed from the losses of this class that they saw considerable service in the minesweeping war.

Destruction by own forces:
The following 'short boats' were under construction in the Far East but destroyed in the face of the Japanese advance on C-in-C's instructions.
At Hong Kong in December 1941, MMSs Nos *95, 96, 123* and *124;*
At Rangoon in April 1942, MMSs Nos *161, 162, 163* and *164;*
At Singapore in February 1942, MMSs Nos *52, 93, 94, 125, 126, 127, 128* and *166.*

Builders (Craft built in the UK)
Adam & Stockman (Brixham): No *6;*
Clapson & Sons (Barton-on-Humber): Nos *50, 135, 181, 263, 280, 305;*

Frank Curtis (Looe): Nos *24, 25, 27, 42, 43;*
Frank Curtis (Par): Nos *26, 28, 74, 75, 139, 140, 149, 150, 167, 168, 169, 170, 204, 205, 224-228, 268-271, 282, 285, 286, 292, 293, 294, 295, 296, 298;*
Frank Curtis (Totnes): Nos *171, 172, 203, 207, 220, 221, 264, 265, 266, 267, 284, 290, 291;*
J. S. Doig (Grimsby): Nos *116-118, 179, 206, 229;*
J. L. Bolson (Poole): Nos *46, 58, 202, 233, 234, 281, 304;*
East Anglian Constructors (Oulton Broad): Nos *71, 72, 73;*
George Forbes (Peterhead): Nos *2, 20, 79, 80, 81, 184, 185, 209, 230;*
J. & G. Forbes (Sandhaven): Nos *12, 33, 59, 60, 190, 208;*
P. K. Harris (Appledore): Nos *9, 38, 92, 165, 183, 210;*
Herd & McKenzie (Buckie): Nos *4, 21, 53, 54, 192, 193, 211, 235, 260, 273;*
Humphrey & Smith (Grimsby): Nos *180, 212, 213;*
Husband Yacht Yard (Marchwood): Nos *7, 22, 23, 65, 66, 67, 137, 138, 262, 309;*
R. Irvine (Peterhead): Nos *3, 55, 136, 186, 187, 261, 278, 299, 302, 308;*
John Morris (Gosport): Nos *5, 49, 89, 90, 91, 109-112, 274, 287, 288, 289;*
MacDuff Eng & Spbdg, (MacDuff): Nos *13, 32, 61, 62, 191, 214, 232, 275, 276;*
Philip & Sons (Dartmouth): Nos *38, 175, 216, 300;*
Walter Reekie (Anstruther): Nos *31, 64;*
Walter Reekie (St Monace): Nos *14, 63, 182, 217, 260;*
Richards Ironworks (Lowestoft): Nos *1, 8, 19, 39, 40, 41, 44, 45, 68, 69, 70, 76, 77, 78, 176, 177, 178;*
Rowhedge Ironworks: Nos *36, 37;*
Thornycroft (Hampton): No *2;*
J. W. & A. Upham (Brixham): Nos *47, 48, 173, 174, 218, 231, 272, 283, 303;*
Wilson Noble (Fraserburgh): Nos *10, 11, 18, 34, 35, 56, 57, 133, 134, 188, 189, 215, 219, 277, 301, 306, 307;*
Wivenhoe Shipyard: Nos *15, 16, 17, 82, 83, 84, 85, 86, 87, 113, 114, 115, 236, 237;*
Wivenhoe Shipyard (Glasgow): No *279;*
Wivenhoe Shipyard (Southampton): Nos *29, 30.*

Builders (Overseas)
Bellmont Dock (Kingston): Nos *222-23;*
Brunton & Co (Cochin): Nos *129-32, 97, 98, 151, 157, 160;*
Clare Shipbuilding (Metaghan): Nos *196, 197, 198, 199, 242, 243, 244, 245, 246, 247;*
Columbo Port Commissioners: Nos *143, 144, 145;*
Colomby Cargo Port Despatch Co: No *146;*
Irrawadi Flotilla Co (Rangoon): Nos *152, 153;*
LeBlanc Shipbuilding: Nos *105, 106, 252, 253;*
Rangoon Dockyard: No *147;*
Royal Bodden (Grand Cayman): Nos *258, 259;*
Shelburne Shipbuilding: Nos *200, 248, 249;*
Symonetty Shipyard (Nassau): Nos *194, 195;*
Steers Ltd (St John's): Nos *141, 142, 238, 239, 240, 241;*
Wagstaff & Hatfield (Port Greville): Nos *99, 100, 101, 102, 103, 104, 201, 250, 251;*
Ch Mar de St Laurent: Nos *254, 255;*
Vaughan SB (Frerickton): Nos *256, 257;*
Vaughan SB (Singapore): Nos *51, 52, 93, 94, 125, 126, 127, 128, 166;*
Vaughan SB (Hong Kong): Nos *95, 96, 123, 124;*
Vaughan SB (Port Quebec): Nos *107, 108, 254, 255;*
H. Stone (Newfoundland): Nos *119, 120, 121, 122;*
H. Stone (Coconada): No *154;*
H. Stone (Mandapan): Nos *148, 155;*
H. Stone (Rangoon): Nos *156, 158, 159, 161, 162, 163, 164;*
A. Wahbad (Beirut): Nos *310, 313;*
Marine Trust (Tel Aviv): Nos *311, 312;*

Note:
The following Short MMSs were completed as Danlayers and named 141 *Burin,* 142 *Cottel,* 238 *Fichot,* 239 *Jude,* 240 *Quirpow,* 241 *St Barbe.*

Admiralty Type Motor Minesweepers 140ft (Long Boats)

This class of Motor Minesweeper, an improvement on the Short 119ft Class, was fitted with the same engine, consequently, although the vessel was an extra 21ft in length, the speed was less by one knot. They were however, more seaworthy, and with their raised forecastle much more spacious.

HM MMS 1044 *was one of the 'long' Motor Minesweepers built with a raised forecastle, funnel similar to the 'short' boats but only powered with the same engine. They were said to be better sea boats and surprisingly were only fitted with one mast.* (Wright & Logan)

SPECIFICATION
Displacement: 255 tons
Dimensions: 126pp 140 × 26 × 10½
Armament: 2 × 20mm on single mtgs
Machinery: 1 shaft diesel engine giving 500bhp
Speed: 10kts
Complement: 21

Building Note:
Likewise to the Short boats, the 140ft version was built at home and overseas.

Numbers Built:
MMS Long boats were built in sequence from 1001-1090, with a small number which were commissioned into the RCN being named.

Losses:
HM MMS *1019* on 2 July 1944 was mined off Cherbourg;
HM MMS *1016* was lost whilst under the Danish flag on 29 January 1946 when off Jutland;
HM MMS *1055* whilst off Ostend on 17 April 1954, caught fire and later sank;

Builders (craft built in the UK)
Frank Curtis (Par): Nos *1032, 1033, 1034, 1040, 1078, 1079, 1080;*
Frank Curtis (Totnes): Nos *1035, 1036, 1075, 1076, 1077, 1087, 1088;*
Camper & Nicholson (Gosport): Nos *1001, 1002;*
J. S. Doig (Grimsby): Nos *1022, 1026, 1081, 1082;*

East Anglian Constructors (Oulton Broad): Nos *1005, 1007, 1008, 1027, 1046, 1074, 1085, 1086, 1089;*
George Forbes (Peterhead): Nos *1013, 1045;*
P. K. Harris (Appledore): Nos *1014, 1031;*
Herd & McKenzie (Buckie): Nos *1015, 1016, 1047;*
Humphrey & Smith (Grimsby): Nos *1023, 1025, 1042, 1043;*
Philip & Sons (Dartmouth): Nos *1030, 1090;*
Walter Reekie (Anstruther): Nos *1018, 1041;*
Richards Ironworks (Lowestoft): Nos *1006, 1037, 1038;*
Rowhedge Ironworks: No *1084;*
J. W. & A. Upham (Brixham): Nos *1019, 1020, 1029;*
Wilson Noble (Fraserburgh): Nos *1017, 1021, 1024, 1048, 1049;*
Wivenhoe Shipyard: Nos *1009, 1010, 1011, 1012, 1028, 1044, 1083;*
Wivenhoe Shipyard (Milford Haven): No *1039;*
Wivenhoe Shipyard (Southampton): Nos *1003, 1004.*

Builders (Overseas)
Clare SB (Methaghan): Nos *1050-56;*
Fairbanks Morse (Montreal): No *1069;*
Wagstaff & Hatfield (Port Greville): Nos *1063, 1064;*
Vaughan SB (Frederickton): No *1070;*
Marine Trust (Canada): Nos *1057-59, 1060-62, 1065-68, 1071-73.*

British Yard Minesweepers (BYMSs) Ex-American Yard Minesweepers (YMS)

The following ships of this Class were allocated to the Royal Navy from vessels building for the United States Navy.

HM BYMS 3-244 was a vessel from the second group of BYMS, having only one funnel.
(Imperial War Museum)

HMS	Completed	Builder
1	1942-44	Associated Car & Foundry Co (Wilmington)
2	1942-44	Associated Car & Foundry Co (Wilmington)
3	1942-44	Associated Car & Foundry Co (Wilmington)
4	1942-44	Associated Car & Foundry Co (Wilmington)
5	1942-44	Wheeler SB (Whitestone)
6	1942-44	Wheeler SB (Whitestone)
7	1942-44	Wheeler SB (Whitestone)

8	1942-44	Wheeler SB (Whitestone)
9	1942-44	Associated SB (Seattle)
10	1942-44	Associated SB (Seattle)
11	1942-44	Associated SB (Seattle)
12	1942-44	Associated SB (Seattle)
13	1942-44	Associated SB (Seattle)
14	1942-44	Associated SB (Seattle)
15	1942-44	Dachel Carter (Benton Harbor)
16	1942-44	Dachel Carter (Benton Harbor)
17	1942-44	Bellingham Marine Railway
18	1942-44	Bellingham Marine Railway
19	1942-44	Bellingham Marine Railway
20	1942-44	Bellingham Marine Railway
21	1942-44	Seattle SB & Dry Dock Co
22	1942-44	Seattle SB & Dry Dock Co
23	1942-44	Seattle SB & Dry Dock Co
24	1942-44	Seattle SB & Dry Dock Co
25	1942-44	Ballard Marine Railway (Seattle)
26	1942-44	Ballard Marine Railway (Seattle)
27	1942-44	Ballard Marine Railway (Seattle)
28	1942-44	Ballard Marine Railway (Seattle)
29	1942-44	Barbour Boats (New Bern)
30	1942-44	Barbour Boats (New Bern)
31	1942-44	Associated Car & Foundry Co (Wilmington)
32	1942-44	Associated Car & Foundry Co (Wilmington)
33	1942-44	Associated Car & Foundry Co (Wilmington)
34	1942-44	Associated Car & Foundry Co (Wilmington)
35	1942-44	Associated Car & Foundry Co (Wilmington)
36	1942-44	Associated Car & Foundry Co (Wilmington)
37	1942-44	Barbour Boats (New Bern)
38	1942-44	Barbour Boats (New Bern)
39	1942-44	Barbour Boats (New Bern)
40	1942-44	Barbour Boats (New Bern)
41	1942-44	Barbour Boats (New Bern)
42	1942-44	Barbour Boats (New Bern)
43	1942-44	Gibbs Gas Engine (Jackson)
44	1942-44	Gibbs Gas Engine (Jackson)
45	1942-44	Gibbs Gas Engine (Jackson)
46	1942-44	Gibbs Gas Engine (Jackson)
47	1942-44	Gibbs Gas Engine (Jackson)
48	1942-44	Gibbs Gas Engine (Jackson)
49	1942-44	Gibbs Gas Engine (Jackson)
50	1942-44	Gibbs Gas Engine (Jackson)
51	1942-44	Gibbs Gas Engine (Jackson)
52	1942-44	Gibbs Gas Engine (Jackson)
53	1942-44	Gibbs Gas Engine (Jackson)
54	1942-44	Gibbs Gas Engine (Jackson)
55	1942-44	Westerguard Boatworks (Biloxi)
56	1942-44	Westerguard Boatworks (Biloxi)
57	1942-44	Westerguard Boatworks (Biloxi)
58	1942-44	Westerguard Boatworks (Biloxi)
59	1942-44	Westerguard Boatworks (Biloxi)
60	1942-44	Westerguard Boatworks (Biloxi)
61	1942-44	Westerguard Boatworks (Biloxi)
62	1942-44	Westerguard Boatworks (Biloxi)
63	1942-44	Westerguard Boatworks (Biloxi)

64	1942-44	Westerguard Boatworks (Biloxi)
65	1942-44	Wheeler Shipbuilding (Whitestone)
66	1942-44	Wheeler Shipbuilding (Whitestone)
67	1942-44	Wheeler Shipbuilding (Whitestone)
68	1942-44	Wheeler Shipbuilding (Whitestone)
69	1942-44	Wheeler Shipbuilding (Whitestone)
70	1942-44	Wheeler Shipbuilding (Whitestone)
71	1942-44	Wheeler Shipbuilding (Whitestone)
72	1942-44	Wheeler Shipbuilding (Whitestone)
73	1942-44	Wheeler Shipbuilding (Whitestone)
74	1942-44	Wheeler Shipbuilding (Whitestone)
75	1942-44	Wheeler Shipbuilding (Whitestone)
76	1942-44	Wheeler Shipbuilding (Whitestone)
77	1942-44	Wheeler Shipbuilding (Whitestone)
78	1942-44	Wheeler Shipbuilding (Whitestone)
79	1942-44	Wheeler Shipbuilding (Whitestone)
80	1942-44	Wheeler Shipbuilding (Whitestone)
137	1942-44	Astoria Marine Con
141	1942-44	Astoria Marine Con
142	1942-44	Astoria Marine Con
148	1942-44	San Diego Marine Con
149	1942-44	San Diego Marine Con
150	1942-44	San Diego Marine Con
152	1942-44	Campbell Machinery (San Diego)
153	1942-44	Campbell Machinery (San Diego)
154	1942-44	Campbell Machinery (San Diego)
155	1942-44	Berger Boat (Manitowac)
156	1942-44	Berger Boat (Manitowac)
157	1942-44	Berger Boat (Manitowac)
161	1942-44	Berger Boat (Manitowac)
162	1942-44	Berger Boat (Manitowac)
167	1942-44	Dachel Carter (Benton Harbor)
168	1942-44	Dachel Carter (Benton Harbor)
171	1942-44	H. C. Grebe (Chicago)
172	1942-44	H. C. Grebe (Chicago)
173	1942-44	H. C. Grebe (Chicago)
174	1942-44	H. C. Grebe (Chicago)
175	1942-44	H. C. Grebe (Chicago)
181	1942-44	H. C. Grebe (Chicago)
182	1942-44	H. C. Grebe (Chicago)
186	1942-44	Greenport Basin (Long Island)
187	1942-44	Greenport Basin (Long Island)
188	1942-44	Greenport Basin (Long Island)
189	1942-44	Greenport Basin (Long Island)
190	1942-44	Greenport Basin (Long Island)
191	1942-44	Greenport Basin (Long Island)
194	1942-44	Greenport Basin (Long Island)
197	1942-44	C. Hiltebrandt Dry Dock (Kingston)
202	1942-44	C. Hiltebrandt Dry Dock (Kingston)
203	1942-44	C. Hiltebrandt Dry Dock (Kingston)
204	1942-44	C. Hiltebrandt Dry Dock (Kingston)
205	1942-44	C. Hiltebrandt Dry Dock (Kingston)
206	1942-44	C. Hiltebrandt Dry Dock (Kingston)
207	1942-44	R. Jacob (City Island)
208	1942-44	R. Jacob (City Island)
209	1942-44	R. Jacob (City Island)

210	1942-44	R. Jacob (City Island)
211	1942-44	R. Jacob (City Island)
212	1942-44	R. Jacob (City Island)
213	1942-44	R. Jacob (City Island)
214	1942-44	R. Jacob (City Island)
217	1942-44	J. M. Martinac SB (Tacoma)
221	1942-44	J. M. Martinac SB (Tacoma)
223	1942-44	Mojean & Erikson (Tacoma)
225	1942-44	Mojean & Erikson (Tacoma)
226	1942-44	F. J. Sample (Boothby)
229	1942-44	F. J. Sample (Boothby)
230	1942-44	F. J. Sample (Boothby)
232	1942-44	F. J. Sample (Boothby)
233	1942-44	F. J. Sample (Boothby)
234	1942-44	F. J. Sample (Boothby)
236	1942-44	Stadium Yacht Basin (Cleveland)
237	1942-44	Stadium Yacht Basin (Cleveland)
238	1942-44	Stadium Yacht Basin (Cleveland)
239	1942-44	Stadium Yacht Basin (Cleveland)
240	1942-44	Stadium Yacht Basin (Cleveland)
244	1942-44	Tacoma Boat Building
246	1942-44	Tacoma Boat Building
252	1942-44	Weaver Shipyard (Orange)
253	1942-44	Weaver Shipyard (Orange)
254	1942-44	Weaver Shipyard (Orange)
256	1942-44	Weaver Shipyard (Orange)
257	1942-44	Weaver Shipyard (Orange)
258	1942-44	Weaver Shipyard (Orange)
261	1942-44	South Coast (Newport Beach)
264	1942-44	South Coast (Newport Beach)
277	1942-44	J. M. Martinac SB (Tacoma)
278	1942-44	J. M. Martinac SB (Tacoma)
279	1942-44	H. C. Grebe (Chicago)
280	1942-44	H. C. Grebe (Chicago)
282	1942-44	San Diego Marine Com
284	1942-44	San Diego Marine Com

Notes:

British Yard Minesweepers were built originally for the United States Navy to an Admiralty design, but the Royal Navy's request for sweepers was deemed to be of such importance that the first 80 (the block of 1-80) were completed as HM ships. The remaining ships of the BYMS class were taken from the second series which commenced at 137 and these ships had one broad funnel, the first 80 having two short funnels. The unlisted numbers of the series were the ships commissioned for the US Navy. In 1943, 2000 was added to these numbers to avoid confusion with the British Motor Minesweepers prior to this date, therefore all BYMS sailed with the pennant letter 'J' followed by three numbers; consequently, the first of class would be J001.

	J001-J080	J137 *et seq*
SPECIFICATION		
Displacement:	207 tons	215 tons
Dimensions:	130pp 135½ × 24½ × 6	
Armament:	1 × 3in AA	
	2 × 20mm AA on single mtgs	
Machinery:	2 shaft diesel engines all giving 1,200 bhp	
Speed:	14kts	
Complement:	30	

Notes:
British Yard Minesweepers were capable of sweeping contact and influence mines and later on, any known type of mine. The fastest building time for one of these ships was three months and 18 days, and they were of timber construction. The 3in gun in the early boats was mounted without a shield, but later numbers were so fitted.

Losses:
HM BYMS *2019* on 19 September 1943 was mined off Salerno and had to be beached;
HM BYMS *2022* on 16 August 1944 was mined South of Marseille;
HM BYMS *2030* was mined off Le Havre on 8 October 1944;
HM BYMS *2053* was mined off the coast of Sicily on 28 April 1945;
HM BYMS *2072* was lost off Beirut in November 1943;
HM BYMS *2074* was mined off Piraeus on 15 October 1944;
HM BYMS *2077* whilst off the coast of Corinth was mined on 25 October 1944;
HM BYMS *2191* was mined off Kos on 15 April 1944;
HM BYMS *2255* on 5 October 1944 was mined off Boulogne.

Transfer Note:
The following BYMSs were transferred to the Greek Navy (as Greek Yard Minesweepers):
GYMS *2033, 2054, 2056, 2065, 2066, 2067, 2068, 2074, 2186* and *2229*.

Ex-Australian 'Bathurst' Class Minesweepers

Bathurst Class Minesweeper HMS Tamworth *with RAN ships company. She is camouflaged even to the shields on the 20mm AA guns, one on each bridge wing and one aft of the main mast. 'A' gun is fully shielded and trained 90 degrees to port.* (Australian War Memorial)

HMS/ HMAS	(Ordered) Commenced	Completed	Builder
Ballarat	1939	1941	Evans Deakin
*Bathurst	1939	1940	Cockatoo
Bendigo	1940	1941	Cockatoo
Broome	1940	1942	Evans Deakin
*Burnie	1940	1941	Morts
*Cairns	1940	1942	Walkers
*Cessnock	1940	1942	Cockatoo
*Gawler (ex-Gambier)	1940	1942	BHP Whyalla
*Geraldton	1940	1942	Poole & Steele
Goulburn	1940	1941	Cockatoo
*Ipswich	1940	1942	Evans Deakin
Kalgoorlie	1940	1942	BHP Whyalla
*Launceston	1940	1942	Evans Deakin

Lismore	1939	1941	Morts
Maryborough			
(ex-*Cairns*)	1939	1941	Walkers
Pirie	1940	1942	BHP Whyalla
Tamworth	1940	1942	Walkers
Toowoomba	1940	1941	Walkers
Whyalla			
(ex-*Glenelg*)	1940	1942	BHP Whyalla
Wollongong	1940	1941	Cockatoo

SPECIFICATION

Displacement:	650 tons
	733 tons for *Ballarat, Bathurst, Bendigo, Goulburn, Maryborough* and *Whyalla.*
Dimensions:	162pp 186 × 31 × 10
Armament:	1 × 4in DP/HA single mtg at 'A' position
	1 × 3in DP/HA single mtg at 'A' position for *Broome,*
Cessnock,	*Ipswich, Launceston, Pirie, Tamworth* and *Wollongong* only in lieu of the 4in piece
	all ships 4 × .303in mg AA and 1 × 2pdr pom-pom AA or 3 × 20mm AA on single mtgs
Machinery:	2 shaft triple expansion engines all giving 1,750ihp for 15kts excepting *Broome, Cessnock, Geraldton, Ipswich, Launceston, Pirie, Tamworth* and *Wollongong* with 2 shaft triple expansion engines all giving 2,000ihp
Boilers:	2
Speed:	16kts (15kts sea)
Fuel:	Oil fuel 180 tons
Anti-submarine:	2 DCT and/or 2 depth charge racks with up to 60 depth charges
Minesweeping:	All ships had the Oropesa, LL, and SA sweeps
Complement:	90

Notes:
The 'Bathurst' minesweepers were an Australian design with some similarity to the 'Bangor' class of the Royal Navy.

   * The 20 ships listed above were ordered by the Admiralty for use by the Royal Navy but eventually only *Bathurst, Burnie, Cairns, Cessnock, Gawler, Geraldton, Ipswich, Launceston, Lismore, Maryborough, Tamworth, Toowoomba* and *Wollongong* were delivered and they were manned by the RAN.

HMS *Bathurst* only had an open bridge, and no gun shield on her 4in gun. Most of the class had fore and main masts although *Geraldton* in Royal Navy service was seen with a foremast only. Overall of this class, 60 ships were built.

Class Note:
Additional hulls of this class would have been *Akbar, Alice, Amelia, Amity, Augusta, Blaze, Brutus, Buffalo, Errant, Espoir, Exploit* and *Sepoy.*

'Catherine' Class (BAM) Ex-American Minesweepers

HMS	Ex-USN	Completed	Builder
Catherine	BAM 2	1943	Associated SB
Cato	BAM 10	1943	Associated SB
Celebrity			
(later *Pique*, ex-BAM 11)		1943	Associated SB
Chamois	BAM 12	1943	Associated SB

Chance	BAM 13	1943	Associated SB
Combatant	BAM 14	1943	Associated SB
Cynthia	BAM 15	1943	Associated SB
Elfreda	BAM 16	1943	Associated SB
Fairy	BAM 25	1944	Lake Washington
Florizel	BAM 26	1944	Lake Washington
Foam	BAM 27	1944	Lake Washington
Frolic	BAM 28	1944	Lake Washington
Gazelle	BAM 17	1943	Savannah
Gorgon	BAM 18	1943	Savannah
Grecian	BAM 19	1943	Savannah
Jasper			
(ex-Garnet)	BAM 29	1944	Lake Washington
Magic	BAM 20	1943	Savannah
Pylades	BAM 21	1943	Savannah
Steadfast	BAM 31	1943	Gulf
Strenuous	AM 129	1943	Gulf
Tattoo	BAM 32	1943	Gulf
Tourmaline	AM 130	1943	Gulf

HMS Gazelle *under tow in a south coast port. She is fully equipped for minesweeping, with the latest radar fitted. The forward 3in gun is enclosed by a* Zareba. (Imperial War Museum)

SPECIFICATION
Displacement:	890 tons (Full load: 1,250 tons)
Dimensions:	215wl 221¼ × 32¼ × 9½/10¼
Armament:	2 × 3in .50 cal DP/AA on single mtgs in 'A' and 'X' positions (designed) 6 × 20mm AA on single mtgs
Anti-submarine:	4 depth charge racks
	4 depth charge throwers
	56 depth charges carried
Machinery:	2 shaft diesel engines all giving 3,532bhp
Speed:	18kts
Fuel:	325 tons oil
Complement:	96

War Losses:
HMS *Cato* on 6 July 1944 was attacked by a German small battle unit off the Normandy beachhead;
HMS *Magic* was sunk by a German small battle unit on 6 July 1944 when off the Normandy beachhead;
HMS *Pylades* on 8 July 1944 when off the Normandy beachhead was torpedoed;
HMS *Chamois* on 21 July 1944 when off the Normandy beachhead was seriously damaged by a German small battle unit and became a constructive total loss.

'Algerine' Class Reciprocating-Engined Minesweepers

ALGERINE CLASS 1942

HMS		Launched	Builder
Bramble		1945	Lobnitz
Cockatrice		1942	Fleming & Ferguson
Disdain			
(later *Niger*)		1945	Lobnitz
Fierce		1945	Lobnitz
Fly		1942	Lobnitz
Hound		1942	Lobnitz
Hydra		1942	Lobnitz
Larne (II)		1943	Lobnitz
Lennox (II)		1943	Lobnitz
Orestes		1942	Lobnitz
Pelorus		1943	Lobnitz
Rattlesnake		1943	Lobnitz
Rowena		1944	Lobnitz
Stormcloud		1943	Lobnitz
Sylvia		1944	Lobnitz
Tanganyika		1944	Lobnitz
Waterwitch		1943	Lobnitz
Wave		1944	Lobnitz
Welcome		1944	Lobnitz

HMS	Ex-USN	Completed	Builder
Antares	AM *325*	1943	Toronto
Arcturus	AM *326*	1942	Redfern
Aries	AM *327*	1943	Toronto
Clinton	AM *328*	1943	Toronto

This is a profile view of what is believed to be HMS Ready. *Being without any 'P' number, it is difficult to identify her.* (Imperial War Museum)

Friendship	AM 329	1943	Toronto
Gozo	AM 330	1943	Redfern
Lightfoot	AM 331	1943	Redfern
Melita	AM 332	1943	Redfern
Octavia	AM 333	1943	Redfern
Persian	AM 334	1943	Redfern
Postillion	AM 335	1943	Redfern
Thisbe	AM 337	1944	Redfern
Truelove	AM 338	1944	Redfern
Welfare	AM 339	1944	Redfern

HMS	Ex-RCN	Completed	Builder
Coquette	Bowmanville	1944	Redfern
Courier	Arnprior	1943	Redfern
Felicity	Coppercliff	1944	Redfern
Flying Fish	Tillsonburg	1944	Redfern
Golden Fleece	Humberstone	1944	Redfern
Lioness	Petrolia	1944	Redfern
Lysander	Hespeler	1944	Port Arthur
Mariner	Kingcardine	1944	Port Arthur
Marmion (II)	Orangeville	1944	Port Arthur
Mary Rose	Toronto	1944	Redfern
Moon	Mimico	1944	Redfern
Prompt	Huntsville	1944	Redfern
Providence	Forest Hill	1944	Redfern
Regulus	Longbranch	1943	Toronto
Seabear	St Thomas	1944	Redfern
Serene	Leaside	1944	Redfern
Skipjack	Scorpion (ex-Solebay)	1944	Redfern

Canadian-built for the RN

HMS	Completed	Builder
Jaseur	1944	Redfern
Laertes	1944	Redfern
Maenad	1944	Redfern
Magicienne	1944	Redfern
Mameluke	1945	Redfern
Mandate	1945	Redfern
Marvel	1944	Redfern

Michael	1944	Redfern
Minstrel	1944	Redfern
Myrmidon	1944	Redfern
Mystic	1944	Redfern
Nerissa	1945	Redfern
Orcadia	1944	Port Arthur
Ossory	1944	Port Arthur
Pluto	1944	Port Arthur
Polaris	1945	Port Arthur
Pyrrhus	1945	Port Arthur
Romola	1945	Port Arthur
Rosamund	1944	Port Arthur

'Algerine' Class Turbine-Engined Minesweepers

HMS	Launched	All built by
Alarm	1942	Harland & Wolff
Albacore	1942	
Alert	1942	
Algerine	1941	
Brave	1943	
Cadmus	1942	
Chameleon	1944	
Cheerful	1944	
Circe	1942	
Espiegle	1942	
Fancy	1943	
Fantome	1942	
Hare	1944	
Jewel	1944	
Liberty	1944	
Mutine	1942	
Onyx	1942	
Pickle	1943	
Pincher	1944	
Plucky	1943	
Rattler		
(later *Loyalty*)	1942	
Ready	1943	
Recruit	1943	
Rifleman	1943	
Rinaldo	1943	
Rosario	1943	
Spanker	1943	
Squirrel	1944	
Vestal	1943	

SPECIFICATION (Reciprocating and turbine-engined ships)
Displacement: 850 tons (Full load: 935 tons)
Dimensions: 212½pp 225 × 35½ × 8½
Armament: 1 × 4in DP, 2 × 20mm on single mtgs, 2 × twin 20mm (2 × 2)
Anti-submarine: 4 depth charge throwers, 2 depth charge racks, 92+ depth charges carried
Machinery: 2 shaft reciprocating engines all giving 2,000ihp *or* 2 shaft turbines all giving 2,000shp

Boilers:	2
Speed:	16½kts
Complement:	105-30

SPECIFICATION (Canadian-built reciprocating-engined ships)

Displacement:	990 tons
Dimensions:	225 × 35½ × 10½
Armament:	As UK-built ships
Anti-submarine:	1 Hedgehog, 2 depth charge racks, 90+ depth charges carried, 4 depth charge throwers
Machinery:	As UK-built ships
Boilers:	2
Speed:	16/17kts
Range:	4,500nm at 12½kts
Complement:	104/138

Notes:
Canadian-built ships destined for the US Navy but transferred on completion were as above, but armed with 2 × 3in DP 50 cal in lieu of the 4in gun.

Cancelled were *Fireball, Gabriel, Happy Return* by Lobnitz; *Larne, Lennox Lysander* by Simons; *Mariner, Marmion, Mary Rose, Moon, Providence, Regulus, Rowena, Seabear* and *Serene* by Harland & Wolff; *Nicator, Niger, Nonpareil, Nox, Odin* and *Styx* by Toronto.

Allocation Note:
The Group commencing with HMS *Antares* were built in Canadian yards for the USN but upon completion were transferred to the Royal Navy; the Group commencing with HMS *Coquette* were built in Canadian yards for the RCN but upon completion were transferred to the Royal Navy; the Group commencing with HMS *Jaseur* were built in Canadian yards for the Royal Navy.

Losses:
HMS *Alarm* on 2 January 1943 whilst off Bone was bombed by German aircraft;
HMS *Algerine* on 15 November 1942 when off Naples was torpedoed by the Italian U-Boat *Asciglia;*
HMS *Fantome* on 20 May 1943 was mined and sank off Malta;
HMS *Hydra* on 10 November 1944 was mined and sank off Ostend;
HMS *Loyalty* on 27 August 1944 was torpedoed by *U-480* in the English Channel;
HMS *Prompt* on 9 May 1945 was mined and became a constructive total loss when off Ostend;
HMS *Regulus* on 12 January 1945 was mined and sank in the Corfu Channel;
HMS *Squirrel* on 24 July 1945 was mined and sank off Puket near the coast of Siam;
HMS *Vestal* on 26 July 1945 was bombed by Japanese aircraft off Puket.

'Bangor' Class Diesel-Engined Minesweepers

HMS	Launched	Builder
Bangor	1940	Harland & Wolff
Blackpool	1940	Harland & Wolff
Bridlington	1940	Denny
Bridport	1940	Denny
Ex-Canadian		
Fort York (ex-*Mingan*)	1942	Dufferin
Parrsboro	1942	Dufferin
Qualicum	1942	Dufferin
Shippigan	1942	Dufferin
Wedgeport	1942	Dufferin

HMS Stornoway *leaving harbour past one of her sisters and a smaller mine warfare vessel.* Stornoway *was powered by reciprocating engines.* (Imperial War Museum)

SPECIFICATION	(Canadian-built ships reciprocating-engined) *Bayfield, Canso, Caraquet, Guysborough Ingonish*	(Canadian-built ships diesel-engined) *Fort York, Parrsboro, Qualicum, Shippigan, Wedgeport*
Displacement:	672 tons	605 tons
Dimensions:	180 × 28½ × 10¼	162 × 28 × 9
Armament:	1 × 12pdr (12cwt or 1 × 3in) 1 × twin 20mm and 2 × 20mm on single mtgs	(As reciprocating engines)
Anti-submarine:	2 × depth charge throwers 2 × depth charge racks 40 depth charges	(As reciprocating engines)
Machinery:	2 shaft reciprocating engines all giving 2,400ihp	2 shaft diesel engines all giving 2,000bhp
Speed:	16kts	16kts
Boilers:	2	
Fuel:	143 tons of oil fuel	
Range:	1,440nm at 16kts 2,950nm at 11kts	2,700nm at 13kts
Complement:	83 (approx)	83 (approx)

'Bangor' Class Reciprocating-Engined Minesweepers

HMS	Launched	Builder
Beaulieu	Incomplete	Hong Kong & Whampoa Dockyard
Looe	Incomplete	Hong Kong & Whampoa Dockyard
Portland	Incomplete	Taikoo Dockyard
Seaford	Incomplete	Taikoo Dockyard
Blyth	1940	Blyth
Bude	1940	Lobnitz
Clydebank	1941	Lobnitz
Cromer	1940	Lobnitz
Eastbourne	1940	Lobnitz
Felixstowe	1941	Lobnitz
Fraserburgh	1941	Lobnitz

Lyme Regis (I)	1941	Lobnitz
Peterhead	1940	Blyth
Rhyl	1940	Lobnitz
Romney	1940	Lobnitz
Seaham	1941	Lobnitz
Sidmouth	1941	Robb
Stornoway	1941	Robb
Tilbury	1942	Lobnitz

Ex-Canadian

Bayfield	1941	North Vancouver
Canso	1941	North Vancouver
Caraquet	1941	North Vancouver
Guysborough	1941	North Vancouver
Ingonish	1941	North Vancouver

The incomplete hulls of the *Portland* and the *Seaford* were captured by the Japanese in December 1941. Neither ship was at launching stage but, nevertheless, the Japanese Naval constructors decided that the hulls were to be completed and with many modifications this was done. *Portland* became *Taitam* with the pennant number 101 and the *Seaford* was named *Waglan,* pennant number 102. 101 was sunk by American aircraft on 12 January 1945 but 102 survived the war and was surrendered to the Allies and rejoined the fleet. She was employed on minesweeping until 1947, being recommissioned into the Royal Navy the same year. But after all her hard work she was condemned and scrapped at Uraga in 1948.

Similarly at Hong Kong, the incomplete hull of *Looe* was found and again she was completed by the Japanese and named *Nanyo* in 1943, being lost on 23 December 1943, the cause and location unknown.

Finally the *Beaulieu* was again completed, but as a mercantile vessel under the name of *Gyosei Maru.* Later the same year, 1943, she was renamed *Kago Shima Maru* and was surrendered in September 1945.

SPECIFICATION

Displacement:	672 tons
Dimensions:	171½pp 180 × 28½ × 8¼
Armament:	1 × 12pdr 2/3 × 20mm AA
Anti-submarine:	2/4 depth charge racks, 2 depth charge throwers
Machinery:	2 shaft reciprocating engines all giving 2,400ihp
Boilers:	2
Speed:	16kts
Fuel:	183 tons of oil fuel
Complement:	60

SPECIFICATION for 'Bangor' class diesel-engined minesweepers (as reciprocating-engined vessels) except:

Displacement:	605 tons
Dimensions:	153½pp 168 × 28 × 9
Machinery:	2 shaft diesel engines all giving 2,000bhp
Speed:	16kts

SPECIFICATION for 'Bangor' class turbine-engined minesweepers (as reciprocating-engined vessels) except:

Displacement:	650 tons
Dimensions:	162pp 174 × 28½ × 9½
Machinery:	2 shaft geared turbines all giving 2,400shp
Speed:	16kts
Boilers:	2

'Bangor' Class Turbine-Engined Minesweepers

HMS	Launched	Builder
Ardrossan	1941	Blyth SB
Beaumaris	1940	Ailsa SB
Bootle	1941	Ailsa SB
Boston	1940	Ailsa SB
Brixham	1941	Blyth SB
Clacton	1941	Ailsa SB
Cromarty	1941	Blyth SB
Dornoch	1941	Ailsa SB
Dunbar	1942	Blyth SB
Greenock	1941	Blyth SB
Hartlepool	1942	Blyth SB
Harwich	1942	Hamilton
Hythe (ex-Banff)	1941	Ailsa SB
Ilfracombe	1941	Hamilton
Llandudno	1941	Hamilton
Middlesbrough	1942	Hamilton
Newhaven	1942	Hamilton
Padstow	1942	Hamilton
Polruan	1940	Ailsa SB
Poole	1941	Stephen
Rothesay	1941	Hamilton
Rye	1940	Ailsa SB
Sunderland (later Lyme Regis (II))	1942	Stephen
Tenby	1941	Hamilton
Whitehaven	1941	Philip
Worthing	1941	Philip

Design Note:
Although all of one class, by reason of three modes of machinery power (triple expansion, diesel and geared turbines) so three different hull lengths evolved. Diesels did not require a boiler room, and turbines are more compact. This applies to other Classes and other types of HM ships.

Transfers:
The following 'Bangor' class Minesweepers were transferred to the Royal Indian Marine during World War II: HMS Clydebank (as Orissa), Greenock (as Baluchistan), Hartlepool (as Kathiawar), Harwich (as Khyber), Lyme Regis (I) (as Rajputana), Middlesbrough (as Kumaon), Newhaven (as Carnatic), Padstow (as Rohilkand), and Tilbury (as Konkan).

Losses:
HMS Cromer was mined on 9 November 1942 off North Africa;
HMS Felixstowe was mined on 18 December 1943 when off Sardinia;
HMS Guysborough was torpedoed by U-878 whilst off Ushant on 17 March 1945 when on loan to the RCN;
HMS Peterhead whilst sweeping off the Normandy beachhead on 8 June 1944 suffered from a near detonation by an enemy mine and was declared to be a constructive total loss;
HMS Clacton when off Corsica on 31 December 1943 was mined;
HMS Cromarty on 23 October 1943 was mined off the Anzio beachhead;
HMS Hythe was torpedoed by U-371 on 11 October 1943 off Bougie;

Allocation Note:
The groups commencing with HMS Fort York and HMS Bayfield were built in Canadian yards for the RCN, but on completion were transferred to the Royal Navy.

'Coniston' ('Ton') Class Minesweepers

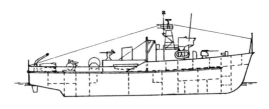

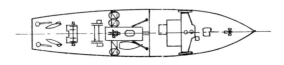

HMS	Commenced	Completed	Builder
Alcaston (ex-Blue Ant)	1951	1953	Thornycroft
Aldington (ex-Pittington)	1953	1956	Camper & Nicholson
Alfriston (ex-Green Ant)	1951	1954	Thornycroft
Alverton (ex-Golden Ant)	1951	1954	Camper & Nicholson
Amerton (ex-Red Aphis)	1951	1954	Camper & Nicholson
Appleton (ex-Blue Aphis)	1951	1954	Goole SB
Ashton	1954	1958	White
Badminton (ex-Ilston)	1953	1955	Camper & Nicholson
Beachampton (ex-Green Aphis)	1951	1954	Goole SB
Belton	1954	1957	Doig
Bevington (ex-Golden Aphis)	1951	1954	White
Bickington (ex-Red Bee)	1951	1954	White
Bildeston (ex-Blue Bee)	1951	1953	Doig

HMS Bronington *was the command of HRH The Prince of Wales KG KT at date of this photograph.* (MOD(N))

Blaxton			
(ex-*Golden Cockchafer*)	1954	1956	Thornycroft
Bossington (ex-*Red Cricket,*			
ex-*Embleton*)	1954	1956	Thornycroft
Boulston (ex-*Golden Bee*)	1951	1954	Richards Ironworks
Brereton (ex-*Red Beetle*)	1951	1954	Richards Ironworks
Brinton (ex-*Blue Beetle*)	1951	1954	CWG
Bronington (ex-*Green Beetle*)	1951	1954	CWG
Burnaston	1951	1954	Fleetlands
Buttington	1951	1954	Fleetlands
Calton (ex-*Blue Butterfly*)	1952	1954	Wivenhoe
Carhampton			
(ex-*Green Butterfly*)	1953	1956	Wivenhoe
Castleton			
(later SANF *Johannesburg*)	1955	1958	White
Caunton (ex-*Golden Butterfly*)	1952	1954	Montrose
Chawton	1955	1958	Fleetlands
Chediston (ex-*Red Centipede*)	1952	1954	Montrose
Chilcompton			
(ex-*Blue Centipede*)	1951	1954	Herd & MaKenzie
Chilton			
(later SANF *East London*)	1956	1958	CWG
Clarbeston			
(ex-*Green Centipede*)	1952	1955	Richards Ironworks
Coniston (ex-*Red Ant*)	1951	1953	Thornycroft
Crichton			
(ex-*Golden Centipede*)			
(ex-*Ossington*)	1952	1954	Doig
Crofton	1956	1958	Thornycroft
Cuxton (ex-*Blue Cicala*)	1952	1954	Camper & Nicholson
Dalswinton (ex-*Red Cicala*)	1952	1954	White
Darlaston (ex-*Green Cicala*)	1952	1954	CWG
Dartington	1955	1958	Philip
Derriton (ex-*Golden Cicala*)	1952	1954	Thornycroft
Dilston	1954	1955	CWG
Dufton	1953	1955	Goole SB
Dumbleton			
(later SANF *Port Elizabeth*)	1956	1958	Harland & Wolff
Dunkerton			
(later SANF *Pretoria*)	1952	1955	Goole SB
(ex-*Golden Firefly*)			
Durweston			
(later INS *Karinada*)	1954	1956	Dorset Yacht Company
Edderton	1951	1954	Doig
Essington (ex-*Blue Cricket*)	1953	1955	Camper & Nicholson
Fenton (ex-*Green Cricket*)	1953	1955	Camper & Nicholson
Fiskerton	1955	1958	Doig
Fittleton (ex-*Golden Cricket*)	1952	1955	White
Flockton (ex-*Red Dragonfly*)	1953	1955	White
Floriston (ex-*Blue Dragonfly*)	1952	1955	Richards Ironworks
Gavington			
(ex-*Golden Dragonfly*)	1952	1954	Doig
Glasserton (ex-*Red Firefly*)	1953	1954	Doig
Hazleton			
(later SANF *Kaapstad*)			
(ex-*Blue Firefly*)	1953	1955	CWG

Hexton (ex-Green Firefly)	1953	1955	CWG
Hickleton (ex-Green Cockchafer)	1954	1955	Thornycroft
Highburton (ex-Blue Cockchafer)	1953	1955	Thornycroft
Hodgeston	1952	1954	Fleetlands
Houghton	1956	1958	Camper & Nicholson
Hubberston	1953	1955	Fleetlands
Ilmington	1952	1955	Camper & Nicholson
Invermoriston	1952	1955	Dorset Yacht Company
Iveston	1952	1955	Philip
Jackton	1953	1956	Philip
Kedleston	1952	1955	Pickersgill
Kellington	1954	1955	Pickersgill
Kemerton	1953	1954	Harland & Wolff
Kildarton (ex-Liston)	1954	1955	Harland & Wolff
Kirkliston	1953	1954	Harland & Wolff
Laleston	1953	1954	Harland & Wolff
Lanton	1953	1955	Harland & Wolff
Letterston	1954	1955	Harland & Wolff
Leverton	1954	1955	Harland & Wolff
Lewiston	1956	1960	Herd & MacKenzie
Lullington	1954	1956	Harland & Wolff
Maddiston	1955	1956	Harland & Wolff
Maryton	1955	1958	Montrose
Maxton	1955	1957	Harland & Wolff
Monkton (ex-Kelton)	1953	1957	Herd & MacKenzie
Nurton	1955	1957	Harland & Wolff
Oakington (later SANF Mosselbaai)	1956	1959	Harland & Wolff
Oulston (ex-Red Cockchafer)	1953	1955	Thornycroft
Overton (later INS Karwar)	1954	1956	Camper & Nicholson
Packington (later SANF Walvisbaai)	1957	1959	Harland & Wolff
Penston	1954	1956	CWG
Picton	1955	1956	CWG
Pollington	1955	1958	Camper & Nicholson
Puncheston	1954	1957	Richards Ironworks
Quainton	1955	1959	Richards Ironworks
Rennington	1955	1960	Richards Ironworks
Repton (ex-Ossington)	1956	1957	Harland & Wolff
Rodington	1953	1955	Fleetlands
Santon	1954	1956	Fleetlands
Sefton	1953	1955	White
Shavington	1953	1956	White
Sheraton	1954	1956	White
Shoulton	1953	1955	Montrose
Singleton	1953	1956	Montrose
Soberton	1955	1957	Fleetlands
Somerleyton (ex-Gamston)	1953	1956	Richards Ironworks
Stratton (later SANF Kimberley)	1955	1959	Dorset Yacht Company
Stubbington	1954	1957	Camper & Nicholson
Sullington	1953	1955	Doig
Swanston	1953	1955	Doig
Tarlton	1953	1955	Doig
Thankerton	1955	1957	Camper & Nicholson

Upton	1955	1956	Thornycroft
Walkerton	1955	1958	Thornycroft
Wasperton	1954	1957	White
Wennington (later INS *Cuddalore*)	1954	1956	Doig
Whitton (later INS *Cannanore*)	1954	1956	Fleetlands
Wilkieston	1955	1957	CWG
Wiston	1956	1960	Wivenhoe
Wolverton	1954	1958	Montrose
Woolaston	1954	1958	Herd & MacKenzie
Wotton	1954	1957	Philip
Yarnton	1954	1957	Pickersgill

SPECIFICATION

Displacement:	360 tons standard (425 tons full load)
Dimensions:	140pp 153 × 28¼ × 8¼
Armament:	1 × 40mm AA with 2 × 20mm on 1 twin mtg, aft of the funnel
Machinery:	2 Mirrles diesel engines, 2,500bhp or 2 Deltic diesel engines, 3000bhp both 2 shafts, giving 15kts max
Fuel:	45 tons oil
Complement:	39

Note:
All were built with timber hulls.

Losses:
HMS *Fittleton* sank after collision with HMS *Mermaid* (Frigate) on 20 September 1976 off the Island of Texel;
HMS *Nurton* became a constructive total loss on 24 February 1983 after colliding with HMS *Brocklesby* (MCMV) off Portland in poor visibility;
HMS *Belton* in October 1971 ran aground in the Hebrides and was later refloated; however, she became a constructive total loss.

'Thorpe' Class Minesweepers

The successor class to the 'Tons' was to have been the 'Thorpe' class and the following were ordered from J. I. Thornycroft & Co: *Ainthorpe* (ex-*Grey Ant*), *Bilsthorpe* (ex-*Silver Ant*) *Cutthorpe* (ex-*Black Ant*).

However, the orders and the class were cancelled in 1953. The 'Thorpe' Minesweepers would have been of a similar specification to the 'Ton' Minesweepers, but of composite construction.

'Ham' Class Inshore Minesweepers

HMS	Commenced	Completed	Builder
Abbotsham	1955	1957	Blackmore
Altham (ex-*Blue Bantam*)	1951	1953	Camper & Nicholson
Arlingham (ex-*Green Bantam*)	1951	1953	Camper & Nicholson
Asheldham (ex-*Golden Bantam*)	1951	1953	Philip
Bassingham (ex-*Red Bullfinch*)	1951	1953	Vosper

HMS Thornham *in European waters on a courtesy visit, but her armament has been dismounted.* (MOD(N))

Bedham (ex-*Blue Bullfinch*)	1951	1953	Bolson
Birdham	1954	1957	J. Taylor
Bisham (ex-*Green Bullfinch*)	1951	1954	Bolson
Blunham (ex-*Golden Bullfinch*)	1951	1953	Brooke Marine
Bodenham (ex-*Red Chaffinch*)	1951	1953	Brooke Marine
Boreham (ex-*Blue Chaffinch*)	1951	1953	Brooke Marine
Bottisham (ex-*Green Chaffinch*)	1951	1953	Ailsa SB
Brantingham (ex-*Golden Chaffinch*)	1951	1954	Ailsa SB
Brigham (ex-*Red Crow*)	1951	1953	Berthon Boat Co
Bucklesham (ex-*Blue Crow*)	1951	1954	Ardrossan Dockyard
Cardingham (ex-*Green Crow*)	1951	1953	Herd & Mackenzie
Chelsham (ex-*Golden Crow*)	1951	1953	Jones (Buckie)
Chillingham (ex-*Red Cuckoo*)	1951	1953	McLean & Sons
Cobham (ex-*Blue Cuckoo*)	1951	1953	Farlie Yacht
Cranham (ex-*Green Cuckoo*)	1952	1955	White
Damerham	1952	1954	Brooke Marine
Darsham (ex-*Red Dove*)	1951	1953	Jones (Buckie)
Davenham (ex-*Blue Dove*)	1951	1953	Weatherhead
Dittisham (ex-*Green Dove*)	1952	1954	Fairlie Yacht
Downham (ex-*Golden Dove*)	1952	1956	White
Edlingham	1954	1955	Weatherhead
Elsenham	1953	1956	Ailsa SB
Etchingham	1954	1958	Ailsa SB
Everingham	1952	1954	Philip & Sons
Felmersham	1952	1954	Camper & Nicholson
Flintham	1952	1955	Bolson
Fordham (ex-*Pavenham*)	1954	1956	Jones (Buckie)
Frettenham (ex-*Golden Cuckoo*)	1953	1954	White
Fritham	1952	1954	Brooke Marine
Georgeham	1955	1957	P. K. Harris
Glentham	1953	1958	Ardrossan
Greetham	1952	1955	Herd & Mackenzie
Halsham	1952	1954	Jones (Buckie)
Harpham	1952	1954	Jones (Buckie)
Haversham	1952	1954	McLean & Sons
Hildersham	1953	1954	Vosper
Hovingham	1954	1956	Fairlie Yacht
Inglesham	1951	1953	White

Isham	1953	1955	White
Kingham	1953	1955	White
Lasham	1952	1954	Weatherhead
Ledsham	1953	1955	Bolson
Littleham	1953	1954	Brooke Marine
Ludham	1953	1955	Fairlie Yacht
Malham	1956	1958	Fairlie Yacht
Mersham	1953	1955	P. K. Harris
Mickleham	1953	1955	Berthon Boat Co
Mileham	1953	1955	Blackmore
Neasham	1955	1957	White
Nettleham	1955	1958	White
Ockham	1955	1959	Ailsa SB
Odiham	1954	1956	Vosper
Ottringham	1956	1958	Ailsa SB
Pagham	1953	1956	Jones (Buckie)
Petersham	1953	1955	McLean & Sons
Pineham	1953	1955	McLean & Sons
Polsham	1956	1960	M. Giles
Popham (ex-*Hatterley*)	1954	1955	Vosper
Portisham (ex-*Foxley*)	1954	1956	Dorset Yacht Co
Powderham	1957	1960	White
Pulham	1954	1956	Saunders-Roe
Puttenham	1954	1958	Thornycroft
Rackham	1954	1956	Saunders-Roe
Rampisham	1954	1957	Bolson
Reedham	1955	1958	Saunders-Roe
Rendlesham	1953	1955	Brooke Marine
Riplingham	1953	1955	Brooke Marine
Sandringham	1955	1957	McLean
Saxlingham	1954	1957	Berthon Boat Co
Shipham	1954	1956	Brooke Marine
Shrivenham	1954	1956	Bolson
Sidlesham	1953	1955	P. K. Harris
Spakham	1954	1955	Vosper
Sparham	1954	1955	Vosper
Stedham	1953	1955	Blackmore
Sulham	1953	1955	Fairlie Yacht
Thakeham	1955	1957	Fairlie Yacht
Thatcham	1955	1958	Jones (Buckie)
Thornham	1955	1958	J. Taylor
Tibenham	1953	1955	McGruer
Tongham	1954	1957	J. N. Miller
Tresham	1953	1955	M. Giles
Warmingham	1953	1956	Thornycroft
Wexham	1953	1955	J. Taylor
Whippingham	1953	1955	J. Taylor
Winteringham (ex-*Cuffley*)	1954	1955	White
Woldingham (ex-*Downley*)	1954	1957	White
Wrentham (ex-*Edgeley*)	1953	1955	Dorset Yacht Co
Yaxham (ex-*Eversley*)	1956	1959	White

SPECIFICATION
Displacement: 120 tons (Full load: 159 tons)
Dimensions: 106/107 × 21¼/21¼ × 5½/5¼
Armament: 1 × 40mm AA or 1 × 20mm AA on the forecastle

Machinery:	2 shaft diesel engines all giving 1,100bhp
Speed:	14kts, permitting 9kts when sweeping
Fuel:	15 tons of oil
Complement:	16/22

Note:
All built with timber hulls.

Losses:
HMS *Bisham* caught fire on 29 September 1956 at Portsmouth and became a constructive total loss;
HMS *Edlingham* caught fire on 29 September 1956 at Portsmouth and became a constructive total loss.

'Ley' Class Inshore Minesweepers

HMS	Commenced	Completed	Builder
Aveley (ex-*Grey Bantam*)	1952	1954	White
Brearley (ex-*Silver Bantam*)	1951	1955	White
Brenchley (ex-*White Bantam*)	1951	1954	Saunders Roe (Anglesey)
Brinkley (ex-*Black Bullfinch*)	1951	1954	Saunders Roe (Anglesey)
Broadley (ex-*Grey Bullfinch*)	1951	1954	Blackmore
Broomley (ex-*Silver Bullfinch*)	1951	1954	P. K. Harris
Burley (ex-*White Bullfinch*)	1951	1954	Dorset Yacht Co
Chailey	1952	1955	Saunders Roe (Anglesey)
Cradley	1952	1955	Saunders Roe (Anglesey)
Dingley	1951	1954	White

HMS Cradley. *This is a very good quarter aerial view of this ISM.* (MOD(N))

SPECIFICATION

Displacement:	123 tons (Full load: 164 tons)
Dimensions:	100wl 106¼ × 21¼ × 5½
Armament:	1 × 40mm AA or 1 × 20mm AA forward of the wheelhouse
Machinery:	2 shaft diesel engines all giving 1,100bhp
Speed:	14kts, permitting 9kts when sweeping
Fuel:	15 tons oil
Complement:	22

Note:
All built with composite hulls. Cancellations were *Foxley* building with the Dorset Yacht Co and *Hattersley* building with Vospers Ltd.

Loss:
HMS *Broadley* on 29 September 1956 was severely damaged by fire at Portsmouth and became a constructive total loss.

'Wilton' Class Mine Countermeasures Vessel (MCM)

HMS	Commenced	Completed	Builder
Wilton	1970	1973	Vosper Thornycroft

HMS Wilton. *This was the first GRP warship in the world, on builders trials with the broad band of Leader on the funnel.* (Vosper Thornycroft)

SPECIFICATION

Displacement:	450 tons
Dimensions:	153 × 28¼ × 8½
Armament:	1 × 40mm
Machinery:	2 Deltic diesel engines to 2 shafts, giving 3,000bhp at 16kts
Range:	2,300nm at 13kts
Complement:	37

Note:
HMS *Wilton* is the first naval vessel in the world to be constructed largely from non-conventional materials. Her design is based on the 'Ton' class Minesweeper and her hull is of GRP. She cost £2¼ million approximately, even though the propulsion machinery and a considerable quantity of the ship's fittings were reconditioned items from the scrapped *Derriton* of the 'Ton' class.

'Hunt' Class Mine Countermeasures Vessels (MCM)

HMS	Commenced	Completed	Builder
Atherstone	1985	1986	Vosper Thornycroft
Berkeley	1985	1988	Vosper Thornycroft
Bicester	1984	1987	Vosper Thornycroft
Brecon	1975	1979	Vosper Thornycroft
Brocklesby	1980	1982	Vosper Thornycroft
Cattistock	1979	1982	Vosper Thornycroft
Chiddingfold	1982	1984	Vosper Thornycroft
Cottesmore	1981	1983	Yarrow SB
Dulverton	1981	1983	Vosper Thornycroft
Hurworth	1982	1984	Vosper Thornycroft
Ledbury	1977	1981	Vosper Thornycroft
Middleton	1980	1983	Yarrow SB
Quorn	1986	1988	Vosper Thornycroft

HMS Middleton *is on builders trials on the Clyde, flying the Yarrow House Flag, Pilot Flag and the Red Ensign. This was only the second ship of this class built on the Clyde.* (Yarrow SB)

SPECIFICATION

Displacement:	615 tons (Full load: 725 tons)
Dimensions:	187wl 196¼ × 32¼ × 9½
Armament:	1 × 40mm Bofors also GPMGs
Machinery:	2 Ruston-Paxman Deltic diesels, each giving 950bhp to 2 shafts, with a third Deltic for slow running
Speed:	15kts free running, 8kts sweeping
Range:	1,550nm at 12kts
Complement:	45

Notes:
This is a follow-up type of vessel from HMS *Wilton* being of the same hull construction, but which combines the role of minesweeper/minehunter in the one hull.

The diesel engines are constructed of low magnetic content steel. There are three 20kW generators to provide power for auxiliary purposes and to pulse the LL sweep.

Minehunting facilities include a CAAIS system with two PAP mine disposal vehicles, together with the usual wire, magnetic and acoustic sweeps.

'River' Class Fleet Minesweepers

HMS	Commenced	Completed	Builder
Arun	1984	1986	Richards (Lowestoft)
Blackwater	1984	1985	Richards (Great Yarmouth)
Carron	1983	1984	Richards (Great Yarmouth)
Dovey	1983	1984	Richards (Great Yarmouth)
Helford	1983	1985	Richards (Great Yarmouth)
Helmsdale	1984	1985	Richards (Lowestoft)
Humber	1983	1985	Richards (Lowestoft)
Itchen	1984	1985	Richards (Lowestoft)
Orwell	1984	1985	Richards (Great Yarmouth)
Ribble	1984	1986	Richards (Great Yarmouth)
Spey	1984	1986	Richards (Lowestoft)
Waveney (ex-Amethyst)	1983	1984	Richards (Lowestoft)

HMS Carron *at speed on builders trials. Note her 40/60 Bofors gun slightly elevated before the bridge. She is wearing the Builders House flag and the Blue Ensign.* (Richards SB)

SPECIFICATION

Displacement:	850 tons (Full load: 920 tons)
Dimensions:	156¼ × 34½ × 11¼ deep
Armament:	1 × 40/60 40mm Bofors AA at 'A' position also small arms
Machinery:	2 shaft diesel engines all giving 3,040bhp
Auxiliary:	2 × 230kW Dorman/Stamford diesel generators, CP propellers fitted
Fuel:	86 tons fuel oil
Range:	4,500nm at 10kts
Speed:	16kts
Complement:	32

Notes:
These are the first minesweepers to be built of steel for the Royal Navy since World War II, also the first to be designed with two funnels since the wartime MMSs and BYMSs.

Designed for use by the Royal Naval Reserve to replace the ageing 'Ton' class. Originally described as EDATS vessels (meaning Extra Deep Armed Team Sweep minesweepers), a number of this class have already proved their seaworthiness by visiting Canada in 1985. HMS *Blackwater* and *Itchen* were originally allocated to Clelands SB prior to the closure of that yard.

'Sandown' Class Single Role Minehunters

HMS	Commenced	Completed	Builder
Bridport	1987	1993	Vosper Thornycroft
Cromer	1987	1991	Vosper Thornycroft
Inverness (II)	1988	1991	Vosper Thornycroft
Sandown	1985	1988	Vosper Thornycroft
Walney	1988	1992	Vosper Thornycroft

The second of Class, HMS *Inverness* of the Sandown Class of Single Role Minehunters. She has completed builders trials and now wears the White Ensign. (Vosper Thornycroft)

SPECIFICATION

Displacement:	450 tons (Full load: 484 tons)
Dimensions:	172 × 34 × 8
Armament:	1 × 30mm DP Rarden cannon, plus GPMGs
Machinery:	2 × Paxman diesel engines connected to 2 Voith Schneider cycloidal propellers, all giving 3,000bhp with 2 bow-thrusters
Auxiliary:	3 diesel auxiliary generators
Shafts:	(See machinery above)
Range:	3,500nm at 12kts
Speed:	15kts
Complement:	40

Notes:
This design originated from a Staff requirement notified to Vosper Thornycroft in 1983 with the first of class, HMS *Sandown,* being ordered in 1985. Similar to the 'Hunt' class of MCMVs, the hull and majority of the superstructure is constructed of glass reinforced plastic (GRP). For low speed noiseless operation, the cycloidal propulsion will be powered from electric motors. These ships will carry two improved PAP 104 submersibles for identification and disposal of mines in depths down to 100 fathoms.

It was anticipated that up to 20 of this class would be built. In March 1989 it was reported that *Inverness* would be completed for the Royal Saudi Arabian Navy.

5: HM Ships and other Vessels Converted for Minesweeping

'Alarm' Class, *Circe* Type Minesweeper

HMS	Launched	Converted	Builder
Circe	1892	1909	HM Dockyard Sheerness
Jason	1892	1909	Vickers
Leda	1892	1909	HM Dockyard Sheerness
Niger	1892	1909	Vickers
Speedy	1893	1909	Thornycroft

HMS Niger. *This is a photograph of* Niger *painted for tropical service but probably still at* Vickers Yard. *No guns appear to be mounted.* (Vickers SB)

SPECIFICATION

Displacement:	810 tons
Dimensions:	230 × 27 × 12½
Armament:	2 × 4.7in DP on single mtgs, 4 × 3pdr QF
Torpedo:	3 × 18in torpedo tubes
Machinery:	2 shaft triple expansion all giving 3,500hp
Boilers:	4
Speed:	18kts
Fuel:	100/160 tons coal
Complement:	85

Notes:

HMS *Speedy* had three funnels, the remainder of the class having two. The 4.7in gun armament was normally landed when minesweeping. Vessels of this class, when constructed, were described as Torpedo Gunboats, their task being to destroy the emergent torpedo boat destroyers, which of course they were not able to do, being lacking in speed.

Losses:

HMS *Jason* on 7 April 1917 whilst off the west coast of Scotland was mined;
HMS *Niger* on 11 November 1914 whilst off Deal was torpedoed by *U-12;*
HMS *Speedy* on 3 September 1914 was mined in the River Humber.

'Sharpshooter' Class *Gossamer* Type Minesweeper

HMS	Launched	Converted	Builder
Gossamer	1890	1909	HM Dockyard Sheerness
Seagull	1889	1909	HM Dockyard Chatham
Skipjack	1889	1909	HM Dockyard Chatham

HMS Seagull. *This is an excellent photograph of* Seagull *with the 'A' frame right aft of the stern. This was the first proper method of streaming the Oropesa Sweep.* (National Maritime Museum)

Spanker	1889	1909	HM Dockyard Devonport
Speedwell	1889	1909	HM Dockyard Devonport

SPECIFICATION
Displacement:	735 tons
Dimensions:	230 × 27 × 12
Armament:	2 × 4.7in DP, 4 × 3pdr QF
Torpedoes:	5 × 14in torpedo tubes
Machinery:	2 shaft triple expansion all giving 3,500hp
Boilers:	4
Speed:	18kts
Fuel:	100/160 tons coal
Complement:	90

Notes:
Similarly designed vessels as the 'Alarm' class Torpedo Catchers. The 4.7in gun armament was normally landed when minesweeping.

Loss:
HMS *Seagull* on 30 September 1918 sank after collision with the SS *Corrib* in the River Clyde.

'Dryad' Class *Dryad* Type Minesweepers

HMS	Launched	Converted	Builder
Dryad (later			
Hamadryad)	1893	1914	HM Dockyard Chatham
Halcyon	1894	1914	HM Dockyard Devonport
Harrier	1894	1914	HM Dockyard Devonport
Hussar	1894	1914	HM Dockyard Devonport

SPECIFICATION
Displacement:	1,070 tons
Dimensions:	250 × 30½ × 13
Armament:	2 × 4.7in DP, 4 × 3pdr QF
Torpedoes:	5 × 18in torpedo tubes
Machinery:	2 shaft triple expansion all giving 3,500hp
Boilers:	4
Speed:	18½kts
Fuel:	100/160 tons coal
Complement:	120

HMS Halcyon *is shown prior to conversion to a minesweeper.* (Imperial War Museum)

Note:
Ships of a similar design and purpose to the 'Alarm' class for which see above. The main 4.7in gun armament was landed when minesweeping was undertaken.

Purchased Trawlers as Minesweepers 1909-13

HMS	Tons	Completed	Builder
Alnmouth	236	1912	Cochrane
Daisy	510	1911	Duthie
Daniel Stroud	209	1912	Hall
Driver (later *Nairn*)	107	1910	Duthie
Esther	510	1911	Duthie
Jackdaw (later *Excellent,* later *Jackdaw*)	250	1903	Goole SB
Janus (later *Kilda*)	243	1911	Goole SB
Jasper (ex-*Rayvernol*)	221	1912	Smiths Dock
Javelin	205	1913	Hall
Osborne Stroud	209	1912	Hall
Rose (ex-*Nizam*)	243	1907	Smiths Dock
Seaflower (later *Sea Rover*)	275	1908	Goole SB
Seamew (later *Nunthorpe Hall*)	248	1909	Smiths Dock
Sparrow (later *Josephine*)	266	1908	Goole SB
Spider (ex-*Assyrian*)	256	1908	Cochrane
Xylopia	262	1911	Cochrane

Notes:
This group of Trawlers were the first purchased by the Admiralty prior to the commencement of World War I, for conversion to Minesweepers.

The following vessels mounted 1 × 6pdr: *Alnmouth, Driver, Osborne Stroud.* The remaining ships of the group carried 1 × 12pdr.

HMS Seaflower. *This photograph shows* Seaflower *with four dan buoys secured to the foremast shrouds. She is painted uniformly dark grey and is rigged for minesweeping.*

(National Maritime Museum)

Losses:
HMS *Jasper* on 26 August 1915 was mined in the Moray Firth;
HMS *Javelin* was mined on 17 October 1915 off the Longsands Light Vessel;
HMS *Spider* when off Lowestoft in heavy weather took the ground and was wrecked, on 21 November 1914.

Purchased Admiralty Trawlers, 'Military' Class, as Minesweepers

HMS	Launched	Builder
Bombardier	1915	Smiths Dock
Brigadier (later *Bugler*)	1915	Smiths Dock
Carbineer	1915	Smiths Dock
Dragoon (later *Drummer*)	1915	Smiths Dock
Fusilier (later *Carbineer*)	1915	Smiths Dock
Highlander	1915	Smiths Dock
Lancer	1914	Smiths Dock
Sapper	1915	Smiths Dock
Trooper	1915	Smiths Dock

(HMS *Gunner* of this class was fitted-out whilst building as a 'Q' ship.)

SPECIFICATION

	Bombardier *Brigadier*	*Carbineer* *Dragoon* *Fusilier* *Lancer* *Sapper*	*Highlander* *Trooper*
Gross Tons:	303	276	239
Dimensions:	130pp × 24 × 13¼	130pp × 23½ × 12¼	118pp × 22½ × 12½
Armament:	1 × 6pdr AA — *Highlander, Trooper*		
	1 × 12pdr — *Bombardier, Brigadier, Fusilier, Sapper*		
	1 × 12pdr and 1 × bomb-thrower — *Dragoon*		
	1 × 3pdr — *Carbineer, Lancer*		
Machinery:	1 shaft triple expansion		

Losses:
HMS *Carbineer* on 18 May 1916 was wrecked on Crebawethan Point;
HMS *Lancer* whilst off the Brighton Light Vessel was in collision on 18 July 1918;

HMS *Sapper* in bad weather foundered on 29 December 1917 whilst off the Owers Light Vessel.

Purchased Admiralty Trawlers, 'Strath' Class, as Minesweepers — Non-standard Hulls

HMS	Launched	Builder
James Archibald	1917	Duthie
John Abbott	1917	Duthie
Joseph Annison	1917	Duthie
Richard Bennett	1917	Hall Russell
Samuel Baker	1917	Hall Russell

HMS Richard Bennett *leaving harbour at dead slow speed. She is rigged as a trawler/mine-sweeper but appears to be unarmed. Note the extended fore and main masts to carry the wireless aerials.* (National Maritime Museum)

SPECIFICATION
Displacement:	194/237 tons
Dimensions:	115/122¼pp × 22/22½
Armament:	1 × 12pdr *James Archibald, John Abbott, Joseph Annison, Samuel Baker*
	1 × 12pdr and 1 × bomb-thrower *Richard Bennett*
Machinery:	1 shaft triple expansion

Notes:
The above Trawlers at the date of purchase were completing for their normal task of fishing. However, their average tonnage and dimensions approximated them closest to the trawler *Strathlochy* which was the name ship for the following 'Strath' class.

Admiralty Trawlers, 'Strath' Class, as Minesweepers

HMS	Launched	Builder
Edward Barker	1918	Hall Russell
George Borthwick	1917	Hall Russell
George Burton	1917	Hall Russell
James Bentole	1917	Hall Russell
John Barry	1917	Hall Russell
John Corwarder	1917	Fleming & Ferguson
John Jackson	1918	Rennie Forrestt
Thomas Bryan	1917	Hall Russell
Thomas Graham	1918	Scott Bowling
William Biggs	1917	Hall Russell

SPECIFICATION

Gross tons:	215
Displacement:	311 tons
Dimensions:	115½pp 123 × 22 × 12
Armament:	1 × 12pdr *Edward Barker, George Burton, James Bentole, John Barry, John Corwarder, John Jackson, Thomas Bryan, Thomas Graham, William Biggs* 1 × 12pdr and 1 × bomb-thrower: *George Borthwick*
Machinery:	1 shaft triple expansion giving 415ihp
Speed:	10kts

Note:
The above Trawlers are the only known ships of this class to have been completed as Minesweepers. This is not to say that others of the class were not converted later.

Purchased Admiralty Trawlers, 'Castle' Class, as Minesweepers — Non-standard Hulls

HMS	Launched	Builder
Daniel Harrington	1917	Smiths Dock
Festing Grindall	1917	Smiths Dock
Hugh Black	1917	Cook, Welton & Gemmell
James Johnson (later *Thomas Deas*)	1917	Smiths Dock
John Burlingham (ex-*Rehearo*)	1917	Cook, Welton & Gemmell
John Gillman	1917	Smiths Dock
Thomas Blackthorn	1917	Cook, Welton & Gemmell
Thomas Buckley	1917	Cook, Welton & Gemmell

SPECIFICATION

Displacement:	236/276 tons
Dimensions:	117½/125½pp × 22/23½ beam
Armament:	1 × 12pdr *Daniel Harrington, Festing Grindall, Hugh Black, Thomas Blackthorn, Thomas Buckley* 1 × 12pdr and 1 × bomb-thrower *Thomas Deas, John Burlingham, John Gillman*
Machinery:	1 shaft triple expansion

Notes:
The above Trawlers at the date of purchase were completing for their normal task of fishing. However, their average tonnage and dimensions approximated them closest to the Trawler *Raglan Castle* which was the name ship for the following 'Castle' class.

HMS Thomas Dowding *is shown at anchor with a 6-pounder gun on a bandstand aft of the funnel. She is flying the North Cone of a minesweeping trawler.* (National Maritime Museum)

Admiralty Trawlers, 'Castle' Class, as Minesweepers

HMS	Launched	Builder
Alexander Palmer (later *Ness*)	1917	Smiths Dock
Andrew Sack	1917	Smiths Dock
Arthur Lessimore	1917	Smiths Dock
Denis Casey	1918	Ailsa SB
Emmanuel Camelaire	1918	Ailsa SB
George Clark	1917	J. P. Renoldson
James Green	1917	Smiths Dock
John Bomkworth (later *Wear*)	1918	Cook, Welton & Gemmell
John Casewell	1917	Ailsa SB
John Chivers (later *Erne*)	1917	Bow McLachlan
John Collins	1917	Ailsa SB
John Kidd	1917	Smiths Dock
John Pollard	1917	Smiths Dock
John Thorling	1917	Smiths Dock
Peter Blumberry	1917	Cook, Welton & Gemmell
Richard Roberts	1917	Smiths Dock
Robert Davidson	1917	C. Renoldson
Samuel Spencer	1917	Smiths Dock
Thomas Chambers	1917	Bow McLachlan
Thomas Dowding	1917	C. Renoldson
Thomas Goble	1917	Smiths Dock
Thomas Hankins	1918	J. P. Renoldson
Thomas Twiney	1917	Smiths Dock
Valentine Bower	1917	C. Renoldson
William Bunce	1917	Smiths Dock
William Cummins	1917	Bow McLachlan
William Symons	1917	Smiths Dock

SPECIFICATION
Gross tons: 275
Displacement: 360 tons
Dimensions: 125½pp 134 × 23½ × 12¼

Armament:	All had 1 × 12pdr except as below: 1 × 12 pdr and 1 × bomb-thrower. *John Casewell, John Pollard, Samuel Spencer, Thomas Chambers, William Bunce* 1 × 6pdr and 1 × bomb-thrower. *John Bomkworth*
Machinery:	1 shaft triple expansion giving 480ihp
Speed:	10½kts

Notes:

The above Trawlers are the only known ships of this class to have been completed as Minesweepers. This is not to say that others of the class were not converted later.

The previous sentence applies to Trawlers and Drifters of the following classes: 'Strath', 'Military', 'Mersey', Canadian 'Castle', Admiralty Drifters (Wood), Admiralty Drifters (Steel).

Admiralty Trawlers, 'Castle' Class, as Minesweepers — Canadian-Built

HMS	Completed	Builder
TR 1	1917	Port Arthur
TR 2	1917	Port Arthur
TR 3	1918	Port Arthur
TR 4	1918	Port Arthur
TR 5	1918	Port Arthur
TR 6	1918	Port Arthur
TR 7	1918	Collingwood
TR 8	1918	Collingwood
TR 9	1918	Collingwood
TR 10	1918	Collingwood

Canadian 'Castle' Class Trawler TR8, *at anchor with some sweep gear on her stern and flying the White Ensign at the gaff.* (D. Brindle)

SPECIFICATION

Gross tons:	275
Displacement:	360 tons
Dimensions:	125½pp 134 × 23½ × 12¼
Armament:	1 × 12pdr (TR 8)
Machinery:	1 shaft triple expansion giving 480ihp
Speed:	10½kts

Notes:
HMS *TR 8* is the only known armed minesweeping trawler of this class on completion. There were no losses.

Purchased Admiralty Trawlers, 'Mersey' Class, as Minesweepers — Non-standard Hulls

HMS	Launched	Builder
Anthony Aslett (later *Rother*)	1917	Cochrane
Cornelius Buckley	1917	Cochrane
William Abrahams	1917	Cochrane
William Westenburg	1917	Cochrane

SPECIFICATION

Displacement:	248/324 tons
Dimensions:	120½/138½pp 22/23¼ beam
Armament:	1 × 12pdr *Cornelius Buckley, William Abrahams*
	1 × 12pdr and 1 × bomb-thrower *Anthony Aslett*
	2 × 12pdr on single mtgs *William Westonburg*
Machinery:	1 shaft triple expansion

Notes:
The above Trawlers at the date of purchase were completing for their normal task of fishing. However, their average tonnage and dimensions approximated them closest to the Trawler *Lord Mersey* which was the name ship for the following 'Mersey' class.

Admiralty Trawlers, 'Mersey' Class, as Minesweepers

HMS	Launched	Builder
Andrew King (later *Ouse*)	1917	Cochrane
Edward Williams	1917	Cochrane
George Andrew	1917	Cochrane
Henry Cramwell	1918	Lobnitz
Henry Ford (later *Boadicea*, later *Henry Ford*)	1917	Cochrane
Isaac Chant (later *Colne*)	1918	Lobnitz
James Buchanan	1917	Cochrane
Lewis Roatley	1917	Cochrane
Michael Clements	1917	Cochrane
Robert Barton	1917	Cochrane
Robert Bookless	1917	Cochrane
Thomas Atkinson	1917	Cochrane
Thomas Bailey	1917	Cochrane
Thomas Thresher	1918	Cochrane
William Jones (later *Boyne*)	1918	Cochrane
William Rivers	1917	Cochrane

SPECIFICATION

Gross tons:	324
Displacement:	438 tons
Dimensions:	138½pp 148 × 23¾ × 12¾
Armament:	1 × 12pdr on all vessels except as below: 1 × 12pdr and 1 × bomb-thrower *Edward Williams*; 1 × 12pdr AA *George Andrew, Henry Ford, James Buchanan,* *Lewis Roatley, Michael Clements*
Machinery:	1 shaft triple expansion giving 600ihp
Speed:	11kts

Notes:
The above Trawlers are the only known ships of this class to have been completed as Minesweepers. This is not to say that others of the class were not converted later.

Losses:
On 20 February 1941 whilst off Tobruk HMS *Ouse* was mined;
HMS *Michael Clements* was in collision off St Catherines Point on 8 August 1918.

Purchased Admiralty Drifters as Minesweepers, Non-standard Hulls — Wood Construction

HMS	Launched	Builder
Darkness (later *Columbine*)	1918	Fellows
Flat Calm	1918	Forbes
Fogbow	1918	Forbes
Midnight Sun	1918	Richards
Nightfall	1918	Richards
Nimbus	1918	Stephen, Banff
Ray	1918	Stephen, Banff

SPECIFICATION

Gross tons:	86/95
Dimensions:	88pp × 20
Armament:	1 × 6pdr all vessels
Machinery:	1 shaft triple expansion

Notes:
The above Drifters at the date of purchase were completing for their normal task of fishing. However, their average tonnage and dimensions approximated them closest to the Admiralty Wood Drifters then under construction for the Royal Navy.

HMS Midnight Sun *is shown at her moorings. She does not carry any wireless aerials and there is no visible armament.* (National Maritime Museum)

Admiralty Drifters as Minesweepers — Wood Construction

HMS	Launched	Builder
Afterglow	1918	Chambers
Atmosphere	1918	Chambers
Avalanche	1918	Chambers
Backwash	1918	Colby
Blue Sky	1918	Colby
Borealis	1918	Colby
Daylight	1918	Fellows
Etesian	1918	Fellows
Fair Weather	1918	Forbes
Fiery Cross	1918	Forbes
Flame	1918	Forbes
Full Moon	1918	Forbes
Solstice	1918	Herd & Mackenzie

SPECIFICATION
Gross tons: 94
Displacement: 175 tons
Dimensions: 86½pp 94½ × 20 × 10
Armament: 1 × 6pdr
Machinery: 1 shaft triple expansion giving 270ihp
Speed: 9kts

Note:
The above Drifters are the only known ships of this class to have been completed as Minesweepers. This is not to say that others of the class were not converted later.

Loss:
HMS *Blue Sky* in bad weather foundered on 12 June 1922 in the Thames Estuary.

Admiralty Drifters as Minesweepers — Steel Construction

HMS	Launched	Builder
Cascade	1918	Ouse SB
Crescent Moon	1918	Duthie
Dawn	1918	Duthie
Fork Lightning	1918	Brooke
Freshet	1918	Hall
Halo	1918	Hall
Harmatton	1918	Hall
Iceberg	1918	Hall
Icefloe	1918	Hall
Icicle	1918	Hall
Landfall	1918	Lewis
Levanter	1918	Hall
Lunar Bow	1918	Lewis
Mist	1918	Lewis
Moonbeam	1918	Lewis
Moonshine	1918	Lewis
Overfall	1918	Colby
Sea Fog	1918	Webster & Bickerton
Seabreeze	1918	Hall
Spectrum	1918	Brooke

HMS Cascade *is shown in Plymouth Sound. She has no wireless aerial and appears to be unarmed.* (National Maritime Museum)

SPECIFICATION

Gross tons:	94
Displacement:	198 tons
Dimensions:	85pp 93¼ × 18½ × 9¼
Armament:	1 × 6pdr where fitted
Machinery:	1 shaft triple expansion giving 270ihp
Speed:	9kts

Note:
The above Drifters are the only known ships of this class to have been completed as Minesweepers. This is not to say that others of the class were not converted later.

Loss:
HMS *Levanter* went ashore on 13 October 1926 near Peterhead and was later sold out of the Service.

Ex-Mercantile Vessels as Minesweepers

HMS Reindeer *clearly showing her lines as an ex-Railway Steamer, but painted grey with the 'A' frame at the stern for minesweeping. She appears to be well armed.* (Imperial War Museum)

HMS	Tons	Completed	Armament	Converted for M/S	Remarks/ Losses
Atalanta II	486	1906	2 × 6pdr AA	1915	
Clacton	820	1904	2 × 12pdr	1914	Torpedoed by U-73 on 3 August 1916 at Chai Aghizi
Folkestone	496	1903	2 × 12pdr	1914	
Gazelle	613	1889	2 × 12pdr	1914	In 1915 was converted for Mine Laying (see page 28)
Hythe	509	1905	2 × 12pdr	1914	Collided with Sarnia on 28 October 1915 off Cape Helles
Lynn (ex-Lynx)	608	1889	2 × 12pdr	1914	
Newmarket	833	1907	2 × 12pdr	1914	Torpedoed by UC-38 on 16 July 1917 in the Eastern Mediterranean
Reindeer	1101	1897	2 × 12pdr	1914	
Roedean (ex-Roebuck)	1094	1897	2 × 12pdr	1914	In bad weather foundered after collision with the harbour service repair hulk Inperieuse at Longhope on 13 January 1915 after dragging her anchor
St Seiriol	928	1914	2 × 6pdr AA	1915	On 25 April 1918 was mined when off the Shipwash LV
Whitby Abbey	1188	1908	2 × 12pdr	1915	

Notes:
All requisitioned/purchased merchant vessels from the coasting trade converted for Minesweeping.

Ex-Mercantile Paddle Vessels as Minesweepers

HMS	Tons	Completed	Armament	Converted for M/S	Remarks/ Losses
Aiglon (ex-Eagle)	647	1898	2 × 6pdr AA	1915	
Albyn (ex-Albion)	363	1893	1 × 6pdr & 1 × 6pdr AA	1915	
Balmoral	473	1900	1 × 6pdr	1915	
Belle	147	1892	1 × 6pdr	1917	
Bickerstaffe	213	1879		1917	
Bourne (ex-Bournemouth Queen)	353	1908	2 × 6pdr AA	1915	
Brighton Queen	553	1897	2 × 6pdr	1914	Was mined on 6 October 1915 off Nieuport
Britain (ex-Britannia)	459	1896	1 × 6pdr AA	1915	
Caledonia	244	1889	1 × 3pdr	1917	
Cambridge (ex-Cambria)	420	1895	1 × 3pdr & 1 × 6pdr both AA	1914	

HMS Snowdon, *converted similarly to* Greyhound II, *with HMS* Bourne *of a similar type alongside.* (R. Perkins)

City of Rochester	235	1904	1 × 6pdr	1917	
Clacton Belle	458	1890	2 × 6pdr AA	1915	
Devonia	520	1905	1 × 12pdr	1914	
Duchess (ex-*Duchess of Fife*)	336	1903	2 × 6pdr	1916	
Duchess of Buccleuch	450	1915	1 × 6pdr & 1 × 6pdr AA	1916	
Duchess of Fife	443	1899	2 × 6pdr AA	1916	
Duchess of Hamilton	553	1890	2 × 6pdr	1915	On 11 September 1915 was mined off the Longsand buoy
Duchess of Kent	399	1897	1 × 6pdr AA	1916	
Duchess of Montrose	322	1902	1 × 6pdr	1915	Was mined on 18 March 1917 off Dunkirk
Eagle III	432	1910	1 × 6pdr & 1 × 6pdr AA	1916	
Erin's Isle	633	1912	1 × 6pdr	1915	On 7 February 1919 was mined off the Nore in the Edinburgh Channel
Fair Maid	432	1915	1 × 6pdr	1915	Mined on 9 November 1916 near the Cross Sands Buoy
Glen Avon	509	1912	1 × 6pdr & 12pdr AA	1914	
Glen Cross (ex-*Glen Rosa*)	306	1893	1 × 6pdr	1917	
Glen Rosa	323	1877	1 × 3pdr	1917	
Glen Usk	524	1914	1 × 6pdr AA	1915	
Grenade (ex-*Grenadier*)	357	1885	1 × 6pdr AA	1916	
Greyhound II	542	1895	2 × 6pdr AA	1915	
Helper (ex-*Sir Francis Drake*)	173	1873	1 × 3pdr	1917	
Her Majesty	235	1885	1 × 3pdr	1917	
Isle of Arran	313	1892	1 × 3pdr	1917	
Junior (ex-*Juno*)	592	1898	1 × 6pdr AA	1915	
Jupiter II	394	1896	1 × 6pdr AA	1915	
Kenilworth	390	1898		1917	
Kylemore (ex-*Vulcan*)	319	1897	1 × 6pdr AA	1915	

Lady Clare	234	1891	1 × 3pdr	1917	
Lady Evelyn	320	1900	1 × 6pdr	1917	
Lady Ismay	495	1911	2 × 6pdr	1914	Mined near the Galloper LV on 21 December 1915
Lady Moyra (ex-*Gwalia*)	519	1905	2 × 6pdr AA	1915	
Lady Rowena	332	1891		1917	
London Belle	738	1893	2 × 6pdr AA	1916	
Lorna Doone	410	1891	1 × 6pdr AA	1915	
Marchioness of Breadalbane	246	1890		1917	
Marchioness of Fife	246	1890	1 × 6pdr & 1 × 6pdr AA	1915	
Marmion II	403	1906	1 × 6pdr AA	1915	
Marsa (ex-*Mars*)	317	1902	1 × 6pdr & 1 × 6pdr AA	1916	When entering Harwich Harbour on 18 November 1917 was in collision and sank
Melcombe Regis (ex-*Lune*)	253	1892	1 × 3pdr	1917	
Mercury	378	1892	2 × 6pdr AA	1915	
Monarchy (ex-*Monarch*)	315	1888	1 × 6pdr	1917	
Nepaulin (ex-*Neptune*)	378	1892		1914	Mined on 20 April 1917 near the Dyck LV
Princess Beatrice	253	1880	1 × 3pdr	1917	
Queen Empress	411	1912	2 × 6pdr AA	1915	
Queen of the North	590	1895	2 × 6pdr AA	1916	Mined on 20 July 1917 off Orford Ness
Ravenswood	345	1891	1 × 6pdr AA	1915	
Redgauntlet II	278	1895		1916	
Royal Pearl (ex-*Pearl*)	171	1897		1917	
Royal Ruby (ex-*Ruby*)	171	1897		1917	
Royal Sapphire (ex-*Sapphire*)	223	1898		1917	
St Elvies	567	1896	2 × 6pdr AA	1915	
St Trillo (ex-*Rhos Trevor*)	164	1876	1 × 3pdr	1917	
Slieve Bearnagh	383	1894	1 × 6pdr	1915	
Snowdon	338	1892	1 × 6pdr AA	1915	
Southern Belle	570	1896	2 × 6pdr AA	1915	
Talla (ex-*Talisman*)	279	1896		1917	
Verdun (ex-*Paris*)	804	1888	1 × 6pdr AA	1916	
Walton Belle	465	1897	2 × 6pdr AA	1915	
Waverley	449	1899	1 × 6pdr & 1 × 6pdr AA	1915	
Way (ex-*Waverley*)	240	1885	1 × 6pdr	1917	
Westward Ho	438	1894	1 × 12pdr AA & 1 × 6pdr AA	1914	Intended to be named *Westhope*

| *William Muir* | 412 | 1879 | 1 × 12pdr | 1917 |
| *Yarmouth Belle* | 522 | 1898 | 2 × 6pdr AA | 1915 |

Notes:
Many of these paddlers were aged, yet they had the required speed and shallow draught for their new task of Minesweeping. They would also have ample accommodation space for the ship's complement and deck space for the sweep gear.

Other Paddle vessels being equipped for M/S were *Cloghmore* (ex-*Greenore*) 217 tons of 1896, and *Earl of Dunraven,* 174 tons of 1888, but were not so completed. Some of the above served in World War II.

The Ex-Mercantile Vessels as Minesweepers were of screw (propeller) propulsion. In general they would be able to sweep in harsher weather than the paddlers and in conditions similar to those expected for the Trawlers and Drifters engaged in Minesweeping.

Patrol Paddle Vessels as Minesweepers

HMS	Tons	Completed	Armament	Converted for M/S	Remarks/ Losses
Cleethorpes	273	1903	1 × 6pdr & 1 × 6pdr AA	1919	Converted from a Paddle Air Service Scout
Duchess of Norfolk	381	1911	1 × 6pdr AA	1919	
Duchess of Richmond	354	1910	1 × 6pdr AA	1919	Mined on 28 June 1919 in the Aegean Sea
Duchess of York	302	1896	1 × 6pdr AA	1916	
Duke (ex-*Duke of Devonshire*)	257	1896	2 × 6pdr AA	1916	
Emperor of India II (ex-*Princess Royal*)	482	1906	2 × 6pdr AA	1919	
Marchioness of Lorne	295	1891	1 × 6pdr & 1 × 6pdr AA	1919	
Minerva II	315	1893	1 × 6pdr & 1 × 6pdr AA	1919	
Princess Mary	326	1911	1 × 6pdr AA	1916	Sank on 2 August 1919 after striking the wreck of HMS *Majestic* off Cape Helles
Queen IV	345	1902	1 × 6pdr AA	1919	

Notes:
All taken into service as Paddle Patrol Vessels to serve as escorts and A/S vessels. HMS *Cleethorpes* carried aircraft off the Humber on anti-Zeppelin patrols with *Brocklesby* and *Killingholme.* Converted to PMSs after the war to clear the numerous mines.

Requisitioned Patrol and other Vessels as Minesweepers

| HMS *Dirk*: | **Gross tons:** | 181 |
| | **Built:** | 1909; served as a Minesweeper and was armed with 1 × 12pdr and 1 × 6pdr AA. On 28 May 1918 was torpedoed by a U-Boat whilst off Flamborough Head. |

HMS Harlequin *is shown bereft of all minesweeping gear.* (National Maritime Museum)

HMS *Harlequin*
Gross tons: 838
Built: 1897 by Russell
Dimensions: 200pp × 24 × 6
Armament: 1 × 3pdr gun
Machinery: Diagonal compound of 1,000ihp to paddles giving 16kts;
Service: Was in commission as a Minesweeper from early 1917 until May 1919.

HMS *Wanderer*
(later *Warden*)
Gross tons: 589
Built: 1895 by McMillan
Dimensions: 210pp × 25 × 6½
Armament: Served as a Minesweeper and was armed with 2 × 6pdr on single mtg
Machinery: Diagonal compound of 1,400ihp to paddles giving 16kts
Service: Was converted for minesweeping and served off the River Tyne from June 1917 until the termination of hostilities.

HMS *Daisy*
Gross tons: 510
Built: 1911 by Duthie
Dimensions: 125pp × 22½ × 10
Armament: 1 × 12pdr gun
Machinery: Triple expansion of 500ihp giving 10kts
Service: Purchased for survey duties but equipped for minesweeping.

HMS *Ester*   Details as for *Daisy* and similar service.

Ex-American/Canadian Motor Launches 75ft & 80ft (MLs)

Builder:	Electric Boat Co	Canadian Vickers
Motor Launch Nos:	*1-50* inc	*51-550* and *551-580* inc
SPECIFICATION		
Displacement:	34 tons	37 tons
Dimensions:	75 × 12 × 4	80 × 12¼ × 4

Armament:	1 × 13pdr	1 × 3in
	or 1 × 3pdr	
	1 or 2mg	1 or 2mg
Machinery:	2 shaft petrol engines all giving 440bhp	
Anti-submarine:	Depth charges were carried	Depth charges were carried
Range:	1,000nm at 15kts	
Speed:	18-20kts	
Complement:	8	10

HM M/L 6. This is a 75 ft version of the ex-American M/Ls which were used for minesweeping.
(Imperial War Museum)

Notes:
The Motor Launch (ML) was a new type of craft for the Royal Navy and was used for many and varied tasks including inshore minesweeping, coastal minelaying, hydrophone vessels, smokescreen generators and anti-submarine tasks. The evolution of the ML was as a direct result of the great success achieved from the patrols of requisitioned Motor Boats. These had been formed into the Motor Boat Reserve and were mainly craft of ex-private ownership varying from three to 75 tons displacement and armed according to capacity. The first 50 MLs were ordered from Elco in the USA with a length of 75ft with further orders for 530 launches of 80ft length from Canadian Vickers. They were too small for transatlantic delivery and so crossed to the UK on merchant ships as deck cargo.

For details of losses of these motor launches see 'Ex-American/Canadian Motor Launches 75ft & 80ft (MLs) as Minelayers', page 35

Whalers as Minesweepers World War I

HMS	Tons	Completed	Converted for M/S
Fair Helga	175	1912	1917
Fair Magda	175	1912	1917

Notes:
Both vessels purchased.
Armament is not known, however other Whalers were armed with 1 × 12pdr and 2 × 3pdr.
Whalers were reported to be inferior to Trawlers and Drifters for minesweeping duties,
particularly in the matter of seakeeping.

Ex-Russian Trawlers as Minesweepers

HMS	Ex-Russian	Completed	Builder
Battleaxe	T 16	1916	Smiths Dock
Goldaxe	T 13	1916	Smiths Dock
Iceaxe	T 17	1916	Smiths Dock
Poleaxe	T 19	1917	Cochrane
Silveraxe (ex-*Tres*)	T 33	1908	Hall Russell
Stoneaxe	T 14	1916	Smiths Dock

This photograph of HMS Iceaxe *shows her with the modified 'A' frame on the stern for mine-sweeping, plus Dan buoys, two on the shrouds of the fore and mainmast. She carries a six-pounder on the small bandstand on the forecastle.* (Wright & Logan)

SPECIFICATION

	Battleaxe, Goldaxe Iceaxe, Stoneaxe	Poleaxe	Silveraxe
Displacement:	520 tons	540 tons	272 tons
Dimensions:	130pp × 23½ × 12	135½pp × 23½ × 12½	?
Armament:	1 × 75mm	1 × 12pdr	1 × 12pdr
Machinery:	1 shaft triple expansion giving 490ihp	1 shaft triple expansion giving 500ihp	? ? ?

Speed:	10½kts	11kts	?
Fuel:	140 tons of coal	140 tons of coal	?
Complement:	20	20	?

Notes:
These Trawlers were acquired in the White Sea by certain of HM ships circa August 1917 and later, probably with the acquiescence of Tsarist naval officers due to conditions in the Imperial Russian Navy (IRN). They were all built in the UK with strengthened forecastles for navigation in ice. Other IRN ships were acquired, but only the above were commissioned as Minesweepers by the Royal Navy from a total of 17.

Ex-German (Prize) Trawlers as Minesweepers

HMS	**Tons**	**Built**	**Captured by**	**Builder**
Censin 1 × 6pdr AA	145	1894	HMS *Conquest* 30 September 1915 ex-*Burgermeister Smidt*	Seebeck
Chirsin 1 × 6pdr AA	218	1912	Detained 4 Aug 1914 at Aberdeen	Unterweser
Churchsin 1 × 6pdr AA	142	1900	HMS *Conquest* 30 Sept 1915 ex-*St Georg*	Smiths Dock
Classin 1 × 3pdr	182	1889	HMS *Arethusa* 20 Aug 1915 ex-*Sophie*	Wencke
Clersin 1 × 6pdr AA	155	1891	HMS *Aurora* 7 Oct 1915 ex-*Resie*	Wencke
Clonsin 1 × 6pdr	202	1911	Detained 4 Aug 1914 at Aberdeen ex-*Dr Robitzsch*	Seebeck
Coalsin 1 × 6pdr AA	130	1892	HMS *Mentor* 7 Oct 1915 ex-*Toni*	Tecklenborg
Cooksin 1 × 6pdr AA	149	1896	Unknown warship 7 Oct 1915 ex-*Herbert*	Seebeck
Craigsin 1 × 6pdr AA	141	1895	Unknown warship 7 Oct 1915 ex-*Blumenthal*	Bremer Vulkan
Cromsin 1 × 6pdr AA	138	1895	HM S/M S1 24 June 1915 ex-*Ost*	W & G Cooke

Notes:
These Trawlers were either taken over in port or captured at sea early in World War I. Approximately 30 were thus acquired, but only the vessels named above were converted to Minesweepers.

Mechanically-Propelled Yacht as a Minesweeper — World War I

HMS	**Tons**	**Completed**	**Converted for M/S**	**Armament**
Adventuress	342	1913	1914	2 × 12pdr DP LA

Ex-Italian Trawlers as Minesweepers

HMS	Tons	Completed	Converted for M/S	Origin
Kumariham (ex-*Minato Maru No 3*)	259	1913	1917	All of these ex-Italian trawlers had been
Kakshimi (ex-*Daitoku Maru*)	249	1913	1917	purchased by the Royal Italian Navy from the
Lankdys (ex-*Nishioso Maru No 1*)	255	1911	1917	Japanese fishing industry. Due to the shortage of M/S
Parvati (ex-*Naniwa Maru*)	208	1912	1917	in the Indian Ocean, on their delivery voyage to
Ranmenika (ex-*Nishiso Maru*)	224	1913	1917	Italy they were loaned to the RN for some months,
Sarasvati II (ex-*Chokai Maru*)	204	1911	1917	given Indian names and eventually returned to the Italian Navy.

Ex-Indian Trawlers as Minesweepers

HMS	Launched	Builder
*Bombay**	1919	Bombay DY
*Calcutta**	1919	Burn & Co
Colombo	1919	Burn & Co
Kennery	1919	Bombay DY
*Kidderpore**	1919	Bombay DY
Madras	1919	Burn & Co
Salsette	1919	Bombay DY
*Sealdah**	1919	Bombay DY

SPECIFICATION
Gross tons: 265
Dimensions: 125pp × 33½ × 12
Armament: 1 × 12pdr DP LA
Machinery: 1 shaft triple expansion giving 480ihp
Speed: 10½kts

* Armament was only fitted in these vessels.

Notes:
Jubbulpore by Bombay DY was cancelled. Only *Madras* was actually commissioned.

Motor Drifters as Minesweepers — World War I

HMS	Tons	Completed	Converted for M/S	Remarks
Abana	44	1902	1917	Later converted to a water carrier
Agnes Irvine	52	1905	1917	
Annie Mathers	56	1905	1917	
Blossom	49	1903	1917	
Comely	51	1904	1917	

Miscellaneous Indian Vessels as Minesweepers — World War I

HMS	Tons	Completed	All taken up for M/S	Remarks
Balgay	303	1897	1917	All local coasting and
Ban Whatt	361	1885		river steamers excepting
Curlew	305	1876		* which were tugs
Elephanta	?	?		
General Brackenbury	127	?		
General Elles	154	?		
*Goliath**	310	1902		
Jattra	371	1896		
Lady Inchcape	93	1911		
*Rose**	308	1904		
*Samson**	310	1902		
Sarasvati	962	1907		
Tamil	93			

Ex-Persian Vessel as a Minesweeper — World War I

HMS *Lewis Pelly* — Ex-Government yacht taken up in 1914 as an armed launch with 2 × 3pdr QF and 1 × mg, disarmed in 1915 and converted for M/S.

Ex-Canadian Coasters as Minesweepers — World War I

HMS	Ex	Tons	Completed	Converted for M/S	Remarks/ Armament
PV I	*William B Murray*	390	1912	1917	All ex-US registry; all armed with 1 × 12pdr
PV II	*Amagansett*	390	1912		
PV III	*Herbert N. Edwards*	323	1911		
PV IV	*Martin J. Marran*	308	1911		
PV V	*Rollin E. Mason*	323	1911		
PV VI	*Leander Wilcox*	205	1903		
PV VII	*Rowland H. Wilcox*	247	1911		
	Baleine	418	1907		1 × 3pdr QF
	Deliverance	280	1914		1 × 3pdr QF

Ex-West Indies Vessel as a Minesweeper — World War I

HMS	Tons	Completed	Converted for M/S	Remarks/ Armament
Lady Hay	75	1900	1917	Registered at Barbados; 1 × 6pdr QF

Hired Paddle Tugs as Minesweepers — World War I

HMS	Tons	Completed	Converted for M/S	Remarks/ Armament
Earl Roberts (ex-*Lord Roberts*)	199	1900	1916	
Ireland	245	1891	1918	Became a Mine-layer later in 1918

'Dance' Class Minesweepers – World War I (ex-Tunnel Tugs)

HMS	Launched	Builder
Cotillion (ex-T92)	1917	Day Summers
Coverley (ex-Roger de Coverley)	1917	Ferguson
Fandango (ex-T98)	1917	Lytham SB
Gavotte	1918	Goole SB
Hornpipe	1917	Murdoch & Murray
Mazurka	1917	Murdoch & Murray
Minuet (ex-T93)	1917	Day Summers
Morris Dance (ex-T99)	1918	Lytham SB
Pirouette	1917	Rennie Forrestt
Quadrille	1917	Ferguson
Sarabande	1918	Goole SB
Step Dance (ex-ET11)	1918	Lytham SB
Sword Dance (ex-ET10)	1918	Lytham SB
Tarantella (ex-T95)	1917	Hamilton

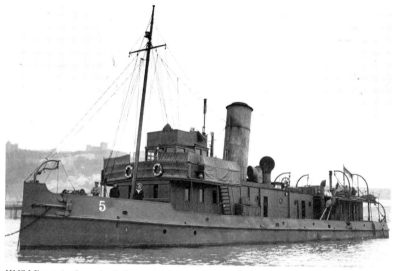

HMS Minuet *is shown in dark naval grey. Fully converted from the original design of Tunnel Tug, she carries No 5 on the bow but is without wireless aerials. Two or three Dan buoys lean on the after port davits and the M/S davits will be seen at the stern.* (National Maritime Museum)

SPECIFICATION

Displacement:	290 tons Cotillion, Coverley, Hornpipe, Mazurka, Minuet, Quadrille.
All others of this class:	265 tons
Dimensions:	130 × 26¼ × 3¼
Armament:	1 × 12pdr and 1 × 6pdr for Gavotte and Tarantella; 1 × 3pdr for Cotillion, Coverley, Pirouette, Quadrille and Sarabande; 1 × 6pdr all other ships of this class
Machinery:	2 shaft compound engines all giving 450ihp
Boilers:	1

Fuel: 40 tons of oil
Speed: 9/10½kts
Complement: 26

Note:
These minesweepers were built for shallow water navigation with the shafts and propellers in tunnels. Intended to be used by the Army (RE) in Mesopotamia, towing barges on the rivers.

Losses:
HMS *Fandango* was mined in the Dvina river on 3 July 1919;
HMS *Sword Dance* was mined in the Dvina river on 24 June 1919.

'Insect' Class River Gunboats as Minesweepers

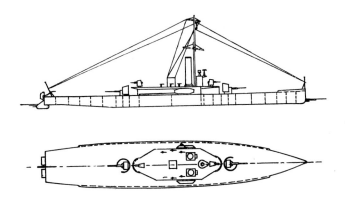

INSECT CLASS 1915

HMS	Launched	Builder
Aphis	1915	Ailsa SB
Bee	1915	Ailsa SB
Cicala	1915	Barclay Curle
Cockchafer	1915	Barclay Curle
Cricket	1915	Barclay Curle
Glowworm	1916	Barclay Curle
Gnat	1915	Lobnitz
Ladybird	1915	Lobnitz
Mantis	1915	Sunderland SB
Moth	1915	Sunderland SB
Scarab	1915	Wood Skinner
Tarantula	1915	Wood Skinner

SPECIFICATION
Displacement: 625 tons
Dimensions: 230pp 237½ × 36 × 4
Armament: 2 × 6in on single mtgs (in 'A' and 'Y' positions)
2 × 3in AA single superimposed and positioned as 'B' and 'X' guns (see diagram)
10 × 1 mg

HMS Ladybird. *Clearly discernable are the twin funnels with the 6in gun at 'A' position and the 3in gun at 'B' position, superimposed with 'X' and 'Y' guns just visible aft of the structure. The old* Dreadnought *to the rear makes interpretation of this photograph difficult.*

(Imperial War Museum)

Machinery:	2 shaft triple expansion engines all giving 2,000ihp. The propellers were in tunnels due to the shallow draft of these vessels
Fuel:	35 tons coal and 54 tons oil
	HMS *Moth* — 76 tons oil only
Trial Speed:	*Jane's 1931* states '18kts on trials was easily obtained'
Speed:	14kts
Boilers:	2
Complement:	55

Notes:

Also from *Jane's* 'These vessels were ordered in February 1915 and built to a design by Yarrow's. Originally intended for service in Salonika, to be dismantled, transported in sections overland and re-erected and re-floated on a tributary of the Danube to fight the Austro-Hungarian Danube Flotilla. To conceal their objective they were ordered as River Gunboats for the Chinese rivers. Some were towed out to Malta and some made their own way but they were never used for their intended purpose.' However, HMS *Glowworm* was mined and suffered damage in 1919 on the Dvina river in North Russia.

Others of the class were, for a short time, in service on the Shatt-el-Arab, the Shatt-el-Bahr (Tigris and Euphrates). They all arrived for some period at the Yangtse Kiang serving on the lower middle, north and west rivers. They were the only Gunboats with twin funnels, one port and one starboard.

After the commencement of the undeclared war between China and Japan from 1932 and later, all our River Gunboats were adapted for minesweeping against mines sown by the Chinese Navy to protect the boom/s which they built across the river.

HMS *Aphis* was employed as a minelayer in the Mediterranean on at least one occasion off Bomba in World War II.

The 3in and 6in guns were mounted in shields and the mg had bullet-proof plating guards retrofitted as required. Sniper-proof plating was also fitted as and when occasion demanded on all Royal Navy River Gunboats.

Losses:

HMS *Cicala* whilst at Hong Kong was lost after Japanese aircraft attack on 21 December 1941;

HMS *Ladybird* on 12 May 1941 was bombed by Italian aircraft whilst off Tobruk;

HMS *Moth* was taken at Hong Kong by the Japanese Navy at the surrender, having been scuttled by own forces on 12 December 1941. She was, however, raised and salved by the Japanese Navy and became *Him Suma* and was mined off Singapore on 19 March 1945.

HMS *Cricket* was mined off Mersa Matruh on 30 June 1941, prior to her conversion for minesweeping.

HMS *Cockchafer* was converted for minesweeping at Hong Kong during 1940. Although HMS *Ladybird* was lost to the Royal Navy, she had settled in shallow water and units of our Army used her weapons and her hull as an anti-aircraft platform;

HMS *Gnat* became a constructive total loss after being torpedoed by *U-79* off Bardia on 21 October 1941, but she was not scrapped until 1945.

'Seamew' Class River Gunboats as Minesweepers

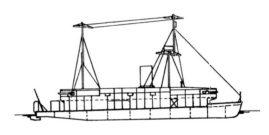

SEAMEW CLASS 1927

HMS	Launched	Builder
Seamew	1928	Yarrow SB
Tern	1927	Yarrow SB
Gannet	1927	Yarrow SB
Peterel	1927	Yarrow SB

HMS Tern *is shown on trials. Note the 'spotting top' on the foremast and the forward gun is unshielded; also on the starboard side, abeam of the mainmast in davits, is the motor sanpan.*

(Yarrow SB)

SPECIFICATION

	Seamew *Tern*	*Gannet* *Peterel*
Displacement:	287 tons	345 tons
Dimensions:	160WL × 167½ × 27 × 3¼	177WL × 184¼ × 29 × 3¼
Armament:	2 × 3in AA on single mtgs and 8 mg (all 4 ships)	
Machinery:	2 shaft geared turbines, 1,370shp	2 shaft geared turbines 2,120shp
Speed:	14kts	16kts
Fuel:	50 tons oil	60 tons oil
Complement:	55	60

Notes:

HMS *Peterel,* due to an error in the shipyard, was so named but should have been named *Petrel.*

After the commencement of the undeclared war between China and Japan from 1932 and later, all our River Gunboats were adapted for minesweeping against mines sown by the Chinese Navy to protect the boom/s which they built across the rivers.

Losses:

HMS *Peterel* on 8 December 1941 was the sole remaining Royal Navy vessel at Shanghai and news of the Japanese attack on Pearl Harbor was not received aboard until two hours after the event. The Chief of Staff to the C-in-C on *Him Idzumo* requested the surrender of *Peterel* but was refused by her Commanding Officer and minutes later the Japanese heavy cruiser opened fire. After blazing fiercely from stem to stern, HMS *Peterel* slowly keeled over and sank beneath the flames of the burning oil from her fuel tanks. The Japanese also directed small arms fire at the survivors in the water.

HMS *Tern* on 19 December 1941 was scuttled by own forces at Hong Kong, in the face of the Japanese advance.

'Falcon' Class River Gunboats as Minesweepers

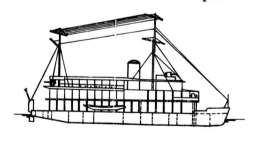

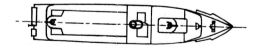

FALCON CLASS 1931

HMS	**Launched**	**Builder**
Falcon	1931	Yarrow SB

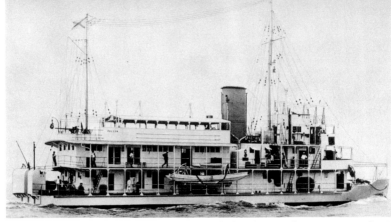

HMS Falcon *is shown proceeding at speed. She is built with a complex superstructure but is fully equipped for wireless telegraphy. Note the seamen's 'heads' overhanging the stern and on the upper deck just aft of the mainmast is a single unshielded 6-pounder.* (Yarrow SB)

SPECIFICATION

Displacement:	354 tons
Dimensions:	146pp 150 × 28¼ × 4¼
Armament:	1 × 3.7in howitzer
	2 × 6pdr on single mtgs
	10 × mg
Machinery:	2 shaft geared turbines all giving 2,250shp
Speed:	15kts
Fuel:	84 tons oil
Complement:	58

Note:
After the commencement of the undeclared war between China and Japan from 1932 and later, all our River Gunboats were adapted for minesweeping against mines sown by the Chinese Navy to protect the boom/s which they built across the river.

'Sandpiper' Class River Gunboats as Minesweepers

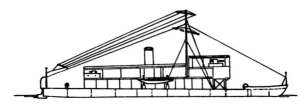

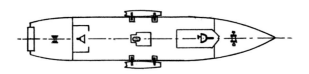

SANDPIPER CLASS 1933

HMS Robin *is shown on trials flying the builders flag. Unlike the* Falcon, *she only has a fore-mast. One of the pieces of the main armament is mounted above the wheelhouse.* (Yarrow SB)

HMS	**Launched**	**Builder**
Sandpiper	1933	Thornycroft
Robin	1934	Yarrow SB

SPECIFICATION	*Robin*	*Sandpiper*
Displacement:	226 tons	185 tons
Dimensions:	150pp × 26¼ × 3	160pp × 30¼ × 1¼
Armament:	1 × 3.7in howitzer	
	1 × 6pdr single mounting, (both ships)	
	8 × mg	
Machinery:	2 shaft VTE reciprocating (both ships)	
	800shp	650shp
Speed:	12¾kts	11¼kts
Complement:	35	32

Note:
After the commencement of the undeclared war between China and Japan from 1932 and later, all our River Gunboats were adapted for minesweeping against mines sown by the Chinese Navy to protect the boom/s which they built across the river.

Loss:
HMS *Robin* was scuttled by own forces at Hong Kong on 25 December 1941 in the face of the Japanese advance.

'Dragonfly' Class River Gunboats as Minesweepers

DRAGONFLY CLASS 1938

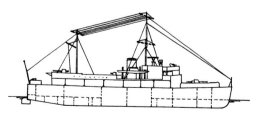

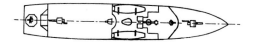

HMS	Launched	Builder
Dragonfly	1938	Thornycroft
Grasshopper	1939	Thornycroft
Locust	1939	Yarrow SB
Mosquito	1939	Yarrow SB
Scorpion	1937	White

HMS Locust *is shown moored mid-stream. Just above the bullet-proof plating on the bow can be seen the top of the 4in gun. On the afterpart of the boat deck is what appears to be a pom-pom and on the stern is a 20mm gun.* (Yarrow SB)

SPECIFICATION		*Scorpion*
Displacement:	585 tons	670 tons
Dimensions:	197 × 35 × 5	208¼ × 34½ × 5
Armament:	2 × 4in on single mtgs	2 × 4in on single mtgs
	1 × 3.7in Howitzer	2 × 3pdr on single mtgs
	8 × mg	1 × 3.7in Howitzer
		8 × mg
Machinery:	2 shaft geared turbines	2 shaft geared turbines
	3,800shp	4,500shp
Speed:	17kts	17kts
Complement:	74	93

Notes:
Bee of this class, building at the yard of J. S. White, was cancelled in March 1940.

After the commencement of the undeclared war between China and Japan from 1932 and later, all our River Gunboats were adapted for minesweeping against mines sown by the Chinese Navy to protect boom/s which they built across the river.

Losses:
HMS *Mosquito* on 1 June 1940 was bombed by German aircraft whilst off Dunkirk;
HMS *Dragonfly* and HMS *Grasshopper* were bombed and sunk by Japanese aircraft on 14 February 1942, south of Singapore;
HMS *Scorpion* was sunk in a surface action with a Japanese destroyer in the Banka Straits on 13 February 1942.

Thornycroft Type (Straits) Motor Minesweepers

HM MMS	Completed	Builder
Pahlawan (later *ML1102*)	1939	Thornycroft
Panglima (later *ML1103*)	1939	Thornycroft
Panji	1939	Thornycroft
Peningat (later *ML1104*)	1939	Thornycroft

This somewhat indistinct photograph of HMS Peningat *shows the Jack of the Straits Settlements being flown at the bow. The 3-pounder forward of the wheelhouse is clearly visible, but the minesweeping gear is right aft and not to be seen.* (Imperial War Museum)

SPECIFICATION

Displacement:	60 tons
Dimensions:	76½ × 13½ × 4¼
Armament:	1 × 3pdr
	1 × .303 mg
Machinery:	Thornycroft petrol and diesel motors 780bhp to 3 shafts
Speed:	16kts
Complement:	10

Notes:
All four craft were designed and constructed for the Admiralty by Messrs Thornycroft to be used by the officers and men of the Royal Naval Volunteer Reserve Division at Singapore.

Loss:
HM MMS *Peningat* was lost on the occupation of Singapore by Japanese forces in December 1942.

'Lake' Class Whalers as Minesweepers

HMS	Launched	Builder
Buttermere (ex-*Kos XXV*)	1939	Smiths Dock
Ellesmere (ex-*Kos XXIV*)	1939	Smiths Dock
Grasmere (ex-*Kos XXVIII*)	1939	Smiths Dock
(later *Wastwater*)		
Thirlmere (ex-*Kos XXVI*)	1939	Smiths Dock
Ullswater (ex-*Kos XXIX*)	1939	Smiths Dock
Windermere (ex-*Kos XXVII*)	1939	Smiths Dock

This photograph of HMS Grasmere *shows her overtaking to starboard a submarine on the surface. (Unfortunately the stern is unclear, but she is wearing her later name of* Wastwater.) *In front of the foremast is the unshielded 4in gun.* (National Maritime Museum)

SPECIFICATION

Displacement:	560 tons
Dimensions:	138½pp 147½ × 26½ × 14¼
Armament:	1 × 12pdr AA
	1 × 20mm AA
	2 × .5in AA on one twin mtg
Machinery:	1 shaft reciprocating engine giving 1,400ihp
Speed:	13¼kts
Complement:	35

Note:
Ex-commercial Whalers requisitioned for Minesweeping.

Losses:
HMS *Ellesmere* on 24 February 1945 was torpedoed by *U-1203* in the English Channel;
HMS *Ullswater* when in the English Channel on 19 November 1942 was torpedoed by an E-Boat.

Whalers as Minesweepers — World War II

HMS	Tons	Completed	Converted for M/S	Remarks/Losses
Atmosphere (ex-*Gos 2*)	247	1938	1940	
Billow (ex-*Gos 3*)	247	1928	1941	
Blizzard (ex-*Gos 4*)	217	1928	1941	
Borealis (ex-*Gos 6*)	264	1935	1941	
Bouvet 1	245	1930	1940	
Bouvet 2	245	1930	1940	
Bouvet 3	245	1930	1940	
Bouvet 4	245	1930	1940	
Busen 3 (later *Icicle*)	210	1924	1940	
Busen 7 (later *Silhouette*)	254	1926	1940	
Busen 11 (later *Snowdrift*)	279	1931	1940	
Calm (ex-*Gos 7*)	264	1935	1940	
Daybreak (ex-*Kos VII*)	248	1929	1941	
Daylight (ex-*Globe 1*)	206	1925	1941	
Domino (ex-*Sabra*)	245	1930	1940	
Egeland	153	1912	1941	Danlayer. Lost on 29 November 1941 being wrecked on the Palestine coast
Firmament (ex-*Kos IX*)	248	1930	1941	Lost on 30 May 1944 being wrecked near Alexandria
Flash (ex-*Globe II*)	206	1925	1941	
Flicker (ex-*Kos X*)	260	1932	1941	
Full Moon (ex-*Kos XI*)	258	1932	1941	
Hailstorm (ex-*Kos XIII*)	258	1932	1941	Later employed as a Danlayer
Hektor 7	233	1929	1940	
Packice (ex-*Vestfold VII*)	273	1927	1941	
Rainstorm (ex-*Busen 6*)	266	1928	1941	
Roydur	174	1911	1939	
Sandstorm (ex-*Vestfold III*)	312	1925	1941	
Santa	355	1936	1941	Mined on 23 November 1943 off Sardinia
Sarna	355	1936	1941	
Sarna	268	1930	1940	Mined on 25 February 1941 in the Suez Canal
Semla	217	1924	1941	Later employed for A/S

Sevra	253	1929	1940	Mined on 6 November 1940 off Falmouth
Shooting Star (ex-*Vestfold VI*)	312	1925	1941	
Shova	180	1912	1940	Dan-layer
Signa	190	1926	1940	Day-layer
Silva	221	1924	1940	
Sirra	251	1929	1940	
Skudd 3	245	1929	1940	Bombed on 27 August 1941 at Tobruk
Skudd 4	247	1929	1940	
Skudd 5	265	1929	1940	
Skudd 6	323	1929	1940	
Sluga	251	1929	1940	
Soika	313	1925	1940	
Sotra	313	1925	1939	Torpedoed by *U-431* off Bardia on 29 January 1942
Southern Field	250	1929	1940	
Southern Foam	295	1926	1940	
Spina	190	1926	1940	Dan-layer
Squall (ex-*Vestfold X*)	299	1935	1941	
Stina	251	1928	1940	
Stormwrack (ex-*Busen 4*)	266	1925	1942	
Sukha	251	1929	1940	
Svana	268	1930	1940	Bombed on 8 April 1942 by Italian aircraft at Alexandria
Svega	253	1929	1940	
Swona	313	1925	1940	

Notes:
Whalers were initially taken up for use as A/S, M/S, boom defence and gate vessels. Many more than the M/S and Dan-layers listed above flew the White Ensign (see below for the 'Tam' and page 144 for 'Lake' classes). Armament was normally 1 × 12pdr and lighter weapons with depth charges and UP projectiles for AA use in the early part of the war.

'Tam' Class Ex-Norwegian Converted Whalers — Auxiliary Minesweepers

HMS	Completed	Converted to Minesweepers	Builder
Hav	1931	1940	Akers Mek Verkstad (Oslo)
Shera	1929	1940	Smiths Dock
Shika	1929	1940	Smiths Dock
Shusa	1929	1940	Smiths Dock
Silja	1929	1940	Smiths Dock
Stefa	1929	1940	Smiths Dock
Sulla	1929	1940	Smiths Dock
Sunba	1929	1940	Smiths Dock
Vega	1929	1940	Smiths Dock

This is believed to be the Whaler HMS Shusa, *wearing No 88. She has the SA sweep gear on her bow and a single 20mm surmounting the forward deckhouse. Note the plastic armour below the bridge and at other points; also the low freeboard of this type of vessel.*

(Imperial War Museum)

SPECIFICATION

Displacement:	250 tons (average)
Dimensions:	116pp × 23¼ × 13½ (*Hav*)
	116pp × 24½ × 21¼ (all others of this class)
Machinery:	1 shaft triple expansion giving 800ihp
Speed:	13½kts
Boilers:	1
Fuel:	Oil
Armament:	1 × 76mm AA
	3 × mg on single mtgs

Notes:

These Minesweepers were requisitioned Whalers converted for magnetic minesweeping. They served up to two years in the Royal Navy prior to transfer to the USSR.

Losses:

HMS *Shusa* whilst in commission with the Russian Fleet on 12 November 1942 foundered due to ice pressure in the Barents Sea;

HMS *Vega* whilst in Russian service was torpedoed by *U-995* on 5 December 1944 whilst off the Kola Inlet;

HMS *Shera* whilst on her delivery voyage to Kola foundered on 9 March 1942 due to stress of weather off the North Cape;

HMS *Sulla* whilst on her delivery voyage to Kola foundered on 25 March 1942 due to stress of weather off the North Cape.

'Basset' Class Naval Trawlers

HMS	Launched	Builder
Basset	1935	Robb
Mastiff	1938	Robb

HMS Basset. *This trawler is shown fitted with the LL sweep and depth charge throwers. She also has an enclosed wheelhouse.* (Imperial War Museum)

SPECIFICATION

Displacement:	460 tons (*Basset*)	520 (*Mastiff*)
Dimensions:	160½ × 27½ × 10½	163½ × 27½ × 10½
Armament:	1 × 4in DP	1 × 4in DP
	2 × .303in mg	2 × .303in mg
Machinery:	1 shaft triple	1 shaft triple
	expansion giving	expansion giving
	850ihp	950ihp
Boilers:	1	1
Speed:	12kts	13kts
Fuel:	180 tons of coal (both)	
Complement:	33 (both)	

Notes:
The above are the first two of this class built for the Royal Navy. Another 52 were built in India for the Royal Indian and Royal Ceylonese Navies.

Loss:
HMS *Mastiff* was mined on 20 November 1939 in the Thames Estuary.

Paddle Vessels Converted to Minesweepers — Group 1

HMS	Tons	Completed	Converted for M/S	Remarks/ Losses
Ambassador (ex-*Embassy*, (ex-*Duchess of Norfolk*)	381	1911	1939	

Brighton Belle	320	1900	1939	*Brighton Belle* on 28 May 1940 was wrecked in the Downs
(ex-*Lady Evelyn*) *Brighton Queen* (ex-*Lady Moyra*, ex-*Gwalia*)	519	1905	1939	*Brighton Queen* on 1 June 1940 was sunk by Wehrmacht gunfire from the shore at Dunkirk
City of Rochester	235	1904	1939	*City of Rochester* was bombed at HM Dockyard, Chatham, on 19 May 1941
Devonia	520	1905	1939	*Devonia* on 31 May 1940 was bombed at Dunkirk
Duchess of Fife	336	1903	1939	
Duchess of Rothesay	338	1894	1939	
Essex Queen (ex-*Walton Belle*)	592	1897	1939	
Gracie Fields	393	1936	1939	*Gracie Fields* on 29 May 1940 was bombed off Dunkirk
Marmion	409	1906	1939	*Marmion* on 9 April 1941 was bombed at Harwich and became a constructive total loss
Medway Queen	318	1924	1939	
Mercury	621	1934	1939	*Mercury* on 25 December 1940 was mined south of Ireland
Oriole (ex-*Eagle III*)	441	1910	1939	
Queen of Thanet (ex-HMS *Melton*)	792	1916	1939	
Snaefell (ex-*Waverley*, ex-*Barry*)	477	1907	1939	*Snaefell* on 5 July 1941 when off the Tyne sank after aircraft attack
Southsea	825	1930	1939	*Southsea* on 16 February 1941 was mined off the Tyne
Waverley	537	1899	1939	*Waverley* on 29 May 1940 1940 was bombed at Dunkirk

Notes:

All taken up from the Merchant Navy in 1939 and converted to Paddle Minesweepers, some of the above had already served in this role in World War I.

There were sufficient to form six minesweeping flotillas which largely served in UK waters. As the Fleet Minesweepers under construction were commissioned, the Paddle Minesweepers in this section were mostly converted to Auxiliary Anti-Aircraft vessels for protection of the east coast convoys.

The majority were armed with 1 × 12pdr AA and lighter AA weapons. HMS *Marmion*, during conversion from civilian use, was armed with the following weapons: 1 × 12pdr AA, 8 × .5in mg AA, on 2 quad mtgs, 4 × .303in mg AA on 1 quad mtg and 2 × .303in mg Lewis with 1 twin mtg. Other ships of this category 'collected' weapons as best they could.

Paddle Vessels Converted to Minesweepers — Group 2

HMS	Completed	Converted for M/S	Builder
Emperor of India (ex-*Princess Royal*) (ex-*Mahratta*)	1906	1939	Thornycroft

BRIEF SPECIFICATION
Displacement:	534 tons
Dimensions:	217¼pp × 25 × 8½
Machinery:	Paddle reciprocating giving 1,422ihp
Speed:	14½kts

Glen Avon	1912	1939	Ailsa SB

BRIEF SPECIFICATION
Displacement:	509 tons
Dimensions:	220pp × 27 × 9
Machinery:	Paddle reciprocating giving 1,650ihp
Speed:	17kts

Loss:
HMS *Glen Avon* on 2 September 1944 foundered off the Normandy beachhead in heavy weather.

Glen Usk	1914	1939	Ailsa SB

BRIEF SPECIFICATION
Displacement:	524 tons
Dimensions:	224¼pp × 28 × 9
Machinery:	Paddle reciprocating giving 1,650ihp
Speed:	17kts

Glen More (ex-*Glen Gower*)	1922	1939	Ailsa SB

BRIEF SPECIFICATION
Displacement:	553 tons
Dimensions:	242 × 28½ × 9
Machinery:	Paddle reciprocating giving 1,800ihp
Speed:	17½kts

Goatfell (ex-*Caledonia*)	1934	1939	Denny

BRIEF SPECIFICATION
Displacement:	624 tons
Dimensions:	229½ × 30 × 6½
Machinery:	Paddle reciprocating giving 1,750ihp
Speed:	16½kts

| *Helvellyn* | 1937 | 1939 | Fairfield |
| (ex-*Juno*) | | | |

BRIEF SPECIFICATION
Displacement: 642 tons
Dimensions: 230½ × 30 × 9¼
Machinery: Paddle reciprocating giving 2,000ihp
Speed: 17kts

Loss:
HMS *Helvellyn* was bombed at London whilst refitting and became a constructive total loss on 20 March 1941.

| *Jeannie Deans* | 1931 | 1939 | Fairfield |

BRIEF SPECIFICATION
Displacement: 635 tons
Dimensions: 257½ × 30 × 9½
Machinery: Paddle reciprocating giving 3,380ihp
Speed: 18¼kts

| *Laguna Belle* | 1896 | 1939 | Denny |
| (ex-*Southend Belle*) | | | |

BRIEF SPECIFICATION
Displacement: 617 tons
Dimensions: 249pp × 30 × 10
Machinery: Paddle reciprocating giving 2,500ihp
Speed: 16kts

| *Lorna Doone* | 1891 | 1939 | Napier Shanks & Ball |

BRIEF SPECIFICATION
Displacement: 410 tons
Dimensions: 220½pp × 26 × 9¼
Machinery: Paddle reciprocating giving 2,480ihp
Speed: 16kts

Plinlimmon	1895	1939	McIntyre
(ex-*Cambria*,			
ex-*Cambridge*)			

BRIEF SPECIFICATION
Displacement: 438 tons
Dimensions: 233 × 26 × 9½
Machinery: Paddle reciprocating giving 2,600ihp
Speed: 20kts

Loss:
In 1946, *Plinlimmon* became a constructive total loss, cause, location and date are not known.

| *Princess Elizabeth* | 1927 | 1939 | Day Summers |

BRIEF SPECIFICATION
Displacement: 388 tons
Dimensions: 195pp × 24¼ × 8

| **Machinery:** | Paddle reciprocating giving 940ihp |
| **Speed:** | 12½kts |

| *Queen Empress* | 1912 | 1939 | Murdoch & Murray |

BRIEF SPECIFICATION

Displacement:	411 tons
Dimensions:	210pp × 25½ × 8½
Machinery:	Paddle reciprocating giving 1,780ihp
Speed:	15kts

| *Ravenswood* | 1891 | 1939 | McKnight |

BRIEF SPECIFICATION

Displacement:	391 tons
Dimensions:	215pp × 24 × 8½
Machinery:	Paddle reciprocating giving 2,050ihp
Speed:	18kts

| *Ryde* | 1937 | 1939 | Denny |

BRIEF SPECIFICATION

Displacement:	603 tons
Dimensions:	223 × 29 × 7¼
Machinery:	Paddle reciprocating giving 1,000ihp
Speed:	14kts

| *Sandown* | 1934 | 1939 | Denny |

BRIEF SPECIFICATION

Displacement:	684 tons
Dimensions:	223 × 29 × 10
Machinery:	Paddle reciprocating giving 1,000ihp
Speed:	14kts

| *Scawfell* | 1937 | 1939 | Fairfield |
| (ex-*Jupiter*) | | | |

BRIEF SPECIFICATION

Displacement:	642 tons
Dimensions:	230½ × 30 × 9¾
Machinery:	Paddle reciprocating giving 2,000ihp
Speed:	17kts

Skiddaw	1896	1939	McKnight
(ex-*Britannia*)			
(ex-*Britain*)			

BRIEF SPECIFICATION

Displacement:	459 tons
Dimensions:	230pp × 26½ × 9½
Machinery:	Paddle reciprocating giving 3,040ihp
Speed:	20kts

Thames Queen (ex-*Queen of Southend* ex-*Yarmouth Belle*)	1898	1939	Denny

BRIEF SPECIFICATION
Displacement:	517 tons
Dimensions:	240pp × 28 × 9¼
Machinery:	Paddle reciprocating giving 1,250ihp
Speed:	17kts

Westward Ho (ex-*Westward Queen* ex-*Westhope*)	1894	1939	McKnight

BRIEF SPECIFICATION
Displacement:	438 tons
Dimensions:	225 × 26 × 9½
Machinery:	Paddle reciprocating giving 2,770ihp
Speed:	17kts

Whippingham	1930	1941	Fairfield

BRIEF SPECIFICATION
Displacement:	825 tons
Dimensions:	250 × 30 × 7
Machinery:	Paddle reciprocating giving 1,960ihp
Speed:	16kts

Note:
As these are all mercantile vessels, there is no true warship displacement tonnage and in fact all tonnage figures are tons gross.

Mechanically-Powered Yachts as Minesweepers

HMS	Tons	Completed	Remarks/Losses
Aronia	193	1933	
Bluebird	148	1938	
Boy Pat	100	1915	
Brinmaric	106	1938	
Bunting (ex-*Merlin*)	181	1896	
Calamara (ex-*Cala Mara*)	313	1898	
Grey Mist	197	1920	
Gulzar	201	1934	*Gulzar* was bombed by German aircraft at Dover on 29 July 1940
Hinba	154	1903	
Lexa	133	1936	
Ombra	275	1902	
Sargosso (ex-*Atlantis*)	216	1926	*Sargosso* was mined off the Isle of Wight on 6 June 1943
Seaflower (ex-*Boadicea*)	447	1882	
Spitfire III	142	1938	

Sylvana	487	1907	
Taransay	175	1930	
Thalia (ex-*Protector*)	185	1904	*Thalia* was lost by collision on 11 October 1942 in the Clyde
Umbriel (ex-*Haussa*)	?	1939	
Yarta	357	1898	

Notes:

These yachts, although acquired for minesweeping, were later used for a variety of tasks such as Anti-Submarine, Examination Service and Firefloats etc. Upon commissioning most were used as Senior Officers' M/S base ships and some were used as Danlayers.

Some acquired 20mm DP AA and mg of various types.

'Berberis' Class Requisitioned and Purchased Trawlers as Minesweepers

HMS Magnolia *shown alongside another requisitioned trawler of the same design.* Magnolia *wears the letters MG on the bow and on the foredeck is an unshielded 4in gun. She has two or three Dan buoys secured to the shrouds of the foremast.* (National Maritime Museum)

HMS	Tons	Built	Converted
Alder (ex-*Lord Davidson*)	500	1929	1939
Beech (ex-*Lord Dawson*)	540	1929	1939
Berberis (ex-*Lord Hewart*)	540	1928	1939
Cedar (ex-*Arab*)	649	1933	1935
Cypress (ex-*Cape Finisterre*)	548	1930	1935
Hawthorn (ex-*Cape Guardufiu*)	593	1930	1935
Holly (ex-*Kingston Coral*)	590	1930	1935

Hornbeam (ex-*Lord Trent*)	530	1929	1939
Larch (ex-*St Alexandra*)	550	1928	1939
Laurel (ex-*Kingston Cyanite*)	590	1930	1935
Lilac (ex-*Beach Flower*)	593	1930	1935
Magnolia (ex-*Lord Brentford*)	557	1930	1935
Maple (ex-*St Gerontius*)	550	1929	1939
Myrtle (ex-*St Irene*)	550	1928	1939
Oak (ex-*St Romanus*)	545	1928	1939
Redwood (ex-*St Rose*)	545	1928	1939
Sycamore (ex-*Lord Beaverbrook*)	573	1930	1935
Syringa (ex-*Cape Kanin*)	574	1930	1935
Tamarisk (ex-*St Gatien*)	540	1929	1939
Willow (ex-*Cape Spartivento*)	574	1934	1935

Notes:
All requisitioned from the fishing fleets for conversion to Minesweepers. All of this class carried 1 × 4in AA plus depth charges; speed was 11kts.

Losses:
HMS *Alder* on 22 October 1941 was wrecked off Cromer;
HMS *Beech* was bombed in Scrabster Harbour on 22 June 1941;
HMS *Myrtle* on 14 June 1940 struck a mine and sank in the Thames Estuary;
HMS *Tamarisk* on 12 August 1940 was bombed in the Thames Estuary.

Ex-Mercantile Vessels as Auxiliary Minesweepers

HMS	Tons	Completed	Converted for M/S	Remarks/Losses
Aik Lam	155	1941	1941	
Azania	375	1926	1939	
Banka	623	1914	1940	Sunk, cause unknown, on 10 December 1941 off the east coast of Malaya
Chinthe (later *Hathe*)	688	1932	1942	
Circe	778	1912	1939	
Gemas	207	1925	1939	Sunk by HMAS *Ballarat* on 2 March 1942 to avoid capture by the Japanese
Huatong	280	1927	1939	Bombed by Japanese aircraft on 13 February 1942 in the Palembang river
Jarak	208	1927	1941	Bombed by Japanese aircraft off Singapore on 17 February 1942
Jeram	210	1927	1939	Taken by the Japanese at Singapore and renamed *Suikei 21* on or about 15 February 1942
Jerantut	217	1927	1941	Scuttled by own forces at Palembang on 8 March 1942
Kai	1,746	1921	1940	
Klias	207	1927	1941	Scuttled by own forces at Palembang on 15 February 1942

Malacca	211	1927	1939	Scuttled by own forces at Sumatra on 18 February 1942
Medusa	793	1913	1940	
Pangkor	1,250	1929	1939	
Rahman	209	1926	1939	Sunk, cause unknown, on 1 March 1942 at Batavia
Scott Harley	620	1913	1940	Sunk, cause unknown, on 3 March 1942 in the Gulf of Sumatra
Sin Aik Lee	198	1928	1939	Lost, cause unknown, in February 1942 in the Singapore area
Tapah	208	1926	1939	Lost, cause unknown, in February 1942 in the Singapore area
Titan	574	1928	1940	
Trang	205	1912	1939	Abandoned on 14 February 1942 off Singapore

Ex-Mercantile Tugs as Auxiliary Minesweepers

HMS	Tons	Completed	Converted for M/S	Remarks/Losses
Alarm (ex-*St Ewe*)	432	1919	1941	
Alcis			1940	
Andromeda	658	1910	1941	Bombed at Malta on 18 April 1942
Ansay			1940	
Changthe	244	1914	1940	Bombed by Japanese aircraft off Singapore on 14 February 1942
Conquerante	70	?	1940	Ex-French, seized at Falmouth on 3 July 1940
Control	?	?	1940	Chartered in June 1940 from an Egyptian firm
Dranguet	70	1935	1940	Ex-French, seized at Southampton July 1940
Minnie Moller	377	1909	1940	Bombed on 31 December 1941 by Japanese aircraft at Hong Kong
St Angelo	150	1935	1939	Mined at Malta on 30 May 1942
St Aubin	468	1918	1940	
St Sampson	451	1919	1939	Foundered on 7 March 1942 due to heavy weather in the Red Sea
Salvo	161	1918	1939	Fitted in 1939 for magnetic M/S
Scythe (ex-*Baltic*)	100	1915	1939	Fitted in 1939 for magnetic M/S
Servitor (ex-*Captain A. Letzer*)	44	?	1939	Fitted in 1939 for magnetic M/S

Shako (ex-*Hercules*)	121	1913	1939	Fitted in 1939 for magnetic M/S
Slogan (ex-*Samson*)	110	1926	1939	Ex-Belgian, fitted in 1939 for magnetic M/S
Solitaire (ex-*The Schelde*)	91	1904	1939	Fitted in 1939 for magnetic M/S. Capsized in heavy weather off the Normandy beach on 20 June 1944
Souvenir (ex-*Wrestler*)	120	1914	1939	Fitted in 1939 for magnetic M/S
Thasos	130	1897	1939	
West Cocker	133	1919	1940	Bombed at Malta on 9 April 1942
Wo Kwang	350	1927	1940	Abandoned in the face of the Japanese advance in February 1942 at Singapore

Notes:

Auxiliary Minesweepers comprised many types of vessel from Dredger Hoppers, Tugs, coastal Cargo vessels to Ferries. Their armament varied from sweeper to sweeper, the largest calibre weapon normally being a 12pdr, however *Circe* acquired a 4in from some source. Armament could have included 20mm, .303in mg, 2pdr, 3pdr and 6pdr etc.

The seven tugs, commencing at *Salvo*, were one of the first sweeper groups to be fitted with electric sweeps to de-sensitize the expected magnetic mine.

Acquired world-wide with the Commonwealth nations included and generally used for sweeping in estuaries and approaches to ports and anchorages, and maintaining the clearance of the various war channels around the coast.

'Dance' Class Naval Trawlers as Minesweepers

HMS	Launched	Builder
Cotillion	1940	Ardrossan
Coverley	1941	Ardrossan
Fandango	1941	Cochrane
Foxtrot	1940	Cochrane
Gavotte	1940	CWG
Hornpipe	1940	CWG
Mazurka	1940	Ferguson
Minuet	1941	Ferguson
Morris Dance	1940	Goole SB
Pirouette	1940	Goole SB
Polka	1940	Hall Russell
Quadrille	1941	Hall Russell
Rumba	1940	Inglis
Sarabande	1940	Inglis
Saltarelo	1940	Robb
Sword Dance	1940	Robb
Tango	1940	Smiths Dock
Two Step (ex-*Tarantella*)	1941	Smiths Dock
Valse	1941	Smiths Dock
Veleta	1941	Smiths Dock

HMS Coverley, *looking weather-beaten, but the typical trawler minesweeper of World War II with the large bandstand before the foremast, the large cowelled funnel and the minesweeping davits aft. She wears the number T 106.* (Imperial War Museum)

SPECIFICATION

Displacement:	530 tons
Dimensions:	160½ × 27½ × 10½
Armament:	1 × 4in DP AA, 3 × 20mm AA on single mtgs
Machinery:	1 shaft triple expansion giving 850ihp
Boilers:	1
Speed:	11½kts
Complement:	35

Notes:
Naval Trawlers were used for Anti-Submarine and Minesweeping *inter alia*. Of the various classes of World War II Naval Trawler construction it is likely that the 'Lake' (Whalers), 'Hill', 'Fish' and 'Military' classes were mostly used on A/S duties with all other classes mostly used for M/S employment. Some vessels were dual purpose/interchangeable for A/S and M/S deployment. It is difficult to say which vessels were involved and when.

Mention must be made of the hundreds of Trawlers, Whalers and Drifters taken up from the fishing and whaling industries for the same or similar purpose. Space is not available to list more than a few such craft but, like the vessels of the class construction programme, 'they also served'.

Loss:
HMS *Sword Dance* collided with an unknown vessel in the Moray Firth on 5 July 1942 and did not make port.

'Fish' Class Naval Trawlers

HMS	Launched	Builder
Bonito	1941	All built by Cochrane
Bream	1942	
Grayling	1942	
Grilse	1943	
Herring	1943	
Mullet	1942	
Pollack	1943	
Whiting	1943	

HMS Grayling *is shown in an anchorage, wearing Pennant No T243 and looking the match for any U-Boat. She has a capability for paravane and wire sweeps.* (Cochrane SB)

SPECIFICATION

Displacement:	680 tons
Dimensions:	162 × 25¼ × 12¼
Armament:	1 × 12pdr QF LA, 3 × 20mm AA on single mtgs
Machinery:	1 shaft triple expansion giving 700ihp
Boilers:	1
Speed:	11kts
Complement:	35

Notes:
Virtually all Trawlers and Drifters carried depth charges as anti-submarine weapons, an outfit generally being two depth charge racks (rails) and 2 depth charge throwers, one each port and starboard. However, different classes/vessels varied from time to time.

Loss:
HMS *Herring* collided with an unknown vessel in the North Sea on 22 April 1943 and did not make port.

'Hills' Class Naval Trawlers

HMS Dunkery *on 5 June 1942 at harbour stations, wearing her pennants and lined fore and aft.* (MoD)

HMS	Launched	Builder
Birdlip	All in 1941	All built by Cook, Welton & Gemmell
Butser		
Brecon		
Duncton		
Dunkery		
Inkpen		
Portsdown		
Yestor		

SPECIFICATION

Displacement:	750 tons
Dimensions:	181¼ × 28 × 12
Armament:	1 × 12pdr QF LA, 3 × 20mm AA on single mtgs
Machinery:	1 shaft triple expansion giving 970ihp
Boilers:	1
Speed:	11kts
Complement:	35

Losses:
HMS *Birdlip* was torpedoed by *U-547* on 13 June 1944 off the Gambian coast or thereabouts;
HMS *Brecon* was torpedoed by *U-521* on 8 February 1943 in the North Atlantic.

'Round Table' Class Naval Trawlers

HMS	Launched	Builder
Sir Agravaine	1942	Lewis
Sir Galahad	1941	Hall Russell
Sir Gareth	1942	Hall Russell
Sir Geraint	1941	Lewis
Sir Kay	1942	Hall Russell
Sir Lamorack	1942	Hall Russell
Sir Lancelot	1941	Lewis
Sir Tristram	1942	Lewis

HMS Sir Geraint, *shown as a minesweeping trawler.* (Imperial War Museum)

SPECIFICATION

Displacement:	440 tons
Dimensions:	137½ × 23½ × 11½
Armament:	1 × 12pdr QF LA, 3 × 20mm AA on single mtgs
Machinery:	1 shaft triple expansion engine giving 600ihp
Boilers:	1
Speed:	12kts
Complement:	35

Notes:
Naval Trawlers employed as Minesweepers were equipped with one or more of a variety of mine sweeps including the Oropesa, SA hammer, acoustic, magnetic etc.

'Shakespearian' Class Naval Trawlers

HMS	Launched	Builder
Celia	1940	Cochrane
Coriolanus	1940	Cochrane
Fluellen	1940	Cochrane
Hamlet	1940	CWG
Horatio	1940	CWG
Juliet	1940	CWG
Laertes	1940	CWG
Macbeth	1940	Goole SB
Ophelia	1940	Goole SB
Othello	1941	Hall Russell
Romeo	1941	Inglis
Rosalind	1941	Inglis

This is a photograph of HMS Coriolanus *fitted out as a Dan-layer.* (Imperial War Museum)

SPECIFICATION

Displacement:	545 tons
Dimensions:	164 × 27½ × 10½
Armament:	1 × 12pdr QF LA, 3 × 20mm AA on single mtgs
Machinery:	1 shaft triple expansion giving 950ihp
Boilers:	1
Speed:	12kts
Complement:	35

Losses:

HMS *Coriolanus* on 5 May 1945 was mined in the Adriatic Sea;
HMS *Horatio* was torpedoed by an Italian MA/SB on 7 January 1943 in the Scarpanto Channel;
HMS *Laertes* was torpedoed off Freetown by *U-201* on 25 July 1942.

'Tree' Class Naval Trawlers

HMS Bay. *This is a photograph of* Bay *fitted out as a Dan-layer. She wears Pennant No T 77 on her bow. Minesweeping davits are fitted aft.* (Wright & Logan)

HMS	Launched	Builder
Acacia	1940	Ardrossan
Almond	1940	Ardrossan
Ash	1939	Cochrane
Bay	1939	Cochrane
Birch	1939	CWG
Blackthorn	1939	CWG
Chestnut	1940	Goole SB
Deodar	1940	Goole SB
Elm	1939	Inglis
Fir	1940	Inglis
Hazel	1939	Robb

Hickory	1940	Robb
Juniper	1939	Inglis
Mangrove	1940	Ferguson
Olive	1940	Hall Russell
Pine	1940	Hall Russell
Rowan	1939	Smiths Dock
Walnut	1939	Smiths Dock
Whitethorn	1939	Smiths Dock
Wisteria	1939	Smiths Dock

SPECIFICATION

Displacement:	530 tons
Dimensions:	164 × 27½ × 10½
Armament:	1 × 12pdr QF LA, 2 × .5in on a twin mtg
	4 × Lewis mg on two twin mtgs
Machinery:	1 shaft triple expansion giving 850ihp
Boilers:	1
Speed:	11½kts
Complement:	35

Note:
HMS *Mangrove* was transferred to the Portuguese Navy.

Losses:
HMS *Almond* was mined off Falmouth on 2 February 1941;
HMS *Ash* was mined on 5 June 1941 in the Thames Estuary;
HMS *Chestnut* was mined off the North Foreland on 30 November 1940;
HMS *Hickory* was mined in the English Channel on 22 October 1940;
HMS *Juniper* was engaged by the *Admiral Hipper* on 8 June 1940 in the Barents Sea;
HMS *Pine* was torpedoed by an E-Boat on 31 January 1944 off Selsey Bill.

Brazilian-Built Naval Trawlers

HMS	Launched	Builder
Pampano	All launched 1942	All built by Nac Nav Costeira
Papatera		
Parati		
Pargo		
Paru		
Pelegrime		

HMS Pelegrime *as completed and making way.* (Brazilian Navy Archives)

SPECIFICATION
Displacement:	920 tons
Dimensions:	176½ × 28 × 14
Armament:	1 × 12pdr QF LA, 4 × 20mm AA on single mtgs
Machinery:	1 shaft triple expansion giving 1,000ihp
Boilers:	1
Speed:	12½kts
Complement:	40

Notes:
These six Naval Trawlers were built in a neutral state, such was the shortage of shipbuilding facilities in the UK. Brazil later joined the cause of the Allies and these Trawlers were returned to commission in the Brazilian Navy.

Portuguese-Built Naval Trawlers
GROUP 1 OF TIMBER HULL CONSTRUCTION

HMS	Launched	Builder
Prophet (ex-*Portobello*)	1942	A. Monica, British Auxiliaries
Protest (ex-*Port Patrick*)	1941	MMB Monica
Prowess (ex-*Portreath*)	1943	MMB Monica
Proof (ex-*Port Royal*)	1942	A. Monica, British Auxiliaries
Property (ex-*Portrush*)	1942	A. Monica, British Auxiliaries
Prong (ex-*Port Stanley*)	1942	A. Monica, British Auxiliaries

HMS Port Stanley *(as* Prong*) is the wooden version of the Portuguese-built Naval Trawler, shown stopped in the water. She carries an LL sweep aft and is armed with three single 20mm AA and a 3in 12-pounder on a bandstand before the foremast.* (D. Brindle)

SPECIFICATION
Displacement:	523 tons
Dimensions:	139 × 27¼ × 11
Armament:	1 × 12pdr QF LA, 3 × 20mm AA on single mtgs
Machinery:	1 shaft diesel engine giving 550bhp

Speed:	11kts	
Complement:	30	

GROUP 2 OF STEEL HULL CONSTRUCTION

HMS	Launched	Builder
Proctor (ex-*Portadown*)	1942	Alfeite, Ruston & Hornsby
Probe (ex-*Portaferry*)	1942	Alfeite, Ruston & Hornsby
Product (ex-*Port Jackson*)	1941	Uniao Fabril
Prodigal (ex-*Porthleven*)	1941	Uniao Fabril
Professor (ex-*Portmadoc*)	1942	Uniao Fabril
Promise (ex-*Port Natal*)	1941	Uniao Fabril

HMS Port Natal *(as* Promise*) is the steel version of the Portuguese-built Naval Trawler, shown dead slow in a swell. She carries the SA hammer sweep on the bow and the LL sweep on the stern. She is armed with depth charges, 3 single 20mm mg and a 3in 12-pounder in a bandstand before the foremast. She also has an enclosed bridge which may be compared with the open bridge of HMS* Prong. *(D Brindle)

SPECIFICATION

Displacement:	550 tons
Dimensions:	148 × 27¼ × 11
Armament:	1 × 12pdr QF LA, 3 × 20mm AA on single mtgs
Machinery:	1 shaft diesel engine giving 550bhp
Speed:	10½kts
Complement:	30

Notes:
Similar to the Brazilian-built Naval Trawlers, the above were built in a neutral country. The Group 1 hulls have an appearance similar to the UK-built Motor Minesweepers.

'Western Isles' or 'Isles' Class Naval Trawlers as Minesweepers and Dan-layers etc

HMS	Completed	Builder
Ailsa Craig	1943	Cook, Welton & Gemmel (CWG)
Annet	1943	CWG
Arran	1941	CG
Balta	1941	CWG
Bardsey	1943	Fleming & Ferguson
Benbecula	1944	CWG

HMS Foula *is shown as a minesweeper but completed with depth charge armament.*

(Imperial War Museum)

Bern	1942	CWG
Biggal	1944	Ferguson
Bressay	1942	CWG
Brora	1941	CWG
Gweal (ex-*Broreray*)	1942	CWG
Bruray	1942	CWG
Bryher	1943	CWG
Burra	1941	Goole SB
Bute	1941	Goole SB
Caldy	1943	Lewis
Calvay	1944	CWG
Canna	1941	Cochrane
Cava	1941	Cochrane
Coll	1942	Ardrossan
Colsay	1943	CWG
Copinsay	1941	Cochrane
Crowlin	1944	CWG
Cumbrae	1941	Cochrane
Damsay	1942	Brown
Earraid (ex-*Gruna*)	1942	Crown
Eday	1941	Cochrane
Egilsay	1943	CWG
Ensay	1942	CWG
Eriskay	1942	CWG
Fara	1941	CWG
Farne	1943	CWG
Fetlar	1941	Cochrane
Fiaray	1942	Goole SB
Filla	1942	Crown
Flatholm	1943	CWG
Flotta	1941	Cochrane
Foula	1942	Cochrane
Foulness	1943	Lewis
Fuday	1944	CWG
Gairsay	1943	Ardrossan
Ganilly	1944	CWG
Harris (ex-*Gilsay*)	1944	CWG
Gillstone	1943	Cochrane
Gorregan	1944	Ardrossan
Graemsay	1943	Ardrossan

Grain	1943	Cochrane
Grassholm	1943	Lewis
Gruinard	1943	Crown
Gulland	1943	CWG
Hannaray	1944	CWG
Hascosay	1944	CWG
Hayling	1942	CWG
Hellisay	1944	Cochrane
Hermetray	1944	Cochrane
Hildasay	1941	CWG
Hoxa	1941	CWG
Hoy	1941	CWG
Hunda	1942	Ferguson
Imersay	1944	Cochrane
Inchcolm	1941	CWG
Inchkeith	1941	Lewis
Inchmarnock	1941	Lewis
Islay	1941	Smiths Dock
Jura	1941	Ardrossan
Kerrera	1941	Fleming & Ferguson
Killegray	1941	CWG
Kintyre	1942	Ardrossan
Kittern	1943	CWG
Lindisfarne	1943	CWG
Lingay	1945	Cochrane
Longa	1944	Cochrane
Lundy	1943	CWG
Mewstone	1943	CWG
Minalto	1943	CWG
Mincarlo	1944	Ardrossan
Mousa	1942	Goole SB
Mull	1941	CWG
Neave	1942	CWG
Orfasy	1942	Hall
Oronsay	1944	Cochrane
Orsay	1945	Cochrane
Oxna	1943	Inglis
Pladda	1941	CWG
Sheppey (II) (ex-*Raasay*)	1942	CWG
Ronaldsay	1941	Cochrane
Ronay	1945	Cochrane
Rosevean	1943	CWG
Rousay	1942	Goole SB
Ruskholm	1942	Goole SB
Rysa	1941	Cochrane
St Agnes	1943	Lewis
St Kilda	1942	Hall
Sanda	1941	Goole SB
Sandray	1944	CWG
Scalpay	1942	CWG
Scaravay	1945	CWG
Scarba	1941	CWG
Shapinsay	1941	Cochrane
Shiant	1941	Goole SB
Shillay	1945	CWG
Skokholm	1943	CWG

Skomer	1943	Lewis
Skye	1942	Robb
Sluna	1941	Cochrane
Staffa	1942	Robb
Steepholm	1943	Lewis
Stroma	1942	Hall Russell
Stronsay	1942	Inglis
Sursay	1945	CWG
Switha	1942	Inglis
Tahay	1945	CWG
Tiree	1942	Goole SB
Tocogay	1945	CWG
Trodday	1945	CWG
Trondra	1942	Lewis
Ulva	1942	CWG
Unst	1942	Ferguson
Vaceasay	1945	CWG
Vallay	1945	CWG
Vatersay	1944	Cochrane
Wallasea	1943	Robb
Westray	1942	Lewis
Whalsay	1942	CWG
Wiay	1945	CWG

SPECIFICATION
Displacement: 545 tons
Dimensions: 164 × 27½ × 10½
Armament: 1 × 12pdr DP, 3 × 20mm on single mtgs
Machinery: 1 shaft reciprocating engine giving 850ihp
Boilers: 1
Speed: 12½kts
Complement: 40

Eight 'Western Isles' Trawlers were built in Canada for the Royal Navy:
Campobello	1942	Collingwood
Dochet	1942	G. T. Davie
Flint	1942	G. T. Davie
Gateshead	1943	G. T. Davie
Herschell	1943	G. T. Davie
Porcher (ex-*Procher*)	1942	Midland
Prospect	1942	Midland
Texada	1942	Midland

SPECIFICATION (Canadian-built ships)
Displacement: 530 tons
Dimensions: 164 × 27¾ × 8½ mean
Armament: 1 × 12pdr (12cwt) DP, 2-4 × 20mm AA on single mtgs
Anti-submarine: 2 depth charge throwers, 2 depth charge racks
Other details: as UK-built ships

The following ships of this Class were fitted out as Day-layers:
Fuday	*Gilsay*	*Hannaray*	*Hascosay*
Hellisay	*Hermetray*	*Imersay*	*Lingay*
Orsay	*Ronay*	*Sandray*	*Shillay*
Sursay	*Tahay*	*Tocogay*	*Trodday*
Vaceasay	*Vallay*	*Wiay*	

Losses:

HMS *Brora* on 6 September 1941 went ashore in the Hebrides;

HMS *Canna* was lost in the Port of Lagos after an accidental explosion on 5 December 1942;

HMS *Colsay* on 2 November 1944 whilst off Ostend, was attacked by a German human torpedo;

HMS *Eriskay* whilst on loan to the Portuguese Navy foundered on 12 November 1945 off Sao Gorge in the Azores;

HMS *Flotta* on 6 November 1941 took the ground off Buchan Ness in bad weather and was abandoned;

HMS *Gairsay* on 3 August 1944 was hit by a German radio-controlled explosive motor boat, sinking off the Normandy beachhead;

HMS *Ganilly* was mined in the English Channel on 5 July 1944;

HMS *Hildasay* on 21 June 1945 was wrecked near Kilindini;

HMS *Jura* on 7 January 1943 was torpedoed by *U-371* when off Malta;

HMS *Orfasy* was torpedoed by *U-68* off the West African coast on 22 October 1943;

HMS *Rysa* was mined off Maddalena on 8 December 1943;

HMS *Stronsay* on 5 February 1943 was torpedoed by the Italian U-Boat *Avorio* off Philippeville;

HMS *Wallasea* was torpedoed during an action with E-Boats on 6 January 1944 in Mounts Bay;

HMS *Campobello* on 16 June 1943 during severe weather, foundered in the North Atlantic.

Dan-layer Armament:

Some of this class had two single 20mm port and starboard in small bandstands in front and below the bridge, with a single 20mm in a bandstand on the centreline aft of the main mast on the upper deck.

Others had one single 20mm in a bandstand on the centreline level, but aft of the forecastle, with one single 20mm in a bandstand on the centreline aft of the main mast on the upper deck.

Transfers During World War II:

The following 'Western Isle' class Naval Trawlers were transferred:

To the Portuguese Navy: HMS *Eriskay* (as *P8*), *Gruinard* (as *P7*), and *Whalsay* (as *P4*);

To the Royal New Zealand Navy: HMS *Inchkeith*, *Killegray*, *Sanda* and *Scarba* under their own names;

To the Royal Norwegian Navy: HMS *Inchmarnock* (as *Karmoy*), *Mincarlo* (as *Tromoy*) and *Shiant* (as *Jeloy*).

'ZZ' Class Motor Minesweepers

SPECIFICATION

Displacement:	360 tons
Dimensions:	145 × 30 × 2½/4
Machinery:	2 shaft diesel engines all giving 200/240bhp
Speed:	7½kts
Complement:	7

Notes:

All 'ZZ' M/S were converted Army 'A' Lighters, probably built by local contractors or the Royal Engineers in the Middle East.

A total of 30 'A' Lighters were transferred to the Royal Navy and named from *ZZ1-ZZ30*. They were fitted for shallow water sweeping and deployed the LL sweep and were used against pressure mines.

Operationally they swept rivers and canals in Europe, and the Canals of Venice.

HM MMSs *ZZ3*, *ZZ6* and *ZZ14* were transferred to the Royal Netherlands Navy.

Losses:
HM MMS *ZZ12* capsized in bad weather on 5 May 1946 whilst transitting the Firth of Forth;
HM MMS *ZZ13* capsized in heavy weather in UK waters on 27 December 1945, but was
later raised and broken up.
HM MMS *ZZ16* caught fire at Port Said in September 1946, being described as a construc-
tive total loss.

Requisitioned Mine Destructor Vessels

HMS	Tons	Built	Converted	Armament
Andelle	1,832	1922	1940	Not known
Borde	2,014	1921	1939	2 × 12pdr AA, 2 × 2pdr AA, 2 × mg, all on single mtgs
Burlington (later *Soothsayer*, later *Fairfax*)	2,068	1940	1940	Not known
Bushwood	2,314	1930	1940	Not known
Corbrae	1,788	1935	1940	8 × 20mm on single mtgs
Corburn	1,786	1936	1940	8 × 20mm on single mtgs
Corfield	1,791	1937	1940	Not known
Queenworth	2,047	1925	1940	Not known
Springdale	1,597	1937	1940	2 × 12pdr AA on single mtgs
Springtide	1,579	1937	1940	2 × 12pdr AA on single mtgs

HMS Fairfax, *mine destructor, in Lundy Roads, 1941. Note the rectangular-shaped magnet at
the stern, forward of the 3in gun in the bandstand. Also the large reels of LL sweep wire at
the stern.* (Lt-Cmdr P. W. Ratcliffe, RNR)

Notes:
These vessels were requisitioned and later purchased to serve as a stop-gap measure for
combatting the magnetic mine as Mine Destructor Vessels (MDVs). The theory for clearing a
lane through a magnetic minefield was that each ship listed above was fitted with a large
magnet, positioned on the stem head, which would radiate a magnetic field of such power
and influence as to enable the average-sized ship to steam safely through the minefield.

However, the magnetic mines notwithstanding, the strong radiation from the stem head electro-magnet on the MDV generally detonated very close to the ship and structural damage was frequently sustained. During this period (early 1940) the LL sweep was being developed and so the MDVs became obsolescent that year.

Further disadvantages were that conventional minesweepers and danlayers had to be deployed on either beam of the MDV to mark the cleared channel. One further unexpected disadvantage arose when the magnet was 'charged up', causing the magnetic compasses of accompanying ships — and even, at times, ships in the MDV's home port — to go completely wild and so pilotage had to be quickly introduced where navigation had been intended.

Losses:
HMS *Corburn* detonated a mine and sank from the resulting explosion on 21 May 1940 whilst off Le Havre;
HMS *Corfield* sank in similar circumstances on 9 April 1941 in the Humber Estuary;
HMS *Queenworth* on 9 May 1941 was bombed and sank in the North Sea.

'Hunt' Class Type 1 as Minesweepers (Destroyers)

HMS	Commenced	Completed	Builder
Cotswold	1939	1940	Yarrow
Hambledon	1939	1940	Swan Hunter
Holderness	1939	1940	Swan Hunter
Quorn	1939	1940	White
Tynedale	1939	1940	Stephen

SPECIFICATION
Displacement: 1,000 tons
Dimensions: 280 × 29 × 17¼
Armament: 4 (2 × 4) 4in DP LA on two twin mtgs
1 × 2pdr quad Pom-Pom
2 (2 × 1) 20mm DP AA
Anti-submarine: 1 × depth charge rack, 2 × depth charge throwers
Machinery: 2 shaft single reduction turbines all giving 19,000shp
Boilers: 2
Speed: 30kts
Fuel: 243 tons of oil fuel
Range: 2,000nm at 12kts
Complement: 243

Notes:
Ships of this type were designed as dual A/S AA vessels and largely used as convoy escorts. However, as this design only had a short range, the convoys involved were mainly on the east coast of the UK which were susceptible to minefields. In consequence the five escorts mentioned above were classed as Destroyer Minesweepers, being fitted with the pneumatic hammer/SA acoustic sweep as well as paravanes.

Losses:
HMS *Quorn* sank after the warhead from a German small battle unit was attached and later detonated when off the Normandy beachhead on 2 August 1944;
HMS *Tynedale* was torpedoed by *U-593* on 12 December 1943 in the Western Mediterranean.

'Fairmile B' Type Motor Launches as Minesweepers

Sequence of MLs completed: Nos: *112-311, 336-500, 511-600, 801-933, 4001-4004, 050-129* (ex *001-80*) built 1940-44 inclusive.

HM ML 2338. This ML is leaving Valetta and has been completely converted for mine-sweeping, with Oropesa and wire sweeps. (Not known)

SPECIFICATION

Displacement:	65 tons (to No *123*, 73 tons thereafter)
Dimensions:	112 × 18¼ × 4¼
Armament:	1 × 3pdr QF, 2 × .303in mg
Anti-submarine:	12 depth charges
Minesweeps:	Lightweight Oropesa sweeps were deployed, also as required acoustic and magnetic sweeps
Machinery:	2 shaft petrol engines all giving 1,200bhp
Speed:	20kts
Range:	1,500nm at 12kts
Complement:	16

Notes:
These MLs were constructed at 43 yards in the UK and 38 overseas.

The 'B' ML was first used for minesweeping against moored mines in the harbours of Malta. At least 100 were converted to the minesweeping role serving in most theatres of war. A later sweep was of wire for use in estuaries and navigable channels. The MLs became so expert that they were used for preliminary sweeping before the Fleet sweepers and continued in this task long after the cessation of hostilities. (For losses of this type see page 45, Fairmile 'B' Type Motor Launches as Minelayers. For shipyards which built these craft see page 45 *et seq.*)

'Fairmile' Harbour Defence Motor Launches (HDML) as Minesweepers

With the advent and success of World War II Coastal Forces the need for a smaller but equally seaworthy craft was quickly realised, and consequently the Harbour Defence Motor Launch (just slightly smaller than the MLs of World War I) was designed and rapidly built. All were built between 1940-44 with numbers in sequence from 1001-1600.

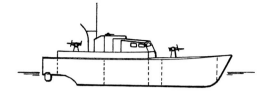

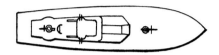

OUTLINE OF H.D.M.L. (72 ft)

SPECIFICATION

Displacement:	46 tons
Dimensions:	72 × 15 × 4¼
Armament:	1 × 2pdr
	2 × twin .303in mg
	1 × Holman Projector for flares
Anti-submarine:	8 depth charges were normally carried.
Minesweeping:	HDMLs landed their depth charges when fitted with the Oropesa minesweeping gear
Fuel:	1,500gals diesel fuel with an additional 200gal deck tanks
Machinery:	2 diesel engines of 150hp each plus an auxiliary lighting set.
Speed:	11/12kts max
Range:	1,000nm at 12kts, 2,000nm at 10kts
Complement:	10

HM HDML 1024. *This HDML is on builders trials and largely unarmed, but a twin .303in Lewis mg is mounted aft of the wheelhouse.* (Imperial War Museum)

Losses:
(The undermentioned HDMLs lost were not necessarily all of the minesweeping version.)
HM HDML *1003* when in transit across the North Atlantic on 20 April 1941 was lost when the merchant ship carrying her was sunk;
HM HDML *1011* on 10 May 1941, whilst off Crete, was bombed by German aircraft;
HM HDML *1015* in October 1943 was wrecked off the breakwater of Alexandria Harbour;
HM HDML *1019* in July 1944 became a constructive total loss after a fire at Freetown;
HM HDML *1030* was lost, cause unknown, north of Alexandria on 28 May 1941;
HM HDML *1039* on 23 June 1942 was lost at Tobruk, cause unknown;
HM HDML *1054* on 23 October 1943 was wrecked off West Hartlepool;
HM HDML *1057* when off Killindini was mined on 13 October 1944;
HM HDML *1060* on 7 August 1944 was lost in an explosion at Poole Harbour;
HM HDML *1062* on 16 February 1942 was engaged by Japanese surface craft in the Banka Strait;
HM HDML *1063* on 1 March 1942 was engaged by Japanese surface craft off Tan Jong Priok;
HM HDML *1069* on 23 June 1942 was mined in Tobruk Harbour;
HM HDML *1083* whilst transitting the Gulf of Kos foundered in bad weather on 20 February 1944;
HM HDML *1100* and *1101* foundered in the Naaf River, April 1942;
HM HDML *1119* on 7 October 1944, took the ground off Ceylon;
HM HDML *1121* on 31 December 1943 in bad weather foundered off Pantellaria;
HM HDML *1147* in July 1944 was lost by fire in Freetown Harbour;
HM HDML *1154* on 14 May 1943 was mined at Bizerta;
HM HDML *1163* on 5 January 1945 was torpedoed in the Western Approaches by a German surface vessel;
HM HDML *1179* on 21 August 1944 in bad weather foundered north of Jamaica;
HM HDML *1226* when off Alexandropolis was mined on 4 October 1945;
HM HDML *1227* was attacked by German surface craft on 5 October 1944 when off Piraeus;
HM HDML *1259* on 31 October 1944 came under shellfire from German shore batteries off Marseille;
HM HDML *1380* on 1 May 1944 in bad weather foundered in the Aegean Sea;
HM HDML *1381* was taken by German forces at Sirina on 26 August 1944;
HM HDML *1388* on 24 December 1943 went ashore and was wrecked off West Hartlepool;
HM HDML *1417* on 15 February 1945 was mined off Flushing;
HM HDML *1037* was lost in transit on 20 April 1941 as HDML *1003;*
HM HDML *1090* was lost in transit from the UK on 11 July 1942;
HM HDML *1153* was lost in transit from the UK in September 1942;
HM HDML *1157* and *1212* were both lost in transit from the UK in April 1943;
HM HDML *1244* and *1289* were both lost in transit from the UK on 11 November 1943;
HDMLs *1092, 1093, 1094* and *1095* were destroyed whilst fitting out at Belfast in 1941 due to a German air attack;
HDMLs *1102, 1103* and *1104* were destroyed incomplete by own forces at Rangoon in April 1942 in the face of the Japanese advance;
HDMLs *1096, 1167, 1168, 1169* and *1170* were lost on the stocks at Singapore in February 1942 in the face of the Japanese advance.

Builders (HDMLs built in the UK)
Anderson, Rigden & Perkins (Whistable): Nos *1009, 1010, 1146, 1147, 1233, 1234, 1273, 1274, 1275, 1382, 1383, 1403, 1404, 1479, 1480;*
Berthon Boat (Lymington): Nos *1013, 1014, 1025, 1026, 1031, 1032, 1037, 1038, 1046, 1047, 1125-1128, 1237-1240, 1255-1260, 1372, 1373, 1390-1393, 1413, 1414, 1465-1468, 1483;*
Wm. Blackmore (Bideford): Nos *1015, 1016, 1065, 1066, 1083, 1084, 1150-1153, 1231, 1232, 1300-1303;*
Graham Bunn (Wroxham): Nos *1019, 1020, 1036, 1055, 1154, 1155, 1308, 1309, 1310;*

Bute Slip Lock (Port Bannatyne): Nos *1156, 1157, 1279, 1280;*
E. F. Elkins (Christchurch): Nos *1080, 1162-1166, 1398, 1399;*
Harland & Wolff (Belfast): Nos *1017, 1018, 1034, 1035, 1092-1095;*
D. Hilyard (Littlehampton): Nos *1005, 1006, 1044, 1056, 1057, 1158, 1159, 1235, 1236, 1269-1272, 1401;*
Lady Bee (Southwick): Nos *1001, 1002;*
McGruer (Clynder): Nos *1029, 1030, 1048-1050, 1229, 1230, 1296-1299, 1380, 1381;*
McLean (Renfrew): Nos *1076-1079, 1241-1244, 1394, 1395, 1407, 1408, 1476, 1477, 1478;*
A. H. Moody (Swannick Shore): Nos *1148, 1149, 1221, 1222, 1276, 1277, 1278;*
Morgan Giles (Teignmouth): Nos *1039, 1051, 1052, 1053;*
Alfred Mylne (Port Bannatyne): Nos *1027, 1028;*
R. A. Newman (Hamworthy): Nos *1011, 1012, 1040-1043, 1225, 1226, 1384, 1385, 1386, 1387, 1590;*
Leo. Robinson (Lowestoft): Nos *1021, 1022, 1075, 1137, 1138, 1247, 1248, 1396, 1397;*
 (Tewkesbury): Nos *1073, 1074, 1139, 1245, 1246;*
Sittingbourne Sbdg.: Nos *1023, 1024, 1071, 1072, 1160, 1161, 1227, 1228, 1281, 1282, 1388, 1389;*
Sussex Sbdg. (Shoreham): Nos *1023, 1024, 1292, 1293, 1294, 1295;*
Thornycroft (Hampton): Nos *1129-1136, 1211, 1212, 1283-1291;*
Watercraft (East Molesey): Nos *1003, 1004, 1069, 1070;*
Herbert Woods (Potter Heigham): Nos *1142-1145, 1304-1307;*
 (Shoreham): Nos *1007, 1008, 1085-1087, 1211-1214;*
 (Poole): Nos *1033, 1045, 1064, 1081, 1082, 1140, 1141, 1209, 1210, 1249-1254;*
 (Yarmouth): Nos *1058, 1059, 1060, 1061;*
 (Southampton): Nos *1067, 1068;*
 (Dumbarton): Nos *1088, 1089;*
 (Isle of Wight): Nos *1090, 1091;*
Builders unknown: Nos *1400-1402, 1405, 1406, 1461, 1462, 1469, 1484, 1485, 1501-1589, 1591-1600.*

Builders (HDMLs built abroad)
Ackerman Boat Works (Azusa): Nos *1348, 1349, 1350, 1351;*
African Marine & General Eng. (Mombasa): Nos *1105-1108, 1195, 1196;*
Dodge Boat Works (Newport News): Nos *1171-1182, 1364-1367;*
Elscot Boats (City Island): Nos *1356, 1357, 1358, 1359;*
Everett Marine Rly. (Washington): Nos *1187, 1188, 1189, 1190;*
Freeport Port Shipyard (Long Island): Nos *1352, 1353, 1354, 1355;*
Garden Reach (Calcutta): Nos *1115, 1120;*
Grays Hbr. Shpg. (Aberdeen): Nos *1191, 1192, 1193, 1194;*
Hooghly Dock & Eng. (Calcutta): Nos *1112, 1113;*
Irrawadi Flotilla Co. (Rangoon): Nos *1100, 1101, 1102, 1103;*
E. Jack (Launceston): Nos *1325, 1326, 1329;*
Wm. Edgar John (Rye): Nos *1360, 1361, 1362, 1363;*
Chas. P. Leek (New Jersey): Nos *1338, 1339;*
MacFarlane (Adelaide): Nos *1323, 1324, 1328;*
Madden & Lewis (Sausalito): Nos *1183, 1184, 1185, 1186;*
H. Mohatta (Karachi): Nos *1109, 1110, 1111, 1265, 1266, 1267;*
Frederick Nichol (Durban): Nos *1098, 1099, 1197-1202, 1330-1337;*
Pehara Land Co. (Alexandria): Nos *1315-1320;*
Purdon & Featherstone (Hobart): Nos *1321, 1322, 1327;*
Rangoon Dockyard: No *1104;*
Spradbrow (Durban): Nos *1203, 1204;*
L. S. Thorsen (Ellesworth): Nos *1340, 1341, 1342, 1343;*
Truscott Boat & Dock Co. (St. Joseph): Nos *1348, 1349, 1350, 1351;*

Walker, Son & Co. (Colombo): Nos *1205, 1206, 1207, 1208;*
(Singapore): Nos *1062, 1063, 1096, 1097;*
(Calcutta): Nos *1118, 1119;*
(Bombay): Nos *1114, 1116, 1117, 1261-1264, 1268;*
(Ceylon): Nos *1311, 1312, 1313, 1314;*
Builders unknown: Nos *1167-1170, 1213-1220, 1409-1412, 1415-1460, 1463, 1464, 1470-1475, 1481, 1482, 1486-1500.*

Mine Destructor Hulls

Also known as 'Stirling Craft', in fact only two were built, being named *Cybele* and *Cyrus*. The names were taken from the list of the 'Algerine' Class and were given as security cover.

Cybele and *Cyrus* were operational experimental towed sweeps built as an attempt to combat the pressure or 'Oyster' mine.

SPECIFICATION
Displacement: 3,980 tons (deadweight 1,950 tons)
Dimensions: 359 × 60 × 30 but with a pump-out facility to reduce the draught to 16ft

Steering was by remote electrical control as a Stirling Craft was unmanned. Construction was in steel to form a bouyant triangular and T-shaped sectional framework, secured together forming the dimensions given.

Name	Completed	Builder
Cybele	1943	Denny
Cyrus	1944	Swan Hunter

Losses:
Cyrus broke her tow in the Seine Estuary when sweeping for pressure mines on 5 December 1944;
Cybele was subjected to underwater detonations and was tested to destruction before she was finally broken up in 1946 at Troon.

Steam Gun Boats (SGB) as Displacement Minesweepers

HMS	Launched	Builder
SGB3 (later *Grey Seal*)	1941	Yarrow SB
SGB4 (later *Grey Fox*)	1941	Yarrow SB
SGB5 (later *Grey Owl*)	1941	Hawthorn Leslie
SGB6 (later *Grey Shark*)	1941	Hawthorn Leslie
SGB7	1941	Denny
SGB8 (later *Grey Wolf*)	1941	Denny
SGB9 (later *Grey Goose*)	1942	White

SPECIFICATION
Displacement: 165 tons
Dimensions: 137¼pp 145½ × 20 × 5½
Armament: 2 × 2pdr on single mtgs, 4 (2 × 2) .5in mg
(designed)
Torpedoes: 2 × 21in tubes, 1 port and starboard of the wheelhouse
Machinery: 2 shaft geared turbines giving 8,000shp, but 7,220shp for boats 7, 8 and 9
Boilers: 1
Speed: 35kts

HMS Grey Shark *on builders trials but looking rather neglected. She is not fitted with radar.*

(Swan Hunter)

Fuel:	50 tons of oil fuel
Range:	400nm at 11kts
Complement:	27

Notes:

HM *SGB7* was lost prior to receiving an official name. Designed and constructed as the heaviest RN GB/TB and as a counter to the increasingly speedy and well-armed German 'R' Boats.

Armament in service comprised 1 × 3in LA, 2 × 6pdr QF, 6 × 20mm on twin mtgs.

SGB1 and 2 by Thornycroft were ordered but not laid down.

Loss:

HM *SGB7* whilst on night patrol in the English Channel came into action with enemy light forces on 19 June 1942 and after an exchange of fire was lost.

Displacement Minesweeping:

This system of minesweeping involved water pressure which activated the pressure or Oyster mine. It consisted of high-speed runs over the mined area in the anticipation that the wash of the vessel would activate the pressure seal of the mine, so causing a harmless detonation, but the idea was not very successful. The principle behind the high-speed of the vessel was that a ship produces a decrease in water pressure under the hull, the more so if the vessel is steaming at speed and/or in shallower water. As the Oyster mine was generally laid as a mixture of magnetic and acoustic mines, the SGBs also deployed special acoustic and magnetic sweeps.

Other classes of Displacement Minesweepers included 'Assurance' and 'Bustler' Class Tugs.

'Bustler' Class Rescue Tugs as Displacement Minesweepers

HMT	Launched	Builder
Bustler	1941	All built by Henry Robb
Growler	1942	
Hesperia (ex-*Hesper*)	1942	
Mediator	1944	
Reward	1944	

Samsonia (ex-Samson)	1942
Turmoil	1944
Warden	1945

HMT Growler, *looking as new and probably straight from the builder's yard.* (Imperial War Museum)

SPECIFICATION

Displacement:	1,120 tons
Dimensions:	205 × 38½ × 13
Armament:	1 × 3in DP AA, 1 × 2pdr AA, 2 × 20mm AA on single mtgs, 4 × .303in Lewis mg on two twin mtgs
Machinery:	2 shaft diesel engines all giving 4,000bhp
Speed:	16kts
Fuel:	405 tons of oil fuel
Complement:	42

Notes:
All were large ocean-going tugs with a bollard pull capable of towing large merchant and other vessels. They carried quite a heavy anti-aircraft armament but little in the way of A/S weapons.
   (See Steam Gun Boat section for details of Displacement Minesweeping, page 176.)

Loss:
HMT *Hesperia* in bad weather was wrecked on the Libyan coast on 9 February 1945.

'Assurance' Class Rescue Tugs as Displacement Minesweepers

HMT	Launched	Builder
Adept	1941	All built by Cochrane
Adherent	1941	
Allegiance	1943	
Antic (ex-*Ant*)	1943	
Assidious	1943	

Assurance	1940
Charon	1941
Dexterous	1942
Earner (ex-*Ernest*)	1943
Frisky	1941
Griper	1942
Hengist (ex-*Decision*)	1941
Horsa (ex-*Rescue*)	1942
Jaunty	1941
Prosperous	1941
Prudent	1940
Restive	1940
Saucy (II)	1942
Sesame	1942
Stormking (ex-*Stormcock*)	1942
Tenacity (ex-*Diligent*)	1940

This photograph is of the Rescue Tug HMT Charon *which, similar to* Bustler, *was used as a Displacement Minesweeper.* (Wright & Logan)

SPECIFICATION

Displacement:	700 tons
Dimensions:	157 × 33½ × 11
Armament:	1 × 3in DP AA, 2 × 20mm AA on single mtgs, 2 × .303in Lewis mg on one twin mtg
Machinery:	1 shaft triple expansion giving 1,350ihp
Boilers:	1
Fuel:	282 tons of oil fuel
Speed:	13kts
Complement:	31

Notes:
Some were employed as displacement Minesweepers. A design of sea-going tug more for inshore and coastal waters.

Losses:
HMT *Adept* on 17 March 1942 was wrecked in the Outer Hebrides;
HMT *Adherent* foundered in the North Atlantic on 14 January 1944;
HMT *Assurance* was wrecked in Lough Foyle on 18 October 1941;
HMT *Horsa* was wrecked on the east coast of Iceland on 16 March 1943;
HMT *Sesame* was torpedoed by a E-Boat when off the Normandy beachhead on 11 June 1944.

Motor Fishing Vessels (MFV) 75ft as Assault Minesweepers

Of the four sizes of Motor Fishing Vessels (MFV) produced by the Admiralty during World War II the 75ft version was one of the most successful. All were built in the UK and particulars of a 75ft MFV are as follows:

This is a photograph of MFV 1152, being the same type of MFV which was used as an Assault Minesweeper in World War II. (Not known)

SPECIFICATION
Displacement: 114 tons
Dimensions: 70pp 75 × 19½ × 5½/9½
Armament: 1 × .303in mg
Machinery: 1 diesel engine, 160bhp, to 1 shaft giving 8½kts
Complement: 9

Loss:
HM MFV *1032* whilst being towed in the North Sea in February 1944 was sunk, cause unknown.

Builders
Berthon Boat (Lymington):   Nos *1223, 1224, 1225, 1226, 1229, 1230;*
Clapson & Sons (Barton on Humber):   Nos *1004, 1005, 1006;*
J. S. Doig (Grimsby):   Nos *1051, 1058, 1102, 1103, 1115-1118, 1173, 1174, 1199, 1206, 1221, 1222, 1242;*

George Forbes (Peterhead):	Nos *1021, 1022, 1026, 1076-1078, 1093-1096, 1131-1134, 1161, 1162, 1191;*
J. & G. Forbes (Sandhaven):	Nos *1035-1038, 1081, 1082, 1085, 1086, 1089, 1090, 1121-1126, 1184-1188, 1211;*
P. K. Harris (Appledore):	Nos *1011-1014;*
Herd & McKenzie (Buckie):	Nos *1043-1046, 1087, 1088, 1151, 1152-1154, 1209;*
Humphrey & Smith (Grimsby):	Nos *1031-1034, 1067, 1068, 1100, 1155-1158, 1169-1172, 1177-1180, 1227, 1228;*
Husband Yacht Yard (Marchwood):	Nos *1061, 1062, 1149, 1150, 1201, 1202;*
Richard Irvine (Peterhead):	Nos *1018-1020, 1052, 1074, 1075, 1097, 1098, 1105-1108, 1193, 1194, 1218, 1219, 1233, 1234;*
Mac Duff Eng. & Shbdg. Co (MacDuff):	Nos *1039-1042, 1143-1146;*
James Noble (Fraserburgh):	Nos *1101-1003, 1015-1017, 1053, 1079, 1080, 1091, 1092, 1139-1142, 1189, 1190, 1213;*
Philip & Son (Dartmouth):	Nos *1083, 1084, 1135-1138, 1175, 1176, 1207, 1208, 1239, 1240;*
Walter Reekie (Anstruther):	Nos *1104, 1110, 1111, 1113, 1163, 1164, 1166, 1196;*
Walter Reekie (St Monace):	Nos *1027-1030, 1109, 1112, 1114, 1165, 1195;*
J. W. & A. Upham (Brixham):	Nos *1007-1010, 1203, 1204, 1205;*
Wilson Noble & Co (Fraserburgh):	Nos *1054, 1127-1130, 1215-1217.*

Cancellations:
Nos *1014, 1047, 1231* and *1232,* builders not known.

Notes:
Assault Minesweeping MFVs were more heavily-built than MLs and had a better pull. However, they were used for a similar purpose using influence sweeps for tidal and freshwater areas, eg: rivers and canals.
    A good account of their use with other M/Ss can be found in *Allied Minesweeping in World War 2* by Peter Elliott.

Minesweeping LCA(HR) Landing Craft Assault ('Hedgerow')

These Landing Craft Assault (LCA) were commissioned with strengthened frames and stringers for the purpose of beaching in the process of landing; and the 'Sweep', which detonated the mines on the beach, consisted of a Squid-type weapon, carrying 24 bombs fired ahead of the craft to explode ground mines buried in, or fixed to, structures on the beach. Details of the LCA were:

SPECIFICATION
Displacement:	9-13 tons
Dimensions:	41½ × 10 × 1/2¼
Armament:	2 × 2in mortars, 3 × .303in mg, 1 single and 1 twin
Machinery:	2 petrol engines, 130bhp, to 2 shafts, giving 6-10kts
Complement:	4

Losses:
HM LCA *689* (Hedgerow) on 13 March 1944 foundered in Loch Fyne;
HM LCA *672* and *811* foundered off the east coast of Scotland on 2 April 1944, whilst on exercise in Pentland Firth;
HM LCA *671, 690, 965* and *1072* were lost in the period June-July 1944 during Operation 'Neptune', off the coast of Normandy.

HM LCA *183* and *802* on 1 July 1944 were lost in the Mediterranean;
HM LCA *678* and *803* were lost, cause and place unknown.

HM LCA. This is a Hedgerow version of the LCA, looking aft to the machinery space. Note the 12 Hedgerow bombs inclined forrard, port and starboard. Also the reload bombs outboard of same. (Imperial War Museum)

Notes:
Although Landing Craft Assault were the most common hulls adapted for the 'Hedgerow' weapon, an unknown number of Landing Craft (Tank) LC(T) Mks 4 and 5 were also converted.

Landing Craft Mechanised (LCM) as Minesweepers — Mks 1, 3 and 7

SPECIFICATION

LCM	*Mk1*	*Mk3*	*Mk7*
Displacement:	21/36 tons	22/53 tons	27/62 tons
Dimensions:	48 × 14 × 2½/3½	40 × 14 × 3½/4½	58pp 16 × 4 × 5
Armament:	2 × .303in mg single	As Mk1	As Mk1
Machinery:	2 petrol engines, 120bhp, to 2 shafts giving 7½kts	2 diesel engines, 220+bhp, to 2 shafts giving 9½kts	2 diesel engines, 290bhp, to 2 shafts giving 9¼kts
Complement:	6	3	6

Note:
Landing Craft Mechanised were used for sweeping as were Fairmile 'B' Type MLs, that is inshore shallow water, using light Oropesa sweeps. Many craft were lost.

HM LCM 7174. This is an LCM(7), many of which were used for forward sweeping into the beaches. (Imperial War Museum)

Landing Craft Personnel (Large) (LCP(L)) as Minesweepers

SPECIFICATION

Displacement:	6½/10½ tons
Dimensions:	37 × 10¼ × 2¼/3½
Armament:	1 × .303in mg
Machinery:	1 petrol or diesel engine to 1 shaft giving 8/10kts. According to the engine fitted, bhp varied from 210 to 260
Complement:	3

Note:
Quite often the first M/Ss into a mined port or harbour, LCP(L)s were used for sweeping snag mines and other similar work.

Losses:
At least 92 of these craft, not necessarily the minesweeping version, were lost on operations and later.

HM LCP(L) 141. This LCP(L) is similar to many that were used for forward minesweeping into the beachhead. (Imperial War Museum)

Landing Craft Tank Mk 4 (LCT(4)) as Minesweepers

HM LC(T)Mk(4) 1319. This is a Landing Craft Tank similar to many that were used for forward minesweeping into the beachhead. (Imperial War Museum)

SPECIFICATION

Displacement:	200/585 tons
Dimensions:	171pp 187½ × 38¼ × 3¼/4¼
Armament:	2 × 20mm on single mtgs
Machinery:	2 diesel engines 920bhp to 2 shafts giving 10kts
Complement:	12

Note:
Used as M/Ss for passage into the beachhead with light Oropesa sweeps.

Losses:
At least 39 of these craft, not necessarily the minesweeping version, were lost on operations and later. These Landing Craft were fitted with a modified version of the old HSMS gear, which enabled each craft to sweep either beam at the same time.

Landing Craft Tank Mk 5 (LCT(5)) as Minesweepers

HM LC(T)Mk(5) 2296. This is a Landing Craft Tank similar to many that were used for forward minesweeping into the beachhead. (Imperial War Museum)

SPECIFICATION
Displacement: 143/311 tons
Dimensions: 112½pp 117½ × 32¼ × 3/4½
Armament: 2 × 20mm on single mtgs
Machinery: 3 diesel engines, 675bhp to 3 shafts giving 8kts
Complement: 13

Notes:
Used in the same way as the LCT(4).

These craft, like the Mk 4s, used a derivation of the destroyer HSMS sweep which gave a clear channel of three-quarters of a cable on either bow.

Losses:
At least 29 of these craft, not necessarily the minesweeping version, were lost on operations and later.

Landing Craft (Vehicle) (LC(V)) for Minesweeping

HM LC(V) 829. This is a minesweeping LC(V) used in numbers for sweeping shallow waters, rivers, canals and docks. (Imperial War Museum)

SPECIFICATION
Displacement: 7/11 tons
Dimensions: 36½ × 10¼ × 1½/3
Armament: 1 × .303in mg
Machinery: 1 shaft diesel or petrol engine giving 225/230bhp
Speed: 9kts (free)
Complement: 3

Note:
Used in a similar way to the MFVs for port and harbour snag minesweeping etc.

Losses:
At least 12 of these craft, not necessarily the minesweeping version, were lost on operations and later.

'Flower' Class Corvettes as Minesweepers

HMS	Completed	Builder
Abelia	1941	Harland & Wolff
Alisma	1941	Harland & Wolff
Amaranthus	1941	Fleming & Ferguson
Aubrietia	1940	Brown
Borage	1942	Brown
Bryony	1942	Harland & Wolff
Buttercup	1942	Harland & Wolff
Candytuft	1940	Grangemouth Dockyard
Delphinium	1940	Robb
Erica	1940	Harland & Wolff
Gloxinia	1940	Harland & Wolff
Hyacinth	1940	Harland & Wolff
Hydrangea	1941	Ferguson
Lotus	1942	Hill
Lotus (II) ex-*Phlox*)	1942	Robb
Nettle (later *Hyderabad*)	1942	Hall
Pennywort	1942	Inglis
Peony	1940	Harland & Wolff
Pink	1942	Robb
Poppy	1942	Hall
Primula	1940	Simons
Salvia	1940	Simons
Snapdragon	1940	Simons
Violet	1940	Simons

HMS Lotus (II). *This is a three-quarter bow view of one of the later Corvettes converted into a full Minesweeper and taken from the Atlantic anti-submarine groups. Her Pennant No is* K 130. (Imperial War Museum)

SPECIFICATION

Displacement:	950 tons (Full load: 1,160 tons)
Dimensions:	190pp 205 × 35 × 8¼/13½
Armament:	1 × 4in DP, 1 × .5in AA on a quad mtg, 2 × .303in Lewis
Anti-submarine:	2 × depth charge racks, 2 × depth charge throwers
Machinery:	1 shaft 4-cylinder reciprocating engine giving 2,750ihp
Boilers:	2
Speed:	16kts
Fuel:	230 tons of oil fuel
Range:	2,630nm at 15kts
Complement:	85 approx

Notes:
These 24 Corvettes were converted from their normal role as convoy escorts and anti-submarine vessels due to the continuing shortage of minesweepers. The M/S Corvettes were equipped to sweep all types of mines, both enemy and Allied. They normally operated in the Mediterranean Sea and Indian Oceans.

Fifty-five Canadian-built Corvettes were fitted for minesweeping but all were RCN-manned.

Losses:
On 9 February 1943 whilst off Benghazi, HMS *Erica* was mined;
HMS *Pink* was mined off Normandy on 27 June 1944 and became a constructive total loss;
HMS *Salvia* when west of Alexandria was torpedoed by *U-568* on 24 December 1941;
HMS *Snapdragon* on 19 December 1942 was attacked by enemy aircraft whilst off Malta.

Ex-German Minesweeping Motor Fishing Vessels

HMS	Ex-German	Builder
	KFK94	Valdemarsviks Slifsverv
	KFK105	Abrahamson-Ramso
	KFK108	A/B Sverre-Gothenburg
	KFK153	Not known
	KFK157	Not known
	KFK158	Not known
	KFK228	Not known
	KFK236	Not known
	KFK240	W Kater-Amsterdam
	KFK309	Gebr Burmester-Swinemunde
	KFK336	Gebr Burmester-Swinemunde
	KFK337	Gebr Burmester-Swinemunde
	KFK356	Gebr Burmester-Swinemunde
	KFK382	Gebr Burmester-Swinemunde
	KFK389	Gebr Burmester-Swinemunde
	KFK392	Gebr Burmester-Swinemunde
	KFK394	Gebr Burmester-Swinemunde
	KFK406	Gebr Burmester-Swinemunde

SPECIFICATION

Displacement:	110 tons
Dimensions:	79½wl × 21 × 8¼
Armament:	1 × 37mm AA, 4 × 20mm AA on single mtgs
Machinery:	1 shaft diesel engine giving 150bhp
Speed:	9kts
Fuel:	Oil fuel
Range:	1,200nm at 7kts

Notes:
The above were allocated to the Royal Navy at the close of World War II. Built in small yards all over Occupied Europe to a navalised design of a commercial fishing boat. Used for minesweeping, patrol and A/S work and as coastal escorts. Quite heavily armed compared to the earlier 'R' Motor Minesweepers.

Ex-German Minesweeper (*Walter Holtzappel*)

HMS	Commenced	Completed	Builder
Deepwater	1939	1940	Norderwerft (Hamburg)
(ex-*Walter Holtzappel*)			

HMS Deepwater *was the ex-German Minesweeper* Walter Holtzappel *but commissioned into the Royal Navy. She is a very handsome ship and was evaluated.* (Wright & Logan)

SPECIFICATION

Displacement:	1,460 tons (Full load: 1,586 tons)
Dimensions:	246wl 260 × 38 × 11½ mean
Armament:	37mm AA (4 × 1)
(as built)	20mm AA (4)
Tubes:	21in (1 quadruple mtg)
Machinery:	Two diesel engines of Sulzer design each giving 3,600bhp to one of two shafts
Speed:	19½kts
Range:	1,500nm at 15kts
Complement:	84 intended

Note:
This ship was built as a trials vessel for torpedo tests but as the war proceeded became more and more used for minesweeping. In 1946 she was ceded to the UK and in 1950 was in use as a Tender to HMS *Vernon* as a Diving Training vessel, later she was relegated to HM Dockyard for Harbour Service duties.

Ex-German 'M' Minesweepers

Ex-German	Completed	Builder
M102	1918	Rickmers Werft, Bremerhaven
M104	1918	Rickmers Werft, Bremerhaven
M131	1941	Lindenau, Memel
M201	1940	Neptun Werft, Rostock
M261	1942	Atlas Werke, Bremen
M272	1942	Rickmers Werft, Bremerhaven
M275	1943	Rickmers Werft, Bremerhaven
M277	1943	Rickmers Werft, Bremerhaven
M302	1941	Unterweser, Bremerhaven
M321	1941	Oderwerke, Stettin
M322	1941	Oderwerke, Stettin
M323	1941	Oderwerke, Stettin
M326	1943	Oderwerke, Stettin
M327	1943	Oderwerke, Stettin
M361	1941	Schichau, Konigsberg
M362	1941	Schichau, Konigsberg
M364	1941	Schichau, Konigsberg
M365	1942	Schichau, Konigsberg
M436	1942	Netherlands Dock & SB
M601	1941	Neptun Werft, Rostock
M602	1944	Neptun Werft, Rostock
M603	1944	Neptun Werft, Rostock
M604	1944	Neptun Werft, Rostock
M605	1944	Neptun Werft, Rostock
M612	1945	Neptun Werft, Rostock
M806	1944	Schichau, Konigsberg

A 1935-type minesweeper which was allocated to the Royal Navy after VE Day 1945. The vessel shown is M 806. (Not known)

TYPE 1935 SPECIFICATION (for *M102, M104, M131* and *M201*)
Displacement:	772 tons (Full load: 878 tons)
Dimensions:	224¼ × 27¼ × 8½
Armament:	2 (2 × 1) 4.1in AA, 2 × 37mm AA on single mtgs
Machinery:	2 shaft triple expansion all giving 3,500ihp
Boilers:	2

Speed:	18¼kts
Fuel:	143 tons of oil fuel
Range:	5,000nm at 10kts
Complement:	104

Notes:
This design had some similarities to the minesweepers of World War I. Ships of this type were also fitted for minelaying with a lay of 30 mines and used as coastal escort vessels. Additional 20mm AA armament was later fitted.

TYPE 1940 SPECIFICATION (for *M261, M272, M275, M277, M302, M321, M322, M323, M326, M327, M361, M362, M364, M365, M436*)

Displacement:	637 tons (Full load: 775 tons)
Dimensions:	204½ × 28 × 9½
Armament:	1 or 2 (2 × 1) 4.1in AA, 6 × 20mm AA on two single and one quad mtg
Machinery:	2 shaft triple expansion all giving 2,400ihp
Boilers:	2
Speed:	16¼kts
Fuel:	162 tons of coal
Range:	4,000nm at 10kts
Complement:	76

Notes:
Due to the general shortage of oil, these Minesweepers were built with coal-fired boilers Some of this class were fitted with two 21in torpedo tubes on the bow for training purposes and were used as Torpedo Recovery vessels. Such vessels only mounted one 4.1in gun.

TYPE 1943 SPECIFICATION (for *M601, M602, M603, M604, M605, M612* and *M806*)

Displacement:	668 tons (Full load: 821 tons)
Dimensions:	224 × 29½ × 8½
Armament:	2 (2 × 1) 4.1in AA, 2 × 37mm AA on single mtgs, 8 × 20mm AA on 4 single and one quad mtg
Machinery:	2 shaft triple expansion all giving 2,400ihp
Boilers:	2
Speed:	16½kts
Fuel:	136 tons of coal
Range:	3,600nm at 10kts
Complement:	107

Notes:
Capable of laying 24 mines and also used as torpedo recovery vessels and coastal escorts. All the above were surrendered to/acquired by the Royal Navy at the close of World War II.

Ex-German 'R' Type Motor Minesweepers

HMS	Ex-German	Completed	Builder
	R18	1937	Abeking & Rasmussen
	R21	1937	Schlicting-Travemunde
	R25	1938	Abeking & Rasmussen
	R26	1938	Abeking & Rasmussen
	R31	1938	Abeking & Rasmussen
	R32	1938	Abeking & Rasmussen
	R47	1943	Abeking & Rasmussen
	R48	1943	Abeking & Rasmussen

ML6115

R49	1943	Abeking & Rasmussen
R83	1943	Abeking & Rasmussen
R115	1943	Abeking & Rasmussen
R124	1943	Abeking & Rasmussen
R143	1943	Abeking & Rasmussen
R152	1943	Burmester Burg Lesum
R153	1943	Burmester Burg Lesum
R154	1943	Burmester Burg Lesum
R155	1943	Burmester Burg Lesum
R156	1943	Burmester Burg Lesum
R157	1943	Burmester Burg Lesum
R160	1943	Burmester Burg Lesum
R167	1943	Burmester Burg Lesum
R168	1943	Burmester Burg Lesum
R170	1943	Burmester Burg Lesum
R173	1943	Burmester Burg Lesum
R174	1943	Burmester Burg Lesum
R175	1943	Burmester Burg Lesum
R176	1943	Burmester Burg Lesum
R181	1943	Burmester Burg Lesum
R220	1944-45	Burmester Burg Lesum
R226	1944-45	Burmester Burg Lesum
R229	1944-45	Burmester Burg Lesum
R230	1944-45	Burmester Burg Lesum
R231	1944-45	Burmerster Burg Lesum
R233	1944-45	Burmester Burg Lesum
R236	1944-45	Burmester Burg Lesum
R240	1944-45	Burmester Swinemunde
R242	1944-45	Burmester Burg Lesum
R244	1944-45	Burmester Burg Lesum
R246	1944-45	Burmester Burg Lesum
R251	1944-45	Burmester Swinemunde
R252	1944-45	Burmester Swinemunde
R255	1944-45	Burmester Burg Lesum
R259	1944-45	Burmester Burg Lesum
R268	1944-45	Burmester Swinemunde
R290	1944-45	Schlicting-Travemunde
R424	1945	Burmester Burg Lesum

SPECIFICATION (for *R18* and *R21*)
Displacement: 115 tons
Dimensions: 121½ × 18 × 4¼
Armament: 2 (2 × 1) 20mm AA
Machinery: 2 shaft diesel engines all giving 1,800bhp
Speed: 21kts
Fuel: 10 tons diesel oil
Range: 1,100nm at 15kts
Complement: 34

Notes:
Both fitted with Voith Schneider propellers and electric motors.

SPECIFICATION (for *R25*, *R26*, *R31* and *R32*)
Displacement: 110
Dimensions: 116¼ × 18¼ × 4½
Armament: 2 (2 × 1) 20mm AA

Machinery:	2 shaft diesel engines all giving 1,800bhp
Speed:	21kts
Fuel:	10 tons diesel oil
Range:	1,100nm at 15kts
Complement:	34

Notes:
As above.

SPECIFICATION (for *R47, R48, R49, R83, R115* and *R124*)

Displacement:	125 tons
Dimensions:	124 × 19 × 4½
Armamant:	1 × 37mm AA
Machinery:	2 shaft diesel engines all giving 1,800bhp
Speed:	20kts
Fuel:	10 tons diesel oil
Range:	1,100nm at 15kts
Complement:	34

SPECIFICATION (for *R143*)

Displacement:	150 tons
Dimensions:	134¼ × 19 × 5½
Armament:	1 × 37mm AA
Machinery:	2 shaft diesel engines all giving 1,800bhp
Speed:	21kts
Fuel:	11 tons diesel oil
Range:	1,000nm at 15kts
Complement:	38

SPECIFICATION (for *R152, R153, R154, R155, R156, R157, R160, R167, R168* and *R170*)

Displacement:	125 tons
Dimensions:	116½ × 18¼ × 4½
Armament:	1 × 37mm AA
Machinery:	2 shaft diesel engines all giving 1,800bhp
Speed:	21kts
Fuel:	10 tons diesel oil
Range:	1,100nm at 15kts
Complement:	34

SPECIFICATION (for *R173, R174, R175, R176, R181, R220, R226, R229, R230, R231, R233, R236, R240, R242, R244, R246, E251, R252, R255, R259, R268* and *R290*)

Displacement:	140 tons
Dimensions:	128½ × 18¼ × 5
Armament:	1 × 37mm AA
Machinery:	2 shaft diesel engines all giving 2,550bhp
Speed:	21kts
Fuel:	15 tons diesel oil
Range:	1,000nm at 15kts
Complement:	38

SPECIFICATION (for *R424*)

Displacement:	140 tons
Dimensions:	128½ × 18¼ × 5
Armament:	1 × 37mm AA, 6 (3 × 2) 20mm AA
Machinery:	2 shaft diesel engines all giving 2,550bhp
Speed:	21kts

Fuel:	16½ tons diesel oil
Range:	1,100nm at 15kts
Complement:	38

Notes:
The 'R' Types of Motor Minesweepers were of similar design to the 'B' Type Fairmile Motor Launch but of heavier build. As the war progressed, the anti-aircraft armament increased to match the many aircraft attacks by the Allies. At the close of the war many of these craft were operated under British control with German crews for clearing the extensive minefields in what had been German-controlled navigable waters. They were also deployed in the Mediterranean, Baltic and North Seas. Later the sweepers numbered above were acquired by the Royal Navy for trial evaluation use and disposal.

Ex-German Auxiliary Minesweeper

Ex-German	Completed
212 (ex-*MFP212*)	1942

BRIEF PARTICULARS:

Tons:	220
Loss:	Whilst in RN service was mined in the Weser Estuary in 1949.

Ex-German Hydrofoils, Minelaying Capability

Ex-German	Completed	Builder
TS1	1940-41	Gebr Saschenburg-Harburg
TS2	1940-41	Gebr Saschenburg-Harburg
TS3	1940-41	Gebr Saschenburg-Harburg
TS4	1940-41	Gebr Saschenburg-Harburg
TS5	1940-41	Gebr Saschenburg-Harburg
TS6	1940-41	Gebr Saschenburg-Harburg

SPECIFICATION

Displacement:	6¼ tons
Dimensions:	39¼ × 12½ × 3
Armament:	1 × 15mm DP
Machinery:	1 shaft petrol engine giving 380bhp
Speed:	40kts
Complement:	4

Note:
All allocated to the Royal Navy at the close of World War II.

'Venturer' Class Ex-Commercial Deep Minesweepers

HMS	Converted	Builder
St David (ex-*Suffolk Monarch*)	1976	Cubow
Venturer (ex-*Suffolk Harvester*)	1976	Cubow

SPECIFICATION

Displacement:	392 tons
Dimensions:	120½ × 29¼ × 12¼
Armament:	Nil
Machinery:	2 diesel engines giving 2,000bhp

HMS St David *entering Portsmouth Channel looking a little sea-worn. Note the two funnels on top of the wheelhouse with the ship's crest.* (M. Lennon)

Propulsion:	2 Kort nozzles
Speed:	14kts
Complement:	20

Notes:
These two trawlers were chartered shortly after completion by the MOD(N) for duties such as offshore patrol in the North Sea. However, it became apparent that they were suitable for trials of the EDATS minesweeping proposals which resulted in the 'Sandown' class (see page 110). After conversion both ships were allocated to Royal Naval Reserve Divisions (Severn & South Wales) as Deep Minesweepers, their hulls and gear enabling the sweep to be shot from the extremity of the stern as in the 'Acacia' class of World War I (see page 66).

VT2 Hovercraft as a Minesweeper

Built by Vosper Thornycroft, a VT2 was chartered by the MOD(N) in 1976 and purchased outright in 1979.

The type (VT2), in common with other makes of hovercraft, has also been tested as a troop carrier, A/S vessel and assault craft. The most efficient use turned out to be minesweeping, being aided by the shallow draught of the VT2 and its great immunity from underwater detonations. The sweep may be streamed from the fore or after part of the hovercraft.

VT2 Hovercraft (artist's impression), viewed from the stern, showing modifications to such a craft as used for minesweeping. (Vosper Thornycroft)

SPECIFICATION
Operating tons: 100
Dimensions: 100¼ × 43½ × 3 (still)
Propulsion/Lift: 2 Proteus gas turbines giving 4,500shp at 60kts
Range: 300nm at full speed
Fuel: 23½ tons of JP4

'Speedy' Class Patrol Craft as MCM Vessel

HMS	Launched	Completed	Builder
Speedy	1979	1979	Boeing Marine Systems

HMS Speedy *(P 296) is shown on trials in the Solent. Note the water jet from the port side after bilge line which, with other jets, is the only propulsion.* (Vosper Thornycroft)

SPECIFICATION
Displacement: 117 tons
Dimensions: 90 × 31 × 4¼ (with foils down)
                    99 × 31 × 16¼ (with foils raised)
Armament: Designed to carry 2 × mg, also 1 × 76mm Compact
Machinery: Two Allison 501/K20 gas turbines giving 6,600hp and two
                    General Motors diesel engines, all powering water jets, giving a
                    speed of 45kts
Radius: 350nm at 5kts and 560nm at 45kts
Complement: 18

Notes:
Speedy was ordered through the US Navy and delivered to the UK but fitted-out by Messrs Vosper Thornycroft. She was largely experimental and has been used for North Sea patrolling, but in November 1980 she was used as a Mine Countermeasures vessel. She was unsuitable for use as a Minelayer due to the light construction of the hull which was very largely of aluminium construction.

It was intended to fit *Speedy* or her follow-up types with surface-to-surface missiles.

BH7 Hovercraft as Minesweepers

BH7 Mk 2A Hovercraft have been in service with the Royal Navy for at least two years from 1979. They have been evaluated by the Hovercraft Trials Unit for a number of tasks, particularly minesweeping, for which the craft appear to be most suited, having a low water-pressure signature combined with the necessary high speed required for this task.

A MCM version of the BH 7 Hovercraft passing the Needles. (British Hovercraft Corporation)

SPECIFICATION	
Builder:	British Hovercraft Corporation (BHC) Ltd
All-up weight:	60 tons
Dimensions:	76¼ × 45½ × 33 on landing pads
Machinery:	One Rolls-Royce Marine Proteus gas turbine to one airscrew for propulsion and hover, giving 4,250shp and 60kts plus at max speed
Fuel:	Up to 11.8 tons of JP4/kerosene can be carried
Endurance/Speed:	8 hours at 58kts
Complement:	14

BH7 Mk 20 Hovercraft as Minehunter/Minesweeper

The BH7 Mk 20 Hovercraft is a development of the Mk 2A, but capable of Minehunting/ Minesweeping *inter alia*. To quote from BHC material 'the minehunter craft with retractable sonars can detect underwater targets and dispose of them with the PAP 104 Remote Control Mine Disposal Vehicle or by the use of divers.'

In the Minesweeping role the craft can tow the wire sweep, acoustic sweep, magnetic sweep or the combined magnetic and acoustic sweep.

A BHC 7 Mark 20 Hovercraft as equipped for minehunting. The Pennant No is, however, P 235.

SPECIFICATION

All-up weight:	82 tons
Dimensions:	94 × 45½ × 6½
Armament:	2 × 30mm Rarden cannon DP
(Designed)	
Machinery:	One Allison 570K gas turbine geared to 1 CP air propeller all giving 4,500shp
Fuel:	7,000gal of JP3
Radius	
Minehunting:	100nm from base plus 16hrs estimating 80nm
Minesweeping:	100nm from base at towing speeds of 12-30kts estimating 200nm
Complement:	Over 4

'Cordella' Class Requisitioned Ex-Fisheries

HMS	Fishery Name	Completed	Requisitioned	Builder
Cordella	*Cordella*	1974	1982	Swan Hunter, Clelands Yard
Farnella	*Farnella*	1972	1982	Swan Hunter, Clelands Yard
Junella	*Junella*	1976	1982	Swan Hunter, Clelands Yard
Northella	*Northella*	1973	1982	Swan Hunter, Clelands Yard

HMS Farnella *as completed for James Marr & Sons prior to her charter by MOD(N).*

SPECIFICATION

PARTICULARS:	Cordella	Farnella	Junella	Northella
Length:	230¼	251¼	180½	230¼
Tons Nett:	427	518	601	427
Tons Gross:	1,238	1,468	1,614	1,238
Machinery:	Mirrlees diesel engines KMR Series			
bhp:	3,246	3,246	2,782	3,246
Shafts:	1	1	1	1
Oil Fuel:	400 tons	400 tons	400 tons	400 tons
Speed:	17kts	17kts	15kts	17kts
Endurance:	60 days	60 days	60 days	60 days
(Normal)				
Complement:	26-30	26-30	26-30	26-30
(Normal)				
Armament:	All fitted with a number of GPMGs and small arms.			

Notes:
All requisitioned by the MOD for the relief of the Falkland Islands and South Georgia in 1982 where they were used to tranship troops and munitions from the RMS *Queen Elizabeth 2* and other vessels. Later they worked on covert landings etc and as minesweepers. All returned safely to the UK by early August 1982 to their owner, J. Marr & Son Ltd of Hull.

HMS	Fishery Name	Completed	Requisitioned	Builder
Pict	*Pict*	1973	1982	Brooke Marine

SPECIFICATION

Tons Nett:	485 Tons Gross: 1,479
Dimensions:	242 × 42 × 17¼ mean
Machinery:	1 Mirrlees Blackstone diesel of 3,246bhp to one shaft
Complement:	47
(Normal)	

Notes:
Further details and service similar to the 'Cordella' Class.

Owned by British United Trawlers of Hull, the five trawlers were designated the 11th Minesweeping Squadron and retrofitted with one or two 20mm Oerlikon weapons for the better sinking of floating mines.

LC(V)P Mk 2 as Minesweepers

LC(V)P Mk 2 with Pennant No H3 is passing HMS Hermes *in Portsmouth Harbour. H3 is on trials and is not rigged for minesweeping.* (MOD(N))

BRIEF SPECIFICATION

Displacement:	8.5 tons (Full load: 13.5 tons)
Dimensions:	41½ × 10 × 2½
Armament:	2 × 7.62mm GPMG may be fitted
Machinery:	2 shaft diesel engines all giving 200bhp
Speed:	8½kts

Notes:

These Landing Craft Vehicle and Personnel (LCVP) normally carry 35 troops or two Land-Rovers plus their own complement of 2-3.

During the Falklands Campaign of 1982, four of these LCVPs from HMS *Fearless* and *Intrepid* were fitted with lightweight minesweeps for local use.

HMS *Northern Horizon* — Chartered

HMS	Completed	Converted	Builder
Northern Horizon (ex-*Marbella*)	1966	1988	Goole SB&E

SPECIFICATION

Gross tons:	1,493
Dimensions:	246 × 40½ × 13¼
Machinery:	1 shaft powered by two diesel engines each giving 2,100bhp, also fitted with a bowthruster
Speed:	16kts
Range:	15,000nm at 14kts
Fuel:	430 tons of diesel oil
Complement:	45 approx

Notes:

Northern Horizon was chartered from her owners in 1988 by MOD(N) and was engaged in the testing of electronic and other equipment to provide prototype data and evaluation prior to outfitting of the *Sandown* of the 'Sandown' Class of SRMH.

Northern Horizon is built with an onboard hospital and has lately been employed as a geophysical survey vessel, having been converted from a North Atlantic stern trawler; MOD(N) have allocated a ship's crest to *Northern Horizon*.

HMS Northern Horizon. *This stern Trawler is shown as built for J. Marr & Sons, prior to her charter by MOD(N).* (J. Marr & Sons)

Bibliography

The War at Sea, Capt S. W. Roskill DSC, RN (HMSO)

Japanese Warships of World War I, A. J. Watts (Ian Allan Ltd)

Jane's Fighting Ships — Various Editions, F. T. Jane (Sampson Low & Marston)

Warships of World War II, H. T. Lenton & J. J. Colledge (Ian Allan Ltd)

Transactions of the Royal Institution of Naval Architects — Various Years (RINA London)

Jane's Pocket Book 9, Denis Archer (MacDonald & Jane's)

British Warships 1914–1919, F. J. Dittmar & J. J. Colledge (Ian Allan Ltd)

Royal Naval Coastal Forces, A. J. D. North (Almark)

German Warships of World War II, J. C. Taylor (Ian Allan Ltd)

Warships of the Royal Navy, Capt J. E. Moore RN (MacDonald & Jane's)

British Escort Ships, H. T. Lenton (MacDonald & Jane's)

Mines Minelayers and Minelaying, Capt J. E. Cowie RN (Oxford University Press)

A Dictionary of Ships of the Royal Navy of the Second World War, John Young (Patrick Stephens Ltd)

Allied Minesweeping in World War II, Peter Elliott (Patrick Stephens Ltd)

Ships of the Royal Navy, J. J. Colledge (David & Charles)

Allied Escort Ships of World War II, Peter Elliott (MacDonald & Jane's)

Fast Attack Craft, Phelan Brice (MacDonald & Jane's)

Combat Fleets of the World 1980–81, J. L. Couhat (Arms & Armour Press)

Destroyers of the Royal Navy 1893–1981, M. P. Cocker (Ian Allan Ltd)

Frigates, Sloops & Patrol Vessels of the Royal Navy 1900 to date, M. P. Cocker (Westmorland Gazette)

Royal Naval Submarines 1901–1982, M. P. Cocker (Frederick Warne (Publishers) Ltd)

Appendix 1:
Brief Particulars and Illustrations of Allied and Enemy Mines of World War I and II

Left: The HII Mk II was manufactured from late 1916 and was used with the Mk VIII sinker. Many of these weapons were used after the outbreak of World War II, such were the stocks that had been built up. The first of this pattern were laid on 24 September 1917. This could be described as an independent-moored contact mine, with a charge of 325 lbs of explosives. It could be laid in up to 200 fathoms, later 600 fathoms, and the below-surface depth was adjustable to a maximum of 300 feet.

Right: The moored magnetic mine known as the M Mk I. In production by 1937.

Left: The XIV type and the follow-up versions were self-compensating depth-keeping mines, which could be laid in depths up to 1000 fathoms.

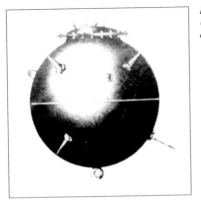

Left: The XIX mine was designed as an anti-U-boat weapon, with switch horns and a charge of 100 lbs of explosives.

Right: The Mk XX Antenna mine, with lower antennae of 80 feet in length. Laid to float 10 feet below the surface.

Overleaf: Examples of German and Italian mines.

Below: Two different types of mines developed by France.

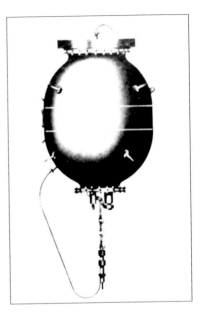

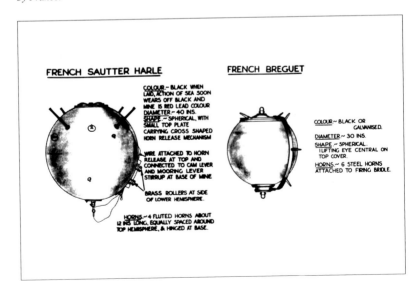

FRENCH SAUTTER HARLE

COLOUR.~ BLACK WHEN LAID, ACTION OF SEA SOON WEARS OFF BLACK AND MINE IS RED LEAD COLOUR
DIAMETER.~ 40 INS.
SHAPE.~ SPHERICAL, WITH SMALL TOP PLATE CARRYING CROSS SHAPED HORN RELEASE MECHANISM

WIRE ATTACHED TO HORN RELEASE AT TOP AND CONNECTED TO CAM LEVER AND MOORING LEVER STIRRUP AT BASE OF MINE

BRASS ROLLERS AT SIDE OF LOWER HEMISPHERE.

HORNS.~ 4 FLUTED HORNS ABOUT 12 INS LONG, EQUALLY SPACED AROUND TOP HEMISPHERE, & HINGED AT BASE.

FRENCH BREGUET

COLOUR~ BLACK OR GALVANISED.
DIAMETER.~ 30 INS.
SHAPE.~ SPHERICAL.
1 LIFTING EYE CENTRAL ON TOP COVER.
HORNS.~ 6 STEEL HORNS ATTACHED TO FIRING BRIDLE.

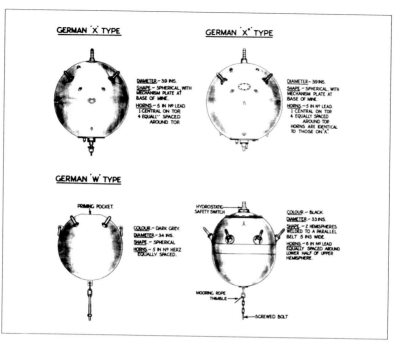

GERMAN 'X' TYPE

DIAMETER - 39 INS.
SHAPE - SPHERICAL, WITH MECHANISM PLATE AT BASE OF MINE.
HORNS - 5 IN Nº LEAD.
1 CENTRAL ON TOP,
4 EQUALLY SPACED AROUND TOP.

GERMAN 'X*' TYPE

DIAMETER - 39 INS.
SHAPE - SPHERICAL, WITH MECHANISM PLATE AT BASE OF MINE.
HORNS - 5 IN Nº LEAD.
1 CENTRAL ON TOP,
4 EQUALLY SPACED AROUND TOP.
HORNS ARE IDENTICAL TO THOSE ON 'X'.

GERMAN 'W' TYPE

PRIMING POCKET.

COLOUR - DARK GREY.
DIAMETER - 34 INS.
SHAPE - SPHERICAL
HORNS - 5 IN Nº HERZ EQUALLY SPACED.

HYDROSTATIC SAFETY SWITCH

MOORING ROPE THIMBLE

SCREWED BOLT

COLOUR - BLACK.
DIAMETER - 33 INS.
SHAPE - 2 HEMISPHERES WELDED TO A PARALLEL BELT 5 INS WIDE.
HORNS - 6 IN Nº LEAD EQUALLY SPACED AROUND LOWER HALF OF UPPER HEMISPHERE.

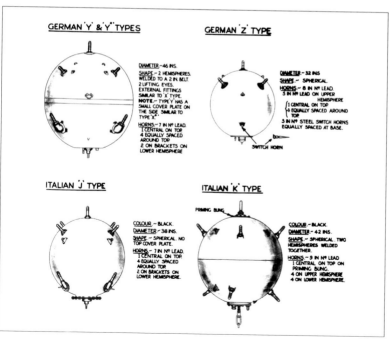

GERMAN 'Y' & 'Y*' TYPES

DIAMETER - 46 INS.
SHAPE - 2 HEMISPHERES WELDED TO A 2 IN. BELT.
2 LIFTING EYES.
EXTERNAL FITTINGS SIMILAR TO 'X' TYPE.
NOTE - TYPE 'Y' HAS A SMALL COVER PLATE ON THE SIDE, SIMILAR TO TYPE 'X*'.

HORNS - 7 IN Nº LEAD.
1 CENTRAL ON TOP.
4 EQUALLY SPACED AROUND TOP.
2 ON BRACKETS ON LOWER HEMISPHERE.

GERMAN 'Z' TYPE

DIAMETER - 32 INS.
SHAPE - SPHERICAL.
HORNS - 8 IN Nº LEAD.
5 IN Nº LEAD ON UPPER HEMISPHERE.
1 CENTRAL ON TOP.
4 EQUALLY SPACED AROUND TOP.
3 IN Nº STEEL SWITCH HORNS EQUALLY SPACED AT BASE.

SWITCH HORN

ITALIAN 'J' TYPE

COLOUR - BLACK.
DIAMETER - 38 INS.
SHAPE - SPHERICAL. NO TOP COVER PLATE.
HORNS - 7 IN Nº LEAD.
1 CENTRAL ON TOP.
4 EQUALLY SPACED AROUND TOP.
2 ON BRACKETS ON LOWER HEMISPHERE.

ITALIAN 'K' TYPE

PRIMING BUNG

COLOUR - BLACK.
DIAMETER - 42 INS.
SHAPE - SPHERICAL. TWO HEMISPHERES WELDED TOGETHER.
HORNS - 9 IN Nº LEAD.
1 CENTRAL ON TOP ON PRIMING BUNG.
4 ON UPPER HEMISPHERE.
4 ON LOWER HEMISPHERE.

Appendix 2:
British Shipbuilders

Company	Location
Ailsa Shipbuilding Co Ltd	Troon, Ayrshire
Ardrossan Dry Dock & Shipbuilding Co Ltd	Ardrossan, Ayrshire
Sir W. G. Armstrong Whitworth & Co Ltd	Newcastle-upon-Tyne
Austin & Pickersgill Ltd	Sunderland, Co Durham
Ayrshire Dockyard Co	Irvine
Barclay Curle & Co Ltd	Glasgow
William Beardmore & Co	Glasgow
Blyth Dry Dock & Shipbuilding Co Ltd	Blyth, Northumberland
Bow McLachlan & Co Ltd	Paisley
J. W. Brooke & Co Ltd	Lowestoft
George Brown & Co (Marine) Ltd	Greenock
Caledon Shipbuilding & Engineering Co Ltd	Dundee
Camper & Nicholson Ltd	Gosport
John Chambers Ltd	Oulton Broad, Lowestoft
Clyde Shipbuilding & Engineering Co Ltd	Port Glasgow
Cochrane Shipbuilders Ltd	Selby, Yorkshire
Colby Bros	Lowestoft
Cook Welton & Gemmell	Hull & Beverley
John Crown & Sons Ltd	Monkwearmouth, Sunderland
William Denny & Brothers Ltd	Dumbarton
Sir R. Dixon & Co Ltd	Cleveland, Middlesbrough
J. S. Doig & Sons Ltd	Grimsby
William Doxford & Sons Ltd	Pallion, Sunderland
Dundee Shipbuilding Co Ltd	Dundee
Dunlop Bremner & Co Ltd	Port Glasgow
J. Duthie Torry Shipbuilding Co	Aberdeen
J. T. Eltringham & Co Ltd	Willington Quay-on-Tyne
Fairfield Shipbuilding & Engineering Ltd	Govan
Fairlie Yacht Slip Ltd	Fairlie
Ferguson Brothers (Port Glasgow) Ltd	Port Glasgow
Fleming & Ferguson Ltd	Paisley
J. & G. Forbes	Sandhaven & Fraserburgh
Rennie Forrest Shipbuilding & Engineering Co Ltd	Wivenhoe
Goole Shipbuilding & Repair Co Ltd	Goole
Greenock & Grangemouth Dockyard Co	Greenock & Grangemouth

William Gray & Co Ltd	West Hartlepool
Alexander Hall & Co Ltd	Aberdeen
Hall Russell & Co Ltd	Aberdeen
William Hamilton & Co Ltd	Port Glasgow
W. Harkness & Sons Ltd	Middlesbrough
Harland & Wolff Ltd	Belfast
P. K. Harris & Sons Ltd	Appledore
R. & W. Hawthorn Leslie & Co Ltd	Newcastle-upon-Tyne & Hebburn
D. & W. Henderson & Co Ltd	Glasgow
Herd & Mackenzie	Findochty
A. & J. Inglis Ltd	Glasgow
John Lewis & Sons Ltd	Aberdeen
Lobnitz & Co	Renfrew
London & Glasgow Co Ltd	Glasgow
Lytham Shipbuilding & Engineering Co Ltd	Lytham
Archibald MacMillan & Sons Ltd	Dumbarton
Murdoch & Murray Ltd	Port Glasgow
Robert Napier & Sons	Govan
Ouse Shipbuilding Co	Hook, Nr Goole
Philip & Son Ltd	Dartmouth
Charles Rennoldson & Sons Ltd	South Shields
John P. Rennoldson & Sons Ltd	South Shields
Richards (Shipbuilders) Ltd	Lowestoft & Great Yarmouth
Henry Robb & Sons	Leith
Saunders Roe (Anglesey) Ltd	Beaumaris
Scott & Sons (Bowling) Ltd	Bowling, Dumbartonshire
William Simons & Co	Renfrew
Smiths Dock & Co Ltd	Middlesbrough
Alexander Stephen & Sons Ltd	Glasgow
W. & F. Stephen	Banff
Sunderland Shipbuilding Co Ltd	Sunderland
Swan Hunter & Wigham Richardson Ltd	Wallsend & Newcastle-upon-Tyne
Thames Iron Works, Shipbuilding & Engineering Co Ltd	Blackwall, London
J. L. Thompson & Sons Ltd	Sunderland
John I. Thornycroft & Co Ltd	Woolston, Southampton
Vickers Ltd	Barrow-in-Furness
Webster & Bickerton Ltd	Goole
Wood Skinner & Co Ltd	Newcastle
J. Samuel White & Co Ltd	Cowes, IOW
Yarrow & Co Ltd	Scotstoun, Glasgow

Appendix 3:
HM Minelayers Lost During World War I and II

CAUSE		TOTAL
Unknown:	ML97, 98, 127, 229; MTB80, 625, 712	7
Surface action:	CMB24A, 33A, 79A, 62BD; ML110, 424, 474; ML129, 130, 132, 310, 311, 358; MTB74, 237, 241, 347, 357, 365, 372; MLB606, 622, 639, 666, 669, 671, 5001	27
Accident:	ML403; MLB715; Princess Irene	3
Wrecked:	ML197, 152, 247, 278, 421; MTB287, 371; ML147, 219, 591, 905; MLB605, 631	13
Aircraft attack:	MTB73, 77, 208; ML160, 352, 353, 579, 835; MLB648; Kung Wo, Latona, Shepperton;	12
Own forces to avoid capture at sea by the enemy:	ML254; MTB287, 371	3
Collision:	CMB18A, 71A; ML121, 356; MTB93, 230, 352; ML183, 251; MLB690, 702	11
Heavy weather:	CMB82C; ML18, 62, 191, 566; MTB242; ML288; Corncrake	8
Lost in transit:	ML230, 253, 255, 540, 541; MTB284, 295;	7
Shore batteries:	ML207, 268, 270, 298, 306, 446, 447, 467; ML156, 157, 192, 262, 562; MLB636, 641, 665, 681	
Caught fire:	CMB114D, 39B, 99ED; ML19, 40, 149, 52, 55, 64, 196, 431, 434, 521, 534; ML169, 242, 265, 282, 301, 387, 385, 444, 460; MLB601, 626, 686, 776, 789, 791, 798; MTB776, 789, 791, 798; Port Napier	35
Expended as target:	CMB90BD; MTB243; MLB635	3
Torpedoed:	ML126, 339; Ariadne, Welshman	4
Mined:	ML561; MTB87, 222; ML103, 108, 109, 111, 144, 210, 216, 252, 443, 466, 563, 870, 890,916; MLB640, 644, 655, 657, 663, 672, 697, 705, 710, 782; Scott, Abdiel, Princess Victoria;	30
Attacked in error by Allied aircraft:	MTB734, MLB708, 734	3
Attacked in error by Allied naval vessel:	MTB732	1
Destroyed by own forces in the face of the Japanese advance at:		
Hong Kong:	ML376, 377; Redstart	3
Rangoon:	ML436, 437	2
Singapore:	ML362, 363, 364, 365, 372, 373,374, 375, 432, 433; HDML 1096, 1167, 1168, 1169, 1170; M7	16

Note:

Minelayers and Minesweepers of World War I, MLs, World War II Fairmile 'A' MLs, 'B' MLs, 'D' MGB/MTBs, and Modified 'D' MGB/MTBs are all included *inter alia.* MLB refers to Fairmile 'D' and Modified 'D' types.

Appendix 4:

HM Minesweepers Lost From World War I to Date

CAUSE		TOTAL
Unknown:	LCA(HR)*183, 678, 802*; MFV*1032*, MMS*1016*, HDML*1030, 1039*; Banka, Plinlimmon, Rahman, Scott Harley, Sin Aik Lee, Tapah	13
Surface action:	SGB7; HDML*1062, 1063, 1227*; Arabis, Bramble, Horatio, Juniper, Peterel, Pine, Scorpion, Sesame, Ullswater, Wallasea	14
Accident:	MMS*1558*; HDML*1060*; Canna;	3
Wrecked:	MMS*278*; HDML*1015, 1056, 1100, 1101, 1119, 1388*; Adept, Alder, Assurance, Belton, Brighton Belle, Brora, Carbineer, Cyrus, Egeland, Firmament, Flotta, Hesperia, Hildasay, Horsa, Levanter, Princess Mary, Saltburn	26
Aircraft attack:	MMS*174*; HDML*1011, 1092, 1093, 1094, 1095*; Abingdon, Alarm, Andromeda, Beech, Changthe, Cicala, City of Rochester, Devonia, Dragonfly, Fermoy, Gossamer, Gracie Fields, Grasshopper, Gulzar, Helvellyn, Huatong, Huntley, Jarak, Ladybird, Marmion, Minnie Moller, Mosquito, Queenworth, Skipjack, Skudd 3, Snaefell, Snapdragon, Sphinx, Stoke, Svana, Tamarisk, Vega, Vestal, West Cocker	40
Own forces to avoid capture at sea by the enemy:	Gemas	1
Collision:	MMS*180*; Begonia, Fittleton, Herring, Hythe, Lancer, Marsa, Michael Clements, Nurton, Roedean, Seagull, Sword Dance, Thalia	13
Heavy weather:	MMS*223*; ZZ*12, 13*; HDML*1083, 1121, 1179, 1380*; Adherent, Blue Sky, Campobello, Eriskay, Glen Avon, Petersfield, St Sampson, Sapper, Shera, Spider, Sulla, Valerian	20
Lost in transit:	HDML*1003, 1037, 1090, 1153, 1157, 1212, 1244, 1289*	8
Shore batteries:	HDML*1259*	1
Caught fire:	HDML*1019, 1147, 2216*; Bisham, Broadley, Edlingham	6
Used as target:	Mallow	1
Torpedoed:	HDML*1163*; Algerine, Arabis, Ascot, Birdlip, Brecon, Clacton, Dirk, Ellesmere, Genista, Gnat, Guysborough, Horatio, Hythe, Jura, Laertes, Lavender, Leda, Loyalty, Newmarket, Niger, Orfasy, Pine, Primula, Pylades, Salvia, Sesame, Sotra, Stronsay, Tynedale, Ullswater, Wallasea	32

Mined:	BYMS*2019, 2022, 2030, 2053, 2074, 2077, 2191, 2255*; MMSs*8, 39, 55, 68, 70, 89, 101, 117, 168, 170, 229, 248, 257, 1016, 1019, 1055*; HDMLs*1057, 1069, 1154, 1226, 1417*; *Almond, Alyssum, Ash, Aster, Bagshot, Blackmorevale, Brighton Queen, Chestnut, Clacton, Corburn, Corfield, Coriolanus, Cricket, Cromarty, Cromer, Cupar, Cyrus, Duchess of Hamilton, Duchess of Montrose, Duchess of Richmond, Dundalk, Dunoon, Erica, Erin's Isle, Fair Maid, Fandango, Fantome, Felixtowe, Fitzroy, Ganilly, Gentian, Hebe, Hickory, Hydra, Jason, Jasper, Javelin, Kempton, Kinross, Lady Ismay, Ludlow, Mastiff, Medway II, Mercury, Mignonette, Myrtle, Nasturtium, Nepaulin, Niger, Ouse, Penarth, Peterhead, Pink, Plumpton, Prompt, Queen of the North, Redcar, Regulus, Rysa, St Angelo, St Seiriol, Santa, Sargasso, Sarna, Sevra, Southsea, Speedy, Squirrel, Sundance, Sword Dance*	67
Attacked in error by Allied aircraft:	*Britomart, Hussar, Salamander*	3
Captured by the Japanese forces:	*Cornflower, Jeram, Peningat, Trang, Wo Kwang*	5
Captured by the German forces:	HMDL*1381*; *Widnes*	2
Gunfire of German tanks/artillery:	*Brighton Queen*	1
Ice pressure:	*Shusa*	1
Foundered:	LCA (HR)*671, 689, 811*	3
Destroyed by own forces in the face of the Japanese advance at:		
Hong Kong:	*Moth, Robin, Tern*	3
Palembang:	*Klias, Jerantut*	2
Rangoon:	HDML*1102, 1103, 1104*	3
Selater:	*Herald*	1
Singapore:	*Laburnum*	1
Sumatra:	*Malacca*	1
Abandoned incomplete to the Japanese at:		
Hong Kong:	MMS*95, 96, 123, 124, Beaulieu, Looe*	6
Rangoon:	MMS*161, 162, 163, 164*	4
Singapore:	MMS*52, 93, 94, 125, 126, 127, 128, 166, Portland, Seaford*	10
Operation 'Neptune':	LCA (HR)*671, 690, 965, 1072*	4
Tested to Destruction:	*Cybele*	1
Small battle unit:	*Cato, Chamois, Colsay, Cairsay, Magic, Quorn*	6
Rammed U-Boat:	*Begonia*	1

Appendix 5:
Axis U-Boat Losses Attributable to HM Mine Warfare Vessels in World War I and II

U-87	25 Dec 1917	Irish Sea	HMS *Buttercup* and *PC56* (Sloops)
UB-71	21 Apr 1918	Straits of Gibraltar	HM ML *413*
UB-110	19 July 1918	Off the Humber and subsequently salvaged by the Royal Navy	HM ML *263* and HMT *Garry*
U-33	12 Feb 1940	Firth of Clyde	HMS *Gladiolus* (Corvette)
U-192	5 May 1943	North Atlantic	HMS *Pink* (Corvette)
U-300	22 Feb 1945	Off Cadiz	HMS *Pincher, Recruit* (M/Ss) and *Evadne* (Armed Yacht)
U-343	10 Mar 1944	South of Sardinia	HMT *Mull*
U-605	7 Nov 1942	Off Algiers	HMS *Lotus* (*II*) and HMS *Poppy* (Corvettes)
U-617	12 Sept 1943	Scuttled off Metilla	HMS *Hyacinth* (Corvette) HMT *Haarlem* and *Wollongong* (RAN Sloop) and aircraft
U-655	24 Mar 1942	North of Hammerfest	HMS *Sharpshooter* (M/S)
U-660	12 Nov 1942	Off Aran	HMS *Lotus* (*II*) and *Starwort* (Corvettes)
Fisalalia	29 Sept 1941	Off Jaffa	HMS *Hyacinth* (Corvette)
Perla	9 July 1942	Captured off Beirut	HMS *Hyacinth* (Corvette)
Bronzo	12 July 1943	Captured off Augusta	HMS *Boston, Poole, Cromarty, Seaham* (M/Ss)

Index

MTB 100   80
Macbeth   161
Macduff   75
Mackerel   159
Maddiston   102
Madras   133
Maenad   94
Magic   92, 93, 209
Magicienne   94
Magnolia   66, 155
Malham   105
Malacca   156
Mallaig   75
Mallow   66, 67, 208
Malvern   75
Mameluke   94
Manchester City   57
Mandate   94
Mangrove   163
Mantis   136
Manxman   22
Maple   155
Marchioness of Breadalbane
   127
Marchioness of Fife   127
Marchioness of Lorne   128
Marguerite   69
Marigold   66
Mariner   94
Marlow   75
Marmion II   94, 127, 149,
   208
Marsa   127, 208
Marticot   81
Marvel   94
Maryborough   91
Maryport   75
Mary Rose   94
Maryton   102
Mastiff   148, 209
Maxton   102
Mazurka   135, 157
Medea   42
Mediator   177
Medlar   30
Medusa   42, 156
Medway Queen   126, 149
Melcombe Regis   94
Melita   94
Melpomene   42

Melton   71, 72
Menestheus   54
Merasheen   31
Mercury   127, 149, 209
Merry Hampton   70, 71
Mersham   105
Mewstone   167
Meynall   72
Michael Clements   208
Mickleham   105
Middlesbrough   99
Middleton   108
Midnight Sun   122
Mignonette   69, 209
Mileham   105
Mimosa   66
Minalto   167
Mincarlo   167, 169
Minehead   75
Minerva II   42, 128
Mines   201
Minnie Moller   156, 208
Minoru   70
Minstrel   95
Minuet   135, 157
Mist   123
Mistley   75
Monaghan   75
Monarchy   127
Monkton   102
Moon   94
Moonbeam   127
Moonshine   123
Morris Dance   135, 157
Mosquito   142, 208
Moth   136, 137, 137, 209
Mousa   167
Mull   167, 210
Mullet   158
Mullion   75
Munlochy   75
Muskerry   73
Mutine   95
Myosotis   69
Myrmidon   95
Myrtle   67, 68, 155, 209
Mystic   95

Nago Shuma Maru   98
Naiad   27

Nailsea   75
Nairn   115
Nanyo   98
Narcissus   67
Nasturtium   69, 209
Nautilus   57
Neasham   105
Neave   167
Nepaulin   127, 209
Nerissa   95
Ness   119
Nettle   186
Nettleham   105
Newbury   71
Newhaven   99
Newlyn   75
Newmarket   125, 208
Newquay   75
Newark   75
Nigella   69
Niger   78, 79, 113, 208
Nightfall   122
Nightingale   42, 43
Nimbus   122
Nizam   115
Northella   197, 198
Northern Horizon   199
Northolt   75
Nunthorpe Hall   115
Nurton   102, 208

Oak   155
Oakington   102
Oakley   73
Ockham   103
Octavia   94
Oderin   81
Odiham   105
Old Colony   28
Olive   163
Ombra   153
Onyx   95
Ophelia   161
Orby   70
Orcadia   95
Orestes   93
Orfasy   167, 169, 208
Oriole   149
Ormonde   79
Oronsay   167